VOLUME 33, NUMBER 1, JUNE 2024

qui parle

CRITICAL HUMANITIES AND SOCIAL SCIENCES

Editors in Chief
Annabel Barry and Robin Manley Mihran
University of California, Berkeley

Published by
Duke University Press

Qui Parle invites submissions from a range of fields, including but not limited to

Aesthetics	History
Anthropology	Literary and Cultural Studies
Critical Race Studies	Philosophy
Critical Theory	Political Theory
Gender and Sexuality Studies	Religion

Submissions of essays and book reviews may be sent directly to the editors at

Qui Parle
Doreen B. Townsend Center for the Humanities
220 Stephens Hall, #2340
University of California, Berkeley
Berkeley, CA 94720-2340
Phone: 510-643-0737
Fax: 510-643-5284
Email: quiparlejournal@gmail.com
Website: quiparle.org

Qui Parle is published twice a year by Duke University Press, 905 W. Main St., Suite 18B, Durham, NC 27701. It is an interdisciplinary journal that publishes works across the humanities and social sciences. *Qui Parle* is edited by graduate students at the University of California, Berkeley, and sponsored by the Doreen B. Townsend Center for the Humanities.

Direct all orders to Duke University Press, Journals Customer Relations, 905 W. Main St., Suite 18B, Durham, NC 27701. Annual subscription rates: print-plus-electronic institutions, $172; print-only institutions, $152; e-only institutions, $134; individuals, $42; students, $25. For information on subscriptions to the e-Duke Journals Scholarly Collections, contact dup_libraryrelations@duke .edu. Print subscriptions: add $8 postage and applicable HST (including 5% GST) for Canada; add $10 postage outside the US and Canada. Back volumes (institutions): $152. Single issues: institutions, $76; individuals, $12. For more information, contact Duke University Press Journals at 888-651-0122 (toll-free in the US and Canada) or 919-688-5134; subscriptions@dukepress.edu.

Direct inquiries about advertising to Journals Advertising Coordinator, journals_advertising@dukeupress.edu.

Visit Duke University Press at dukeupress.edu.

For a list of the sources in which *Qui Parle* is indexed and abstracted, see dukeupress.edu/qui-parle.

Qui Parle is grateful to Stephen Best and Rebecca Egger at the Doreen B. Townsend Center for the Humanities at the University of California, Berkeley, whose continued generosity and support have made publication of the journal possible.

Qui Parle is published by Duke University Press on behalf of the journal's Editorial Board.

ISSN 1041-8385

Printed and bound by CPI Group (UK) Ltd, Croydon, CR0 4YY

Contents

Review Essays

Introducing Ordinariness

ANNABEL BARRY

At the infamous 1982 Barnard Center Conference that would inaugurate the "sex wars," splintering the second-wave feminist movement into "sex positive" and "sex critical" factions, Hortense J. Spillers delivered a talk in which she argued that feminist discourse about sex wasn't really about sex at all. In "Interstices: A Small Drama of Words," later anthologized in essay form, Spillers takes issue with Western feminists' appropriation of a Freudian-Lacanian grammar of sexuality divorced from the material realities of sex and abstracted to a level of pure discursive circularity.[1] If some feminists employ psychoanalytic theory to claim that women are constitutively silenced within a phallocentric symbolic order, they obscure how their own writings doubly silence Black women by enacting a "metonymic playfulness" whereby "a part of the universe of women speaks for the whole of it."[2] In revisionary readings of theoretical texts by men, certain feminists don't so much undo their logic as transpose their rhetorical strategies to make white women the center of a new theoretical system, against which Black women are posited as what humanity and sexual subjectivity are not. To show how this works, Spillers introduces a distinction between "first-order naming"

QUI PARLE   Vol. 33, No. 1, June 2024
DOI 10.1215/10418385-11125454   © 2024 Editorial Board, *Qui Parle*

(immediate description of a community's experience) and "second-order naming" (discussion of that description). Feminism, she argues, had by the 1980s already progressed to a focus on second-order naming—on words about words about sex. The problem is that Black women's self-described experiences as sexual subjects had never even been admitted to first-order naming, at least in nonfiction texts. Thus feminism's "logological disposition" functions as "the subtle component of power that bars black women, indeed, women of color, as a proper subject of inquiry from the various topics of contemporary feminist discourse" (I, 167–68). This confirms Black women's sexual subjectivity as what Spillers calls an "interstice"—a lexical and epistemological gap—within feminist discourse.[3]

Spillers's proposed solution is a return to the ordinary. In particular, she turns to John Gwaltney's 1980 anthropological text *Drylongso: A Self Portrait of Black America*. Gwaltney's title comes from a word for "ordinary" used in African American communities in the South, in a gesture that affirms the connection between vernacular speech and everyday life in the oral interviews whose transcriptions compose the book. For Spillers, the interviews in the "Sex and Work" chapter constitute a repository of working-class Black women's first-order naming of their own sexual experiences in words that "seem to come off the human tongue and need not be referred back to a dictionary in order to be understood" (I, 169). Yet Spillers's return to the ordinary should not be seen as a naive validation of regular people and simple speech as somehow grounding a transparent contact between naming and reality; she has elsewhere influentially elucidated how anti-Blackness is encoded as "an American grammar book."[4] Spillers is careful to note that, despite Gwaltney's tendency to fade into the background as an interviewer, his book still constitutes a translation of women's words "through the medium of the male voice" (I, 169). Furthermore, these words are already removed to the level of second-order naming by the time we encounter them in Spillers's own analysis, which resituates them in a theoretical register. Calling attention to her uneasy task, Spillers admits, "I do not quite know where to fit these women's words about their bodies, or the status of their report" (I, 170). Her project, then, is best described as recuperating an alternative ordinary *"to be interpreted,"* not as announcing ordinariness as a domain that stands alone, beyond critique (I, 173).

The concept of "the ordinary" has surged as an area of critical attention in the last few decades and especially in the last few years—nonexhaustively, in philosophy, with Sandra Laugier's *Why We Need Ordinary Language Philosophy* (2013); in anthropology, with Kathleen Stewart's *Ordinary Affects* (2007) and Veena Das's *Life and Words: Violence and the Descent into the Ordinary* (2006) and *Textures of the Ordinary: Doing Anthropology after Wittgenstein* (2020); in literary studies, with Toril Moi's *Revolution of the Ordinary: Literary Studies after Wittgenstein, Austin, and Cavell* (2017) and Nancy Yousef's *The Aesthetic Commonplace: Wordsworth, Eliot, Wittgenstein, and the Language of Every Day* (2022); in Black studies, with Christina Sharpe's *Ordinary Notes* (2023) and Ianna Hawkins Owen's forthcoming *Ordinary Failure: Diaspora's Limits and Longings*; and in affect theory, with Lauren Berlant's *Cruel Optimism* (2011) and *On the Inconvenience of Other People* (2023). One way of reading this critical interest in the ordinary is as an endeavor to recuperate a sense of normalcy in the face of overwhelming and overlapping crises—genocide, war, pandemic, disruptions of supply chains, climate collapse, systemic erasure of reproductive autonomy. An emphasis on the ordinary might also be seen as a counterbalance to a proliferation of recent volumes and conferences on crisis, apocalypse, disaster, and catastrophe.

This special issue resists seeing the ordinary as a mere respite from the extraordinary; as the work of Spillers shows, the ordinary also emerges out of deep histories of subjugation and injustice. While "the ordinary" is a specific critical category in many of the fields surveyed above, this issue uses the term *ordinariness* to unsettle calcified theoretical assumptions about what it means for language, people, or social, economic, and political conditions to be ordinary.

This special issue demonstrates that ambivalence is central to what "ordinariness" is. In canonical Marxist scholarship on everyday life, the ordinary is alternatively the domain of the ideological (for Henri Lefebvre) and a set of shared materials that can be reappropriated to resist ideology (for Michel de Certeau).[5] For Lauren Berlant, everyday life in late capitalism is defined by a "crisis ordinariness" wherein we are able to stay afloat only by remaining attached to things that impair our ability to thrive.[6] Outside these paradigms, *ordinary* is defined as "normal; customary; usual." Applied to language, "ordinary" means "that most commonly found or attested; everyday, nontechnical" as opposed to "specialized terminology" or "logical symbolism." Applied to people, "ordinary" means "of low social position . . . vulgar; unrefined, low, course."[7] Raymond Williams traces the curious etymological evolution of the term *ordinary* from a word connoting formally invested authority (related to *ordination* and *ordinance*) to a word that suggests resistance to authority, becoming nearly synonymous with *rank and file* and *grassroots*.[8] The "ordinary" also carries the dual valence that Williams attributes to the "common"—both terms are at once markers of inclusion and exclusion, used alternatively to denote vernaculars and experiences shared by everyone and to derogate a segment of the population as particularly unsophisticated.[9] This special issue seeks to find where ordinariness maintains the prevailing social order and where it disorders existing assumptions and positions.

In the service of recalibrating assumptions about who counts as a theorist of "ordinary language," I have begun this introduction with Spillers, although Ludwig Wittgenstein comes more readily to mind as one of the inaugurators of so-called ordinary language philosophy, alongside J. L. Austin and Stanley Cavell. Can we reconcile someone like Spillers, who calls us to close the linguistic gaps that remand Black women to silence, with someone like Wittgenstein, who famously declares, in the final line of his *Tractatus Logico-Philosophicus*, "Whereof one cannot speak, thereof one must be silent?"[10] In other words, is Wittgenstein's sense of the ordinary more quiescent, in contrast with Spillers's transformative vision? While there is a growing body of scholarship that applies Wittgenstein's methodologies for feminist purposes, comparing Spillers's return to the ordinary with Wittgenstein's remains counterintuitive. Philosophy of language has been described as "malestream" and as an "alien hermeneutic circle" hostile to feminist interests.[11] Some feminists have been wary of Wittgenstein's personal misogyny and lack of concern about gender imbalances encoded in language.[12] For feminists who hold that "the personal is political," the ordinary cannot be simply the place where skepticism and critique dissolves; rather, it is a domain that must be continuously subject to scrutiny for the way it develops and perpetuates gendered power dynamics.[13] In a recent essay in *Post45* Bonnie Honig writes, "Both Wittgenstein and Spillers study grammar and embrace the kind of teaching that 'points beyond' given examples, but it is Spillers who presses us past Wittgenstein's view of the given as a refuge, Spillers who confronts the monstrousness of the given and the possibility and necessity of its refusal."[14] That is, Wittgenstein and Spillers each return us to everyday grammar, but only Spillers gives us a sense of what it might mean, ethically, to refuse grammatical and social conventions alike. Following Honig in noticing an affinity between these thinkers, I find ordinariness ambivalently emancipatory and normative, clarifying and confounding, for both. Spillers and Wittgenstein swerve away from problems that are introduced by complicated, self-referential discursive systems—whether psychoanalytic feminist theory or the analytic logic of Gottlob Frege and Bertrand Russell—finding a solution to these problems in a retrieval of language as it is ordinarily used. Both precede methodologically through a "critique of language" (*TLP*, 4.0031). Yet, for both, ordinary grammar ultimately creates as many distortions as it resolves.

One way to understand the divergence Spillers introduces between first-order and second-order naming is as an alternative version of what Frege in 1948 termed "sense and reference." Seeking to answer the question of how we can say that one thing is identical to another thing with which it does not share a name, Frege articulated a distinction between a name's "referent" (the externally existing thing to which it points) and its "sense" (its mode of presentation or expression). In Frege's example, the "morning star" and the "evening star" have different senses but the same referent. Both levels of language are equally important to the meaning of a given phrase.[15] This enables us to conclude that the morning star is the evening star, asserting an identity while adding meaningfully to our knowledge. Furthermore, sense and reference are distinguished from "conception," an individual's idiosyncratic associations with a word based on personal experiences. Unlike conception, sense is objective, because it is an object that can be shared by multiple

people, deriving from "a common store of thoughts which is transmitted from one generation to another."[16] In a similar manner to
Frege, Spillers describes her project as "identifying careers of words
that do different things with regard to a common point of reference"
(I, 168). Her theoretical account, like Frege's, relies on the idea that
language can be split into different levels: second-order naming takes
first-order naming as its referent, estranging language even further
from a referent out there in the world. Likewise, Frege acknowledges
that sometimes, as in reported speech, the referents of our words are
the senses of someone else's words—marking a departure from the
"ordinary way" of speaking where an external referent outside language is assured.[17] Frege's mathematical approach to philosophy is
entirely abstracted from any explicitly political—let alone feminist—
stakes. By contrast, a multilayered picture of language allows Spillers to detail how the senses of words like *woman* and *feminist* in
mainstream feminist discourse obscure the fact that only some women
are really part of the referents. Her critical approach to language prob-
lematizes the alleged objectivity of Frege's notion of sense as opposed
to conception, showing how, as racist and misogynist conceptions
are held and transmitted in common, they introduce subjective bias
insidiously into the very senses of words.

Frege's concern about the abuses engendered by the ambiguous or
missing referents of ordinary words prompted him to dream of the
possibility of a logically complete language in which every proper
name would have an actual and discrete referent.[18] In his 1905 essay
"On Denoting," Russell also suggested that many seemingly philosophical problems were in fact produced by inexactitude in common
language and that these problems would be resolved if names were
rewritten as logically rigorous descriptions. Wittgenstein extended
and then ultimately contested this foundational work in analytic philosophy of language by Frege and Russell in his own return to the
ordinary. In the *Tractatus*, published in 1922, Wittgenstein seems
at first to concur with Russell that "most questions and propositions
of the philosophers result from the fact that we do not understand
the logic of our language" (*TLP*, 4.003). He approaches philosophy not as an assortment of propositions but as the *activity* of dissi-
pating philosophical problems by putting propositions conveyed

imprecisely in language into a purely logical form to reveal their non-sensical natures. This suggests a suspicious orientation toward the language of the everyday. "Colloquial language is part of the human organism and is no less complicated than it," Wittgenstein writes. "Language disguises the thought; so that from the external form of the clothes one cannot infer the form of the thought they clothe, because the external form of the clothes is constructed with quite another object than to let the form of the body be recognized" (*TLP*, 4.004). Uncannily, even as he condemns the obfuscation that colloquial language generates, Wittgenstein reaches for metaphorical language to clarify his point. His chosen idiom poses embodiment both as a marker of authenticity, in contrast with clothing, and as what language tries and fails to reach. Instead of purifying language, he complicates it, moving from mathematical formulas toward a literary device that is equally enabling and confusing. Despite acknowledging in the preface a debt to Frege and to Russell (who wrote an approving introduction), Wittgenstein appears to undermine their logical approach by the end, concluding that "even if *all possible* scientific questions be answered, the problems of life have still not been touched at all" (*TLP*, 6.52). A purely logical language, which cannot touch ethical, aesthetic, or metaphysical questions, ends up feeling impoverished.

In his *Philosophical Investigations*, published posthumously in 1953, Wittgenstein endeavors by contrast to "bring back words from their metaphysical to their everyday use."[19] It is a move that might be read either as a radical rejection or as a continuation of the work of the *Tractatus*. In his later text Wittgenstein turns the "critique of language" he envisioned in his earlier text against philosophical language itself. In the *Investigations* it is philosophy's tendency to take words out of context that generates confusion, because the meanings of words cannot be separated from their use in specific situations. Departing from Russell and Frege's approach, Wittgenstein no longer describes his project as "*striving after* an ideal, as if our ordinary vague sentences had not yet got a quite unexceptional sense, and a perfect language awaited construction by us."[20] However, a movement from the logical notation of analytic philosophy back to the language of the everyday does not settle existing problems without posing new ones. Indeed, Wittgenstein turns to the ordinary because it provides the "rough ground" that produces the friction necessary for difficult philosophical inquiry. The ordinary as he describes it is not the thing of which one has "a clear view" but that which is overlooked "because it is always before one's eyes."[21] Ordinariness, for Wittgenstein, is the opacity of close familiarity. Starting with Spillers and moving to Wittgenstein sets up the varied disciplinary orientations and interpretative moves of the pieces in this special issue. Some contributors offer new interpretations of Wittgenstein, making his version of the ordinary look strange. Others push beyond Wittgenstein as a privileged thinker on the ordinary, looking to feminism, queer theory, film studies, Black studies, affect theory, anthropology, the visual arts, and nonphilosophy to revisit "ordinariness."

This issue begins with a new English translation, by Hannah Cox, of Sandra Laugier's "From the Ordinary to the Everyday," originally published in French as "De l'ordinaire au quotidien" in 2023. Laugier has introduced Anglo-American ordinary language philosophy to France by way of her own work as a translator, and her work has been instrumental in articulating and elaborating the critical and ethical capacities of this area of philosophy, especially for feminism. In this essay Laugier moves us back from Cavell's centralization of "the ordinary" for "ordinary language philosophy" toward Wittgenstein's original call to engage with the "everyday." For Laugier, Das's feminist anthropology emblematizes an investigation tethered to the concept of the Wittgensteinian everyday, which recovers the foreignness of the familiar. Das's work shows how the everyday, with its democratic, Emersonian connotations of "common" and "low," is something that we must endeavor to reach, not an uninterrogated given. Laugier's essay is already important in France, and we are excited to introduce it to the Anglophone world.

In "Wittgenstein in the Moonlight: On the Nonexistence of Riddles," Eesha Kumar also reappraises Wittgenstein's conception of the ordinary by grappling with his underengaged theorization of riddling and enigma. While the famous imperative to "throw away the ladder" of philosophical investigation after climbing up on it in §6.54 of the *Tractatus* has been an interpretive crux dividing "traditionalist" and "resolute" readers of Wittgenstein, Kumar instead directs attention to the less remarked on §6.5, which asserts that "the riddle does not exist." What might this assertion mean, she asks, for a thinker whose best-known formulations can be rephrased as riddles? In a reading of Edgar Allan Poe's story "The Purloined Letter," Kumar draws out the implications of a riddling Wittgenstein for questions of interpretation. In Poe's story, Detective Dupin relocates a valuable letter that has gone missing by recognizing that the letter has not been removed to a new location but is instead ensconced in a different envelope. In what Kumar reads as a Wittgensteinian mode, this story negotiates a middle way between reading for depth and reading for surface—if what we are looking for might be hidden in plain sight, interpretation requires seeing the ordinary differently, neither taking surfaces as a given nor probing beneath them. Yet, unlike other literary scholars who have mobilized Wittgenstein to unsettle the "reading wars," Kumar stresses that if the ordinary is not precisely the realm of depth, it is still defined by concealment as opposed to revelation, riddling as opposed to self-evidence.

Nicholas Baer turns us specifically to gendered language in "The Rumors Are True: Gossip in the Films of F. W. Murnau." In his theorization of speech action in *How to Do Things with Words* (1962), Austin pays little attention to how power delimits speech. Some feminist philosophers have since expanded his work to explore how gendered and racialized power differentials systemically prevent certain speakers from performing the speech acts they intend.[22] By contrast, Baer's approach focuses on the enabling, rather than disabling, dimension of modes of language that are conventionally gendered feminine. His article accords an epistemological value to the ordinary speech acts of rumor and gossip in feminist and queer studies, against a mainstream philosophical tradition that condemns these speech acts as "authorless yet forceful, trifling yet consequential, fickle yet enduring, unfounded yet steadfast." Baer shows that Murnau's films often treat gossip as accurate even if unsubstantiated, enabling characters to make sense of their situations. Furthermore, rumor opens up a queer reading of Baer's own biography that more traditional historical scholarship would foreclose. In recuperating

Murnau's homosexuality as a vague insinuation rather than an archivally documented fact, Baer's project connects to Owen's in a shared commitment to what Saidiya Hartman has called "critical fabulation."[23]

Owen's contribution, "Dead Tired," resists binary frameworks that have positioned the suicide of enslaved women as exemplifying either defeat or resistance. Through a reading of Octavia Butler's *Wild Seed* that draws on research into Butler's archive at the Huntington Library in Los Angeles, Owen asks us to make space for the possibility that Black women's suicidality stems from desirelessness and exhaustion, constituting a failure of relationality rather than a productive negativity that can be enfolded back into collective politics. Owen's essay relates to his larger project of envisioning how the term *diaspora* fails to hail certain subjects. Mobilizing the ambivalence generated by attention to ordinary affects, Owen poses the question of "how to offer ourselves and others one small framework in a sea of possibilities that might maintain the agency of those we've lost without celebrating them and without condemning them but merely continuing to find ways to be present with their irreversible decisions, and with the pieces of us that follow them to wherever they've gone next." His approach amounts to a refusal of, or at least a reticence about, a Black politics of refusal.

The affective entailments of failure in American life are also the subject of Sean Michael Muller's "Ordinary Expectation: Failure on the American Scene." Following methodologically from Stewart's anthropological excavation of the architecture of the everyday in *Ordinary Affects*, Muller unfolds the daily experience of dispossession in rural Washington County, New York, a segment of the so-called heroin highway. Muller's analysis progresses through a detailed attention to the landscape as "a material, psychic, and social geography where contradictions conjoin, strengthen, and obscure one another" before moving into the body as itself a landscape shaped by addiction and impoverished expectations. Although lives that enfold in the economically and ecologically devastated postindustrial spaces of the United States are often configured as extraordinary, Muller demonstrates their inextricability from ordinary structures of American life.

If Muller seeks to reveal the structural character of "the 'trashy-ness' of the rural, the industrial and domestic debris that conjoins in the signature forms of deindustrial ruination," Adrian De Leon pro-vides an alternative emphasis on "trash" in his "Brown Gathering: Archive, Refuse, and Baduy Worldmaking." De Leon analyzes the sculptures of Diane Williams, who crafts artworks out of discarded objects from everyday life in the Filipinx diaspora: packets of soup mix and seasoning, plastic bags from the supermarket chain Seafood City, cans of SPAM. Williams's sculpture *Curtain of Illegibility* is fea-tured on the cover of this special issue. De Leon argues that Williams enacts what he calls "brown gathering," a practice of stewarding and curating the remainders of colonial violence without allowing them to be assimilated fully into aesthetic pleasure or commodification. Both Muller and De Leon trace distortions of ordinary temporal-ity, whether the interminability of addiction as a chronic illness or the long durée of the plastics in William's sculptures, which gesture toward geological as opposed to human time scales. Both move be-tween structural critique and visceral engagement with the body—in De Leon's case, the "gustatory terrain" of colonial consumption in-dexed by the refuse objects of Filipinx cuisine.

In "The Pathos of Finitude: Ordinariness, Solitude, and Individu-ality in Nonphilosophy," Thomas Sutherland takes us to different critical terrain. Sutherland elucidates how François Laruelle's enig-matic "nonphilosophy" seeks to recover the concept of the "ordi-nary Man" who, in his radical immanence, resists a post-Kantian philosophical view of the human as a "doublet" split between empir-ical and transcendental qualities. For Laruelle, the "ordinary Man" is entirely devoid of qualities that would enable him to be assimilated into philosophical investigation. Yet Sutherland argues that the fig-ure of the "ordinary Man" can't be accounted for on Laruelle's own terms; Laruelle's very emphasis on finitude, for example, brings his project back within the domain of traditional academic philosophy. Sutherland's essay ultimately sketches the limits of Laruelle's attempt to rigorously distinguish the ordinary from the philosophical.

Redirecting us from the ungendered "ordinary man" of Laruelle, a new interview with Honig brings us back an explicitly feminist inter-rogation of "ordinariness." We discuss how attention to ordinary language has shaped Honig's work in political theory throughout her career. In her early work, Honig sketched the difference between Austin's emphasis on speech acts as entirely ordinary and Hannah Arendt's positioning of speech as extraordinary political action. Her current book project revisits Austin and Cavell alongside an alternative tradition of philosophy of language that she locates in the Black feminist thought of Spillers, Hartman, Sharpe, Patricia Williams, and others. For Honig, these thinkers exemplify a "care for language," a dedication to unraveling the intertwined "succor" and "horror" of the ordinary through thought and action that takes place in words.

This special issue closes with two reviews of recently published books that critically elaborate ordinariness. What is notable about each of these reviews is their attention to how new explications of ordinariness emerge from a resistance to the ordinary form of the academic monograph. Daryl Maude, reviewing Berlant's *On the Inconvenience of Other People*, describes how Berlant's formulations convict the reader through the force of their laconic, aphoristic style, as much as through their explicit content. Amber Sweat, reviewing Sharpe's *Ordinary Notes*, explores how Sharpe's blackout text undermines the valorization of white supremacy and how her expansive white spaces around the printed words provide a reparative space to breathe in the wake of racial violence. Returning us to the questions of language and silence raised in our consideration of Spillers and Wittgenstein, Sweat praises those of Sharpe's notes that provide "the bare topography of nothing but breath," what Sharpe herself describes as notes that "end in silence."[24]

If a conventional understanding might oppose the ordinary to the extraordinary or to the catastrophic, for Spillers and Wittgenstein the ordinary is specifically opposed to the theoretical. The ordinary, for these thinkers, is what feminist philosophy or analytic philosophy of language, respectively, fails to engage. However, as the essays in this special issue demonstrate, to reach toward the ordinary is not to leave the complications of theory behind but to innovate on existing theoretical modes. Building on a recent expansion of critical attention to the ordinary across humanistic and social sciences disciplines, this special issue introduces the orthogonal term *ordinariness*. If "the ordinary" connotes something monolithic and self-evident, "ordinariness" suggests something plural and diffuse. For example, for the contributors to this issue, ordinariness is the language of riddling and enigma, rumor and gossip; the affective experience of desirelessness, exhaustion, failure, and inconvenience; the phenomenological terrain of the addicted, gustatory, and breathing body. Ordinariness is what infuses and yet unsettles the ordinary.

....

ANNABEL BARRY is a PhD student in English at the University of California, Berkeley. Her research focuses on how Anglo-American ordinary language philosophy is extended both by feminist accounts of how power shapes language use and by formal experiments in Irish women's writing that shed light on the constructed ordinariness of English. Her academic articles appear or are forthcoming in *English Literary History*, the *Keats-Shelley Review*, and *Milton Studies*. With Caroline Godard and Jane Ward, she edited a cluster of essays on "heteropessimism" for *Post45: Contemporaries*.

Notes

1. Although Spillers explicitly targets American feminists, she evidently has in mind the legacy of French feminist writers like Hélène Cixous, who wrote "The Laugh of the Medusa."
2. Spillers, "Interstices," 158 (hereafter cited as I).
3. Spillers's use of *interstice* anticipates the term *intersection*, which Kimberlé Crenshaw would coin in a legal context several years later in "Demarginalizing the Intersection of Race and Sex."
4. Spillers, "Mama's Baby, Papa's Maybe."
5. Lefebvre, *Critique of Everyday Life*; Certeau, *Practice of Everyday Life*.
6. Berlant, *Cruel Optimism*, 10.
7. *Oxford English Dictionary*, s.v. "ordinary, adj." (https://www.oed.com/dictionary/ordinary_adj).
8. Williams, *Keywords*, 225–26.
9. Williams, *Keywords*, 61–62.
10. Wittgenstein, *Tractatus Logico-Philosophicus*, 7 (hereafter cited as *TLP*). I use the online, side-by-side version of the text collated by Kevin C. Klement, which includes the original German alongside English translations by C. K. Ogden and by D. F. Pears and B. F. McGuinness. I quote from Ogden's translation.

11. Hornsby, "Feminism in Philosophy of Language," 87; Nye, "Philosophy of Language," 263.
12. Scheman, introduction, 1–2.
13. Felski, "Invention of Everyday Life," 93.
14. Honig, "Grammars of Refusal."
15. Frege, "Sense and Reference," 215.
16. Frege, "Sense and Reference," 212.
17. Frege, "Sense and Reference," 211.
18. Frege, "Sense and Reference," 222.
19. Wittgenstein, *Philosophical Investigations*, 116.
20. Wittgenstein, *Philosophical Investigations*, 98.
21. Wittgenstein, *Philosophical Investigations*, 122, 129.
22. See, e.g., Langton, "Speech Acts and Unspeakable Acts"; Hornsby, "Disempowered Speech"; and Maitri and McGowan, *Speech and Harm*; as well as Butler's critical response to this area of scholarship in *Excitable Speech*.
23. Hartman, "Venus in Two Acts," 11.
24. Sharpe, *Ordinary Notes*, 3.

References

Austin, J. L. *How to Do Things with Words*. Oxford: Clarendon, 1962.
Berlant, Lauren. *Cruel Optimism*. Durham, NC: Duke University Press, 2011.
Berlant, Lauren. *On the Inconvenience of Other People*. Durham, NC: Duke University Press, 2023.
Butler, Judith. *Excitable Speech: A Politics of the Performative*. New York: Routledge, 1997.
Certeau, Michel de. *The Practice of Everyday Life*. Translated by Steven Rendall. Berkeley: University of California Press, 1984.
Cixous, Hélène. "The Laugh of the Medusa." Translated by Keith Cohen and Paula Cohen. *Signs* 1, no. 4 (1976): 875–93.
Crenshaw, Kimberlé. "Demarginalizing the Intersection of Race and Sex: A Black Feminist Critique of Antidiscrimination Doctrine, Feminist Theory, and Antiracist Politics." *University of Chicago Legal Forum* 1 (1989): 139–67.
Das, Veena. *Life and Words: Violence and the Descent into the Ordinary*. Berkeley: University of California Press, 2006.
Das, Veena. *Textures of the Ordinary: Doing Anthropology after Wittgenstein*. New York: Fordham University Press, 2020.

Felski, Rita. "The Invention of Everyday Life." In *Doing Time: Feminist Theory and Postmodern Culture*, 77–98. New York: New York University Press, 2000.

Frege, Gottlob. "Sense and Reference." *Philosophical Review* 57, no. 3 (1948): 209–30.

Gwaltney, John Langston. *Drylongso: A Self-Portrait of Black America*. New York: Random House, 1980.

Hartman, Saidiya. "Venus in Two Acts." *Small Axe*, no. 26 (2008): 1–14.

Honig, Bonnie. "Grammars of Refusal." *Post45: Contemporaries*, October 27, 2022. https://post45.org/2022/10/grammars-of-refusal/.

Hornsby, Jennifer. "Disempowered Speech." *Philosophical Topics* 23, no. 2 (1995): 127–47.

Hornsby, Jennifer. "Feminism in Philosophy of Language: Communicative Speech Acts." In *The Cambridge Companion to Feminism in Philosophy*, edited by Miranda Fricker and Jennifer Hornsby, 87–106. Cambridge: Cambridge University Press, 2006.

Langton, Rae. "Speech Acts and Unspeakable Acts." *Philosophy and Public Affairs* 22, no. 4 (1993): 293–330.

Laugier, Sandra. *Why We Need Ordinary Language Philosophy*. Chicago: University of Chicago Press, 2013.

Lefebvre, Henri. *Critique of Everyday Life*. Translated by Sacha Rabinovitch. New Brunswick, NJ: Transaction, 1984.

Maitri, Ishani, and Mary Kate McGowan, eds. *Speech and Harm: Controversies over Free Speech*. Oxford: Oxford University Press, 2012.

Moi, Toril. *Revolution of the Ordinary: Literary Studies after Wittgenstein, Austin, and Cavell*. Chicago: University of Chicago Press, 2017.

Nye, Andrea. "Philosophy of Language: Semantics in a New Key." In *Philosophy in a Feminist Voice: Critiques and Reconstructions*, 263–95. Princeton, NJ: Princeton University Press, 1997.

Owen, Ianna Hawkins. *Ordinary Failure: Diaspora's Limits and Longings*. Durham, NC: Duke University Press, forthcoming.

Russell, Bertrand. "On Denoting." *Mind*, no. 56 (1905): 479–93.

Scheman, Naomi. Introduction to *Feminist Interpretations of Ludwig Wittgenstein*, edited by Naomi Scheman and Peg O'Connor, 1–24. University Park: Pennsylvania State University Press, 2002.

Sharpe, Christina. *Ordinary Notes*. New York: Macmillan, 2023.

Spillers, Hortense J. "Interstices: A Small Drama of Words." In *Black, White, and in Color: Essays on American Literature and Culture*, 152–75. Chicago: University of Chicago Press, 2003.

Spillers, Hortense J. "Mama's Baby, Papa's Maybe: An American Grammar Book." *Diacritics* 17, no. 2 (1987): 64–81.

Stewart, Kathleen. *Ordinary Affects*. Durham, NC: Duke University Press, 2007.

Williams, Raymond. *Keywords: A Vocabulary of Culture and Society*. Rev. ed. New York: Oxford University Press, 1983.

Wittgenstein, Ludwig. *Philosophical Investigations*. Translated by G. E. M. Anscombe. Malden, MA: Blackwell, 2001.

Wittgenstein, Ludwig. *Tractatus Logico-Philosophicus*. Translated by C. K. Ogden, D. F. Pears, and B. F. McGuinness, edited by Kevin C. Klement. Amherst: University of Massachusetts, 2018.

Yousef, Nancy. *The Aesthetic Commonplace: Wordsworth, Eliot, Wittgenstein, and the Language of Every Day*. Oxford: Oxford University Press, 2022.

From the Ordinary to the Everyday

SANDRA LAUGIER

Translation by Hannah Cox

In paragraph 116 of Wittgenstein's *Philosophical Investigations*, we find the following statement, which seems to outline the fundamental goal of his philosophy: "What *we* do is to bring words back from their metaphysical to their everyday use."[1] This assertion epitomizes Wittgenstein's conception of philosophy, but it presents some difficulties—our words, having gone astray, must find their "place of origin" (*Heimat*).[2] As Stanley Cavell has consistently shown, themes of loss, foreignness, and exile are at the heart of Wittgenstein's thought: "A philosophical problem has the form: 'I don't know my way about.'"[3] The philosopher presents himself as someone who is lost in his own language, entangled in its rules, even though the rules are our own: "Here the fundamental fact is that we lay down rules, a technique, for playing a game, and that then, when we follow the rules, things don't turn out as we had assumed. So that we are, as it were, entangled in our own rules."[4] But what happens to make language stray off course, from its everyday use to its metaphysical use? How does our language, which says only what we make it say, escape

QUI PARLE   Vol. 33, No. 1, June 2024

DOI 10.1215/10418385-11125464   © 2024 Editorial Board, *Qui Parle*

us to the point of saying something entirely different from what we meant to say, or even saying nothing at all? Cavell poses this fundamental question in his first book, *Must We Mean What We Say?*, when he asserts that "the ordinary" is defined by this indeterminacy of language itself.[5]

Indeed, the everyday use to which Wittgenstein constantly refers is far from self-evident: it is just as elusive and indeterminate as our forms of life. The project of *Philosophical Investigations* is not to replace disqualified logic with the study of use, finding therein a new foundation or new convictions, even purely practical ones. The study of everyday language use presents new problems, arduous in a different way from those of logical analysis, as J. L. Austin and the Oxford School later showed—the same school that, in coining the term *ordinary language philosophy*, formalized the Ordinary rather than the Everyday as a central concept.[6]

Here we will consider several reasons for returning to the concept of the Everyday, Wittgenstein's point of departure, in the philosophy of language.

Categories of the Everyday

Philosophical Investigations, as scholars have argued in multiple ways (notably Pierre Hadot and Jacques Bouveresse, its first French critics),[7] is a critique of *Tractatus Logico-Philosophicus*. We forget, Cora Diamond so judiciously reminds us, that it is precisely a *critique* in the strict sense of the term: taking up the same problem, the same need, with new tools and a change of perspective. Indeed, we must be wary of any reading of Wittgenstein that assumes a rift between the first philosophy, that of the *Tractatus*, and the second, that of ordinary language (though this has long been the official reading, still present in the work of numerous Wittgenstein specialists). According to the traditional interpretation, the first Wittgenstein seeks to establish a logical relationship between language and reality, and the second abandons that project in favor of an (autonomous) grammar of the rules of everyday language use. Cavell, in his renowned work *The Claim of Reason*, then Diamond, in *The Realistic Spirit*, were the first to contest this reading.[8] For Diamond, *Philosophical Investigations* carries on the

Tractatus's realist project through a return to the Everyday, bringing it back to the "rough ground" of ordinary language. When Wittgenstein evokes the rules of "our" language, he does not reinscribe the real into grammar: as he says from the very beginning of *Philosophical Investigations*, we learn from "our elders" how to use words in certain contexts, and throughout our lives—without a safety net as it were, without guarantees, without universals—we must use them in novel contexts, project them, discover new meanings. This forms the basis of human existence, this form of life in everyday language.

But it presents the difficulty of knowing what *we* say. How do *I* know what *we* ordinarily say in a given circumstance? How can the language that I speak, inherited from others, be mine? Herein is the meaning of the skeptical questioning of criteria: who am I to speak with (or on behalf of) others? Wittgenstein writes in a famous passage: "What is true or false is what human beings say; and it is in their language that human beings agree. This is agreement not in opinions, but rather in form of life."[9]

Wittgenstein says that we agree *in* and not *on* language. This means that we are not actors in the agreement, that language precedes this agreement just as much as it is produced by it, and that this circularity constitutes an essential element of the Everyday. There is no prior, given agreement on which to rely. The language agreement can always be broken, and this break is part of its everyday functioning. Skepticism need not be denied, then, by a turn to the ordinary. What is given, as Wittgenstein says here, is not only the world and things but also *forms of life*. By this he means that our form of life itself is a given, at once inevitable and alterable by what we make of it every day. Cavell accounts for this point by simply moving the emphasis: forms of *life* (and not *forms* of life). This biological aspect of form of life is also "the specific strength and scale of the human body and of the human senses and of the human voice."[10]

To realize what we mean to say would be to restore words to their land of origin, their "natural environment," to use the expression in *Philosophical Investigations*; this is how we can "bring words back from their metaphysical to their everyday use." Ordinary language defines the Ordinary, not the other way around. Everyday language (the strange fact of being able to speak with each other) defines the

Ordinary. Recognizing the ordinary nature of language is then discovering the Ordinary in two dimensions: the relationship to "us"
(the common, the agreement), and the Everyday (daily life). The
call to the Everyday is neither a matter of course nor a solution; it
is infused with skepticism, with what Cavell terms the "uncanniness
of the ordinary."[11]

In the community of language the skeptical question, far from
being solved, takes on its most radical sense: What allows me to
speak on behalf of others? How do I know what *we* mean to say,
by a *word* or by a *world*? It is in this context that we should consider
Cavell's return to authors from the American tradition, such as
Ralph Waldo Emerson and Henry David Thoreau, the thinkers/
writers of transcendentalism, who constantly raise the issue of *my*
voice in community and society. Cavell's idea is that the particular-
ity of American thought, its capacity to give philosophy a new beginning in America, may be found in its invention of the Everyday. This
new beginning for philosophy—which is no tabula rasa but has to
do with a second chance, just like the American comedies about remarriage, which constitute a major object of study for Cavell[12]—is
also a reversal of its two deep-rooted tendencies: its pretension to
surpass, and correct, ordinary language, and its denial of the interest
of everyday life. Our words, our everyday lives, have lost their mean-
ing(s), and we must learn to find it (them) again. Emerson says as
much in a famous line from "Self-Reliance": "Every word they say
chagrins us."[13] The notion of the Everyday is inseparable from the
issue of a reappropriation of human speech, the ordinary voice,
the right expression. For Cavell, it is not so much a question of finding the Everyday as it is of *recovering* it.[14]

Emerson's experiential philosophy is political from the outset, with
its democratic demands, echoed in the work of John Dewey:[15] both
advocate for the common, at once through their references to daily
life, shared by all humans, and through their call for a community of
shared ordinary values. The appeal to ordinary experience is of particular relevance to the democratic ideal, from Emerson to Dewey.
For Emerson, access to the world is given to us not by science but
by the close-up experience of everyday life. It is hard to see how the
scientific method could provide us with the elements of everyday
life, as he evokes in "The American Scholar":

I ask not for the great, the remote, the romantic; what is doing in Italy or Arabia; what is Greek art, or Provencal minstrelsy; I embrace the common, I explore and sit at the feet of the familiar, the low. Give me insight into today, and you may have the antique and future worlds. What would we really know the meaning of? The meal in the firkin; the milk in the pan; the ballad in the street; the news of the boat; the glance of the eye; the form and the gait of the body;—show me the ultimate reason of these matters; show me the sublime presence of the highest spiritual cause lurking, as always it does lurk, in these suburbs and extremities of nature; . . . and the world lies no longer a dull miscellany and lumber-room, but has form and order; there is no trifle; there is no puzzle; but one design unites and animates the farthest pinnacle and the lowest trench.[16]

In claiming to "embrace the common," "sit at the feet of . . . the low," Emerson positions himself on the side of what philosophers like George Berkeley and David Hume have positively called "the vulgar" in their project of valorizing ordinary experience over metaphysics. But we might consequently worry about a notion of the Everyday that would aim to "sublimate" and aestheticize it. We must note that Emerson took part in advocating for a distinctly American culture, which would be defined by an essentially democratic experience of everyday life.[17] This claim to the everyday as *low* is thus presented as an alternative to European culture.[18] It proleptically refers to the prized objects of American cinema and to those, closer still to Emerson, of photography:[19] as if Emerson were giving up on the grandiose art of Europe to envision an art of the Everyday, "American" in its own right, which would focus on the details of daily life, traditionally neglected by philosophy. As Cavell points out:

His list in "The American Scholar" of the matters whose "ultimate reason" he demands of students to know—"The meal in the firkin; the milk in the pan; the ballad in the street; the news of the boat; the glance of the eye; the form and the gait of the body"—is a list epitomizing what we may call the physiognomy of the ordinary, a form of what Kierkegaard calls the perception of the sublime in the everyday.[20]

This list is akin to the conception of a series of new categories, those of the Everyday. It is thus a matter not of transforming classical metaphysics through a reversal of its categories, as Charles Sanders Peirce and others will strive to do, but of inventing a new way of relating to the world. The question is no longer that of knowing the "ultimate reason" of phenomena but that of introducing a relationship to the Everyday that might allow us to *approach* it. This use of the Everyday is democratic, and for Emerson, the aesthetic is political:

> One of these signs is the fact that the same movement which effected the elevation of what was called the lowest class in the state, assumed in literature a very marked and as benign an aspect. Instead of the sublime and beautiful, the near, the low, the common, was explored and poetized. That which had been negligently trodden under foot by those who were harnessing and provisioning themselves for long journeys into far countries, is suddenly found to be richer than all foreign parts. The literature of the poor, the feelings of the child, the philosophy of the street, the meaning of household life, are the topics of the time.[21]

The poor, the child, the street, "household life": these are the new objects that will need to be considered, and to do so, the list of categories inherited from Europe will not suffice. The appeal to the Ordinary is thus democratic and practical. Emerson, far from giving up on skepticism to embrace the Everyday, will invent a specific form of tragedy—a tragedy of *ordinary experience*, of the *casual*, both everyday and tragic (*casualty*).

The Everyday is always an object of *inquiry*; it is never a given. The low is always to be *reached*, rather than surpassed—in a reversal of the sublime. It will not suffice to leave behind the Ordinary, Frank Capra's "man in the street." We must give another meaning to inherited words (as to those of experience, idea, impression, understanding, reason, necessity, condition, and constitution) and bring them back to the common or, to use Wittgenstein's expression, from the metaphysical to the Everyday. For Emerson, America can strive to reinvent Kantian transcendental philosophy not by fixing its categories but by inventing an access point to this world of the common, a specific way of approaching this new nature—*this new yet unapproachable America*[22]—for which the categories of transcendental philosophy (the conceptual mode of accessing nature as formulated by Europe) are inoperable. He offers his own version of categories in the epigraph of "Experience," with the list of "lords of life":

> The lords of life, the lords of life,—I saw them pass,
> In their own guise,
> Like and unlike,
> Portly and grim
> Use and Surprise
> Surface and Dream . . .
> Succession swift, and spectral Wrong,—[23]

These "lords of life" resemble the categories that govern our life, our experience, and the Everyday and determine our access to the world, analogous to the categories of causality, substance, and totality in Kant. But the list clearly shows that it cannot refer to *these* categories: use, surprise, surface, dream, succession. . . . Indeed, this ironic usage of categories reveals what is at stake in "Experience." Emerson has the idea that a new group of concepts—but will they still be *concepts?*—must be invented to describe everyday life. These concepts must then be applied to given, diverse, and scattered material that will have to be built and dominated, or, as he says, "domesticated." "This revolution is to be wrought by the gradual domestication of the idea of Culture. The main enterprise of the world for splendor, for extent, is the upbuilding of a man. *Here are the materials strown along the ground.*"[24] By "domestication," we may understand something entirely different than mastery and control. But to do so, we must go beyond categories. In thinking about categories of everyday life, Emerson was driven to rethink the very idea of category. Emerson's work expresses a clear desire to do away with this categorical schema and to redefine experience via everyday life. In the above passage, this idea of the domestication of culture, of the domestic, is not simply an idea about mastering the real. The idea of the *domestic*, which proves to be a central element of everyday life, allows us to reconceive our relationship to the world, not as knowledge but as *proximity* and direct, tactile access to an everyday universe.

The self-confidence and the relationship to the Everyday to which Emerson lays claim are instruments for a radical democracy, in creating a system of thought for democratic experimentation. This experiment called for the invention of a new, ordinary human, a man of democracy, who is also a man of the Everyday. Emerson and Thoreau, through their attention to the Everyday, herald the emergence of Wittgenstein and Austin's Ordinary language philosophy. The Everyday is always an object of *inquiry.*

For these "lords of life" do not govern our perception or experience; they emerge from it, like forms in a background: "I saw them pass." The categories are themselves subjects/objects of observation and exploration. The transcendental question, then, is no longer how to know on the basis of experience (a question which, as we have known since Hume, leads to the response: we know nothing at all—and thus to skepticism) but how to approach the Everyday— how to *have* an ordinary experience. In "Experience" Emerson expresses the difficulty of being close to the world, in the context of the experience of grief. Taken in its whole, this difficulty can be generalized to that of a world itself conceived under the sign (category) of loss. Herein lies the skepticism: not in the impossibility of knowing but in the inability to *have an experience.*

"Experience" does not so much aim to describe or explain experience as it questions its possibility. We believe that we have an experience, for example that of suffering, but this is not the case: suffering does not give us any contact with reality. William James follows this thread of Emersonian thought, for example in *The Will to Believe.* Dewey also takes up the question of experience—of knowing what it is to *have an experience*—in *Art as Experience.* We see the radical transformation of Kantian synthesis at work in Emerson, a transformation made possible not by the transcendental approach but by the opposite approach. Surpassing synthesis from below, not from above, is characteristic of all revalorizations of the Everyday.

From Everyday Language to the Anthropology of Life

To recognize the ordinary nature of language is to discover the Ordinary in the Everyday and in the repetition of days and nights. Exploration of the Everyday is possible only when we gather a variety of tools and approaches to stay as close as possible to the detail of life; we may reapply Austin's description of the observation of ordinary language to the Everyday:

> Our common stock of words embodies all the distinctions men have found worth drawing, and the connexions they have found worth marking, in the lifetimes of many generations: these surely are . . . more subtle, at least in all ordinary and reasonably practical matters, than any that you or I are likely to think up in our armchairs of an afternoon—the most favoured alternative method. When we examine what we should say when, what words we should use in what situations, we are looking again not merely at words (or "meanings," whatever they may be) but also at the realities we use the words to talk about: we are using a sharpened awareness of words to sharpen our perception of, though not as the final arbiter of, the phenomena.[25]

Austin speaks of "fieldwork," and many scholars have noted the anthropological character of his approach.[26] Today, however, this approach seems to be marred by the narrowness of his field (the English language, notably what was in use at Oxford in the discussions he led with his students and colleagues). The work of the anthropologist Veena Das, on the other hand, has given massive (in terms of density, consistency), concrete substance to Cavell's and Wittgenstein's thought about the ordinary. From focusing on our own language as strange—*uncanny*—to examining the ordinary *form of life*, the transition was rather obvious. Both Cavell and Das connect *Lebensform* to an attention to the form of human life as occurring every day: from what Cavell calls "the uncanniness of the ordinary" to what Das designates "the everyday life of the human." In his foreword to Das's *Life and Words*, Cavell notes that the Ordinary is *our* ordinary language insofar as we constantly render it foreign, referencing the Wittgensteinian image of the philosopher as an explorer of a foreign tribe.[27] This tribe is us, as both foreign and strange to ourselves. This intersection of the familiar with the foreign, common to anthropology, psychoanalysis, and philosophy, defines the Everyday. "Wittgenstein's anthropological perspective is one puzzled in principle by anything human beings say and do, hence perhaps, at a moment, by nothing."[28]

Das and Cavell subvert one of philosophy's tendencies, to be attracted to "revelation." They propose not to seek to discover the invisible but first to "see the visible," to discover the Everyday, the unseen. This is the project of *Philosophical Investigations*: to see what escapes us, not because it is hidden but because it is too close to us. "What we are supplying are really remarks on the natural history of human beings; not curiosities, however, but facts that no one has doubted, which have escaped notice only because they are always before our eyes."[29] The Ordinary is thus presented in terms of difficulty in accessing what is just before our eyes, and what we must learn to see precisely because we do not want to or do not know how to see it. In this way, Das's work suggests an alternative reading of Wittgenstein's conception of the Ordinary, tying it back to the Everyday as a specific concept. If the theme of the Everyday is far from new in anthropology, the approach that Das offers is completely distinctive, as we see in her commentary on a passage of *Philosophical Investigations*, which we may read alongside the passage that opened our discussion: "The ideal, as we conceive of it, is unshakable. You can't step outside it. You must always turn back. There is no outside; outside you cannot breathe."[30] This passage, according to Das, evokes not so much a simple return as a *coming home* to inhabit or haunt the same space, now marked as a space of destruction in which we must live again.[31] Hence the meaning of the Everyday in Wittgenstein: something recovered, a way of reinhabiting time and space, day after day. Cavell already noted that the Everyday is what we can only aspire to, since it appears as lost to us. "That is, there is nothing beyond the succession of each and every day; and grasping a day, accepting the everyday, the ordinary, is not a given but a task."[32]

Here Cavell's constant slippage between the Everyday and the Ordinary becomes problematic, since it is indeed a matter of passing (painfully) from one day to the next while pretending as if each day were a *whole*, to be completed or finished off. Michel de Certeau also cites Wittgenstein when he denounces the attempt by scientists to place themselves above ordinary language, and their contempt for the language of "the ordinary man."[33] For Certeau as for Cavell, escape from the Ordinary is impossible, but therein forms a sort of regret, and consequently lines of flight are sought out within the Everyday itself, in stories, movement, and diversion. Cavell and Das, meanwhile, seek the means for a return to the Ordinary and an experience of the Everyday, for a perception of its *texture*. We can contrast Certeau's melancholy with Cavell's romanticism (in a devastated world) and Das's anthropology of suffering (anchored in the catastrophe of partition). This difference is not only one of method or of "world vision"; it is anchored in experiences and physical sites, all distinct from one another.

This inevitably brings us back from the Ordinary to the Everyday—or, so to speak, lower than the Ordinary—an Ordinary that cannot be sublimated or aestheticized, as shown by the idea of *descent* into the Ordinary in Das, and the *infra-ordinary* in Perec:

> What is there under your wallpaper? How many movements does it take to dial a telephone number? Why can't you find cigarettes in grocery stores? Why not? . . . What's really going on, what we're living, the rest, all the rest, where is it? What happens every day and recurs every day, the banal, the everyday, the obvious, the common, the ordinary, the infra-ordinary, the background noise, the habitual, how to account for it, question it, describe it?[34]

What "goes without saying" is what we take for granted, what we do not worry about—tiny and neglected objects, people, and movements. The Everyday thus adds a dimension to the Ordinary that, in a sense, escapes the usage of language: rhythm, work, the passage of days and nights. These are the daily, repetitive actions that make life *continue*. The work of *care* constitutes the central example of this daily effort—at once a practical response to specific needs and a sensibility toward the details that matter in life. *Care* thus ensures the upkeep, the conversation, the preservation, and the texture of both the Everyday and form of life, a life defined in Das's work by violence, poverty, and the vulnerability of women.

The anthropology of the Everyday is *experimental* not in the sense of this adjective's meaning in psychology or pragmatism but in the sense that it aims to describe the *experience* of the Everyday (and not just daily experience) or its texture (the object of Das's more recent book, *Textures of the Ordinary*).[35] From Wittgenstein to Cavell and

Das, this anthropology advocates for new forms of paying attention to human life *as everyday*.

We might think back to how Austin, Cavell's teacher, and Erving Goffman, another of Austin's disciples who is very present in Das's work, stage human vulnerability in social exchanges. In "A Plea for Excuses" Austin draws attention to the vulnerability of human action, which he defines as what can go wrong. Human action, as Austin, Goffman, Cavell, and Das would argue, *is* precisely that at which we fail, which we *do not* exactly do, for which we make up excuses: the meaning of "action" is taken from this *everyday* form of life of excuses, slips, and failures that Freud was the first to analyze. Cavell notes:

> Excuses are as essentially implicated in Austin's view of human actions as slips and overdetermination are in Freud's. What does it betoken about human actions that the reticulated constellation of predicates of excuse is made for them—that they can be done unintentionally, unwillingly, involuntarily, insincerely, unthinkingly, inadvertently, heedlessly, carelessly, under duress, under the influence, out of contempt, out of pity, by mistake, by accident, and so on? It betokens, we might say, the all but unending vulnerability of human action, its openness to the independence of the world and the preoccupation of the mind.[36]

The "vulnerability of human action, its openness to the independence of the world and the preoccupation of the mind"—this may constitute another definition of the Everyday, as the *framework* for the vulnerability of form of life. Here form of life is inseparably biological and social, a linkage for which Cavell and Das have both argued, demonstrating that there are not *two meanings* of *Lebensform* but a linkage between the social and the vital in the texture of life. Wittgenstein's anthropological approach seeks to refer to a shared, vulnerable human experience that interacts with the Everyday. "Shared human behaviour is the system of reference by means of which we interpret an unknown language."[37] Cavell clarifies:

> The biological or vertical sense of form of life recalls differences between the human and so-called "lower" or "higher" forms of

life, between, say, poking at your food, perhaps with a fork, and pawing at it, or pecking at it. Here the romance of the hand and its apposable thumb comes into play, and of the upright posture and of the eyes set for heaven; but also the specific strength and scale of the human body and of the human senses and of the human voice.[38]

It is not surprising that it was around this question of the human body (expressive, vulnerable, and suffering) that Cavell and Das offered their own conceptions of form of life. Das explained that the violence against women during the partition of India and Pakistan could not simply be accounted for as a cultural variation in form of life, but that it rather calls attention to the need to redefine human life. "Life form" engenders a new understanding of biopolitics; in situations of extreme violence, war, breakdown, or disaster, the nature of humans may be changed depending on the actions and suffering that they endure. The fragility of forms of life speaks to a vulnerability in the Everyday itself, to mistakes, awkwardness, indifference, and cruelty. The loss of ordinary life (when confronted with madness, disease, or catastrophic and war-torn environments)[39] reveals the urgency of identifying forms of life and connecting human vulnerability to a radical vulnerability of the Everyday.

In his foreword to *Life and Words*, Cavell draws our attention to the maintenance of the texture of everyday life in *all* circumstances and to the ambivalent creativity of women faced with the fragility of this world and precarious life forms. Cavell thus refers to Das's description of the role of women in preserving/reinventing forms of life in times of catastrophe and violence. "[She recognizes] that in the gender-determined division of the work of mourning the results of violence, the role of women is to attend, in a torn world, to the details of everyday life that allow a household to function, collecting supplies, cooking, washing and straightening up, seeing to children, and so on, that allow life to knit itself back into some viable rhythm."[40] Form of life is no longer a matter of institutions or social structures but of life forms that emerge from everyday temporalities. It is then no longer a question of the Ordinary but of the Everyday as something borne, woven each day by the work of women, the work of grief and restoration. The "texture of life" is neither a given nor self-evident; it is forged by both tragedy and domestic reality. What is given and then threatened by disaster is our forms of life, everything that makes up the texture of human existence and human activity, the form that life takes in a collection of natural routines and habits in which language and affects come to be rooted. Das's entire work carries on, and indeed completes, Cavell's *elucidation* of the concept of form of life, engaging it with an elucidation of the *form* of the *Everyday*. Crucially, this elucidation will be gendered and *pointed toward the low*. Das is careful to distance herself from heroic pretenses and the politicization of the ordinary, the call to "give a voice" to those who do not have one, and so on: "It is often considered the task of historiography to break the silences that announce the zones of taboo. There is even something heroic in the image of empowering women to speak and to give voice to the voiceless. I have myself found this a very complicated task."[41] The women in Das's work have an entirely different access to speech and a particular demand for recognition or reparation—a new form of attention to how suffering and breakdown enter, each day, into the Everyday. By further radicalizing Cavell's reading of Wittgenstein, enacting a transition from "forms of life" to the life of forms, of human pain and of the suffering of women, and finally from the Ordinary to the Everyday, Das brings Wittgenstein into new territory.

....

SANDRA LAUGIER is professor of philosophy at the University of Paris 1 Panthéon-Sorbonne and a senior member of the Institut Universitaire de France. She works in moral philosophy, political philosophy, the philosophy of language, gender studies, and popular culture.

....

HANNAH COX received her MA in French language and literature from the University of California, Berkeley, in 2023. She has researched and translated around themes of language and care, notably in the work of second-wave French feminist authors. She lives in Paris and teaches at the Université Paris Nanterre.

Notes

1. Wittgenstein, *Philosophical Investigations*, 116.
2. What I have translated as "find" comes from the French verb *retrouver*, which may more accurately be translated as "find again." *Retrouver* is to find something familiar; it is also used to refer to meeting with a friend. Because English is a satellite-framing language, relying on adverbial particles like "again" to express a path of motion, while French is verb-framing, I often must sacrifice the nuance that a particle could provide for the sake of a smoother syntax.—Translator.
3. See Cavell, *Une nouvelle Amérique encore inapprochable*, 40–42; and Wittgenstein, *Philosophical Investigations*, 123.
4. Wittgenstein, *Philosophical Investigations*, 125.
5. Cavell, *Must We Mean What We Say?*
6. Here we have the first instance of the nominal form of *le quotidien*, which I have translated as "the Everyday" in keeping with Laugier's own translation in her English summary of this article. In its adjectival form, *quotidien* is variously translatable as "everyday," "daily," "day-to-day," or simply "quotidian," and I oscillate between several of these options in my translation.—Translator.
7. Hadot, *Wittgenstein et les limites du langage*.
8. Cavell, *Claim of Reason*; Cavell, *Les voix de la raison*; Diamond, *Realistic Spirit*; Diamond, *L'esprit réaliste*.
9. Wittgenstein, *Philosophical Investigations*, 241.
10. Cavell, *This New Yet Unapproachable America*, 79.
11. Cavell, *In Quest of the Ordinary*, 171.
12. Cavell, *Pursuits of Happiness*; Cavell, *À la recherche du bonheur*.
13. Emerson, "Self-Reliance," 6.
14. Reappearance of *retrouver* or "finding again" (something familiar). See n. 1.—Translator.
15. Dewey frequently invokes Emerson's name. See Dewey, "Emerson—the Philosopher of Democracy."
16. Emerson, "American Scholar," 49; Emerson, "Le savant américain," 564.
17. The original has *revendication*, which is a French cultural concept, coming from the way social movements form and act. Lacking a direct English equivalent, it has to do with (re)claiming an identity or putting forth demands. In this article I translate *revendication* and its verb form, *revendiquer*, variously as "advocate for," "demands," "(lay) claim to," and "revalorization."—Translator.

18. Cavell, *Senses of Walden*, 149.

19. See Brunet, *La naissance de l'idée de photographie*.

20. Cavell, *Senses of Walden*, 149.

21. Emerson, "American Scholar," 65.

22. Emerson, "Expérience."

23. Emerson, "Expérience," 504.

24. Emerson, "Le savant américain," 562.

25. Austin, "Plea for Excuses," 8.

26. Austin, "Plea for Excuses," 9.

27. Cavell, foreword; Wittgenstein, *Philosophical Investigations*, 206.

28. Cavell, foreword, x.

29. Wittgenstein, *Philosophical Investigations*, 415.

30. Wittgenstein, *Philosophical Investigations*, 103.

31. Here I must signal the nuance and tension between the two French verbs in the original, *retourner* and *revenir*. While both may be translated as simply "return" in English, *retourner* evokes a nondescript return to any location previously visited, while *revenir* (and more canonically *rentrer*) speak of a return to the place of inhabitation, of origin, of home. In honoring the themes around care studies that are of importance to both Laugier and Das, I translate *revenir* as "coming home," passing up the more literal translation "coming back."—Translator.

32. Cavell, *In Quest of the Ordinary*, 107–8.

33. Certeau, *L'invention du quotidien*.

34. Perec, *L'infra-ordinaire*, 9. My translation.—Translator.

35. Das, *Textures of the Ordinary*.

36. Cavell, *Pitch of Philosophy*, 87. See also Laugier, "Vulnerability of the Ordinary."

37. Wittgenstein, *Philosophical Investigations*, 359.

38. Cavell, *Une nouvelle Amérique encore inapprochable*, 45.

39. Lovell et al., *Face aux désastres*.

40. Cavell, foreword, xiii–xiv.

41. Das, *Life and Words*, chap. 1.

References

Austin, J. L. "A Plea for Excuses." In *Philosophical Papers*, edited by J. O. Urmson and G. J. Warnock, 175–204. Oxford: Oxford University Press, 1962.

Brunet, François. *La naissance de l'idée de photographie*. Paris: Presses Universitaires de France, 2012.

Cavell, Stanley. *À la recherche du bonheur: Hollywood et la comédie du remariage*. Translated by Christian Fournier and Sandra Laugier. Paris: Vrin, 2017.

Cavell, Stanley. *The Claim of Reason*. New York: Oxford University Press, 1979.

Cavell, Stanley. *Dire et vouloir dire: Livre d'essais*. Translated by Sandra Laugier and Christian Fournier. Paris: Cerf, 2009.

Cavell, Stanley. Foreword to Das, *Life and Words*, ix–xiv.

Cavell, Stanley. *In Quest of the Ordinary: Lines of Skepticism and Romanticism*. Chicago: University of Chicago Press, 1988.

Cavell, Stanley. *Les voix de la raison: Wittgenstein, le scepticisme, la moralité et la tragédie*. Translated by Sandra Laugier and Judith Balso. Paris: Seuil, 1996.

Cavell, Stanley. *Must We Mean What We Say? A Book of Essays*. Cambridge: Cambridge University Press, 1976.

Cavell, Stanley. *A Pitch of Philosophy*. Cambridge, MA: Harvard University Press, 1996.

Cavell, Stanley. *Pursuits of Happiness: The Hollywood Comedy of Remarriage*. Cambridge, MA: Harvard University Press, 1981.

Cavell, Stanley. *The Senses of Walden: An Expanded Edition*. San Francisco: North Point, 1981.

Cavell, Stanley. *This New Yet Unapproachable America*. Chicago: University of Chicago Press, 1989.

Cavell, Stanley. *Une nouvelle Amérique encore inapprochable: De Wittgenstein à Emerson*. Translated by Sandra Laugier. Combas: Éditions de l'Éclat, 1991.

Certeau, Michel de. *L'invention du quotidien*. 2 vols. Paris: Gallimard, 2012.

Das, Veena. *Life and Words: Violence and the Descent into the Ordinary*. Berkeley: University of California Press, 2007.

Das, Veena. *Textures of the Ordinary: Doing Anthropology after Wittgenstein*. New York: Fordham University Press, 2020.

Dewey, John. "Emerson—the Philosopher of Democracy." In vol. 3 of *The Middle Works, 1899–1924*, edited by Jo Ann Boydston, 184–93. Carbondale: Southern Illinois University Press, 1977.

Diamond, Cora. *L'esprit réaliste: Wittgenstein, la philosophie et l'esprit*. Translated by Emmanuel Halais and Jean-Yves Mondon. Paris: Presses Universitaires de France, 2004.

Diamond, Cora. *The Realistic Spirit*. Cambridge, MA: MIT Press, 1991.

Emerson, Ralph Waldo. "The American Scholar." In *The Complete Essays and Other Writings of Ralph Waldo Emerson*, edited by Brooks Atkinson, 45–67. New York: Random House, 1940.

Emerson, Ralph Waldo. "Expérience." Translated by Christian Fournier. In *Qu'est-ce que la philosophie américaine? De Wittgenstein à Emerson*, edited by Stanley Cavell, 504–27. Paris: Gallimard, 2009.

Emerson, Ralph Waldo. *Self-Reliance*. White Plains, NY: Peter Pauper, 1967.

Hadot, Pierre. *Wittgenstein et les limites du langage*. Paris: Vrin, 2004.

Laugier, Sandra. "The Vulnerability of the Ordinary: Goffman, Reader of Austin." Translated by Wayne Wapeemukwa. *Graduate Faculty Philosophy Journal* 39, no. 2 (2019): 367–401.

Lovell, Anne M., Stefania Pandolfo, Veena Das, and Sandra Laugier. *Face aux désastres: Une conversation à quatre fois sur le "care," la folie et les grandes détresses collectives*. Montreuil-sous-Bois: Ithaque, 2013.

Perec, Georges. *L'infra-ordinaire*. Paris: Seuil, 1989.

Wittgenstein, Ludwig. *Philosophical Investigations*. Translated by G. E. M. Anscombe, P. M. S. Hacker, and Joachim Schulte. Hoboken, NJ: Wiley Blackwell, 2009.

Wittgenstein in the Moonlight
On the Nonexistence of Riddles

EESHA KUMAR

The ordinary slips away from us. If we ignore it, we lose it. If we look too closely, it becomes extraordinary, the way words or names become strange if we keep staring at them. The very notion turns into a baffling riddle. Shall we say the ordinary doesn't exist, or that it exists only when we don't look at it too closely?
  Michael Wood

"If it is any point requiring reflection," observed Dupin, as he forbore to enkindle the wick, "we shall examine it to better purpose in the dark."
  Edgar Allan Poe

In the past thirty years of Wittgenstein scholarship,[1] a disagreement about how to read Wittgenstein's enigmatic *Tractatus Logico-Philosophicus* (1921) has hinged on §6.54:

My propositions are elucidatory in this way: he who understands me finally recognizes them as senseless, when he has climbed out

QUI PARLE   Vol. 33, No. 1, June 2024
DOI 10.1215/10418385-11125474   © 2024 Editorial Board, *Qui Parle*

through them, on them, over them. (He must so to speak throw
away the ladder, after he has climbed up on it.)

He must surmount these propositions; then he sees the world
rightly.[2]

From this passage, "resolute" readers have drawn license to regard
the *Tractatus* as a parody of philosophy that brings about a thera-
peutic disenchantment with philosophical claims. "Traditional" readers, on the other hand, hold that the text makes substantial and meaningful philosophical claims.[3] At stake on both sides of the debate,
as Martin Stokhof observes, is an implicit belief about what constitutes a philosophical argument and the goal of philosophy as such.[4]
This article suggests a different approach to the contested proposition: one that looks beyond the resolute-versus-traditionalist debate
but is nevertheless concerned with philosophical method. A spotlight
on philosophical ladders has obscured the more reclusive proposition to which §6.54 is but a footnote. In §6.5 Wittgenstein declares
the nonexistence of riddles: "For an answer which cannot be expressed the question too cannot be expressed. *The riddle* does not
exist."[5] This proposition is often cited in literary studies of the riddle
as genre,[6] but it is not as often the subject of extended philosophical
study. I argue that an emphasis on riddles not only enables a new approach to the figure of the ladder but also reorients and clarifies
persistent concerns (to do with exposure and concealment) through
the arc of Wittgenstein's career. The problematic of the riddle, and the
dynamic it denotes between the enigmatic and the ordinary, is of enor-
mous consequence in philosophy and literary studies, raising questions about the basic structure of our theoretical investments, treatment of texts, and engagements with others.

Arguably, Wittgenstein himself would have wanted the ladder
proposition (§6.54) to be read as an elaboration of his remark on
riddles (§6.5). Recent projects such as the University of Iowa's inter-
active, subway-style *Tractatus* map and Bazzocchi's 2021 edition of
the *Tractatus* present the text in a new and suggestive visual shape,
inspired by the ranked numbering system explained in the *Tractatus*'s
one and only footnote.[7] However, it is not so much authorial intent
that makes this approach compelling as its hermeneutic advantages:

a different arrangement of the text makes it readable in a way that not only is simpler but also lays out new problems, allows us to make analytic leaps and to see connections previously hidden by the format of the printed book. These new presentations of the *Tractatus* bring the proposition on riddles into prominence, making it available as a point of entry into Wittgenstein's body of work. In emphasizing Wittgenstein's interest in riddles and enigma, I offer a characterization of his thought that is different from that encountered, for instance, in Toril Moi's influential *Revolution of the Ordinary* (2017). Moi is emphatic in her argument that "in Wittgenstein's vision of language there is simply no need to think of texts and language as hiding something."[8] In my view, we do not find in *Revolution of the Ordinary* a thorough exposition of the significance of concealment in Wittgenstein's thought; this is a task that this article takes up, or begins to take up. With an exclusive focus on *Philosophical Investigations* (1953),[9] Moi's book is unable to account for the ideas expressed in and about the *Tractatus*, to say nothing of *Lecture on Ethics* (1929) or posthumous volumes such as *Culture and Value*; this is a limitation that this article seeks to address.

Moreover, I do not share Moi's belief that Wittgenstein's philosophy runs counter to dominant traditions of "theory";[10] indeed, I find—and will attempt to demonstrate—that Wittgenstein's philosophy finds felicitous interlocutors in thinkers associated with "theory" or "suspicion" or both, such as G. W. F. Hegel, Theodor W. Adorno, and Emmanuel Levinas. In fact, this essay builds on efforts in the preceding decades to develop or elaborate a "literary Wittgenstein."[11] These works, however, do not take up (or treat as central) Wittgenstein's remark on riddling or his interest in concealment. Marjorie Perloff makes repeated reference to riddling in her wonderful book *Wittgenstein's Ladder*, but her reading of the relevant passage in the *Tractatus* excises entirely the pronouncement on riddles that precedes it.[12] Similarly, Nancy Yousef has brought necessary attention to "a pitch of emotional intensity" in Wittgenstein's writing, its "tone of alarm, importunate appeals, the willingness to be embarrassingly earnest."[13] Yousef notices an important trace of Wittgenstein's interest in the themes of revelation and exposure; I seek to bring these scenes of embarrassment into conversation with Wittgenstein's philosophical treatment of these themes.

Attending to Wittgenstein's writings on riddles—and his riddle-like writings—inspires, above all, the following questions: What is the mise-en-scène of good analysis? What are the right conditions for posing questions and receiving answers? These are vital considerations for critique and criticism. Wittgenstein offers us a theoretical framework in which ordinariness does not fall outside of or sit next to mystery/wonder/enigma but is interwoven with it, such that the crucial question for all analysis is whether one must be obtained at the cost of the other, and under what circumstances it is possible to access one through the other. I argue that the riddle constitutes a through line in Wittgenstein's philosophical trajectory—the breaks and phases of which have led to no small amount of debate—which can be understood as a search for philosophical modes hospitable to enigma, in contrast with the reigning philosophies of his day that treated objects of knowledge as perfectly available, apparent, and comprehensible to logic and philosophy: (perhaps we might say) "ordinary."

This article contextualizes Wittgenstein's best-known claims about the ordinary by juxtaposing them with more enigmatic aspects of his oeuvre. It reveals a crepuscular, moonlit Wittgenstein, deeply invested in a gentle handling of delicate enigma, at a time when the rising authority of the sciences coincided with a declining respect for the mysterious and the unknown. We think we know Wittgenstein as a founder of ordinary language philosophy, as a proponent of ideas like "There is no such thing as a private language" and "What can be said at all can be said clearly."[14] This can give the impression that Wittgenstein privileges the obvious, the banal, the ordinary. In my reading, this is true only in a highly conditional and qualified sense. When we consider riddles and Wittgenstein's approach to them, we find that what these well-known pronouncements register is not necessarily a rejection of depth or suspicion but a profound and enduring interest in epistemological limits and hermeneutic possibilities, questions famously at home in traditions of depth and suspicion. We will track the riddle and its relation to the transcendent in Wittgenstein, beginning with *Tractatus Logico-Philosophicus*, his first published work.

In an undated letter to Ludwig von Ficker, Wittgenstein revealed a "key" to the *Tractatus*; he said that it had two parts and that the more important one consisted of everything he had not written.[15] This unusual format for a first philosophy book may have been inspired by an exchange with Paul Engelmann, who sent him the poem "Count Eberhard's Hawthorn" with the following note: "Almost all other poems (including the good ones) attempt to express the inexpressible, here that is not attempted, and precisely because of that it is achieved." Wittgenstein agreed. The poem, he wrote to Engelmann, is indeed "really magnificent": "And this is how it is: if only you do not try to utter what is unutterable then nothing gets lost. But the unutterable will be—unutterably—contained in what has been uttered!"[16]

This exchange contains a typical movement in Wittgenstein's thought, of which various expressions are scattered in the text of the *Tractatus*, such as §4.115: "[Philosophy] will mean the unspeakable by clearly displaying the speakable." What is captured here is not merely a radical notion of reference but a program for philosophy and a proposal on philosophical method. If Wittgenstein knew that the *Tractatus* needed to be unlocked—thus recognizing (what several commentators have called) its sibylline quality—why did he insist on the nonexistence of the riddle? While his writing often seems direct to the point of bluntness, it is nevertheless strange and cryptic, and invites unraveling. The *Investigations*, Wittgenstein's other major work (published posthumously), is an unwieldy compendium of observations on mental processes and language use, full of rough transitions, sometimes dilating beyond comfort and other times contracting suddenly and sharply. Its technique has been described as "the uninterrupted question without answer, the question destined to provoke irritation, and not an assertion. This is what one might call the style of the bee: torment and sting."[17] Wittgenstein's works are not just riddle-like (in style) but can be thought to contain riddles (in substance). Taking as a model the famous Zen koan "What is the sound of one hand clapping?," several remarks in the *Investigations* are expressible as riddles: If a lion could speak, would we understand it?[18] What time is it on the sun?[19] Where are the teeth of a rose? "Why can't my right hand give my left hand money?" "How does one point twice to the same image?"[20] The list goes on. These riddles appear to us; we see them, read them, think about them; how, then, are we to understand their nonexistence?

§6.5 holds a clue to its own unraveling. The first sentence of this proposition ("For an answer which cannot be expressed the question too cannot be expressed") tells us how we might read "existence" in the next: as a matter of appearance in language, or the possibility of expression. When we experimentally rephrase the statement as "The riddle cannot be expressed," we find Wittgenstein in the company of Levinas, who thought of enigma and phenomena as fundamentally opposed: "Phenomena, apparition in the full light, the relationship with being, ensure immanence as a totality and philosophy as atheism. The enigma, the intervention of a meaning which disturbs phenomena but is quite ready to withdraw like an undesirable stranger, unless one harkens to those footsteps that depart, is transcendence itself, the proximity of the Other as Other."[21] In this light, Wittgenstein's claim against the existence of riddles seems straightforward: if something can be brought into appearance, it is no longer truly mysterious. The wonder evoked by the transcendent, Wittgenstein once said in a gathering with the Vienna Circle, "cannot be expressed in the form of a question, and there is no answer to it."[22] This may be taken as a reflection not only on the nature of the transcendent but also (conversely) on the riddle's discursive format of question and answer, and philosophy's relationship to it.

Wittgenstein and Levinas seem to have shared an interest in what being keeps from coming into being and how to make that available to thought.[23] While their investments and preferred metaphors are often incompatible, both Wittgenstein and Levinas pursue traces of the transcendent where direct perception of it is impossible. The following line from Levinas's essay would not be out of place in the preface to the *Tractatus*: "What can the attentive ear hear, listening at the doorway of language, which by the signification of which it is made closes its own apertures? It is perhaps reasonable to respect the decency of this closed door."[24] The way to do philosophy, then, is to listen at a closed door. This is how Wittgenstein suggests that we respect its decency: "The correct method in philosophy would really be the following: To say nothing except what can be said, i.e. propositions of natural science—i.e. something that has nothing to do with philosophy."[25] When Wittgenstein says in the preface to the *Tractatus* that all problems have been solved, it is a statement not of hubris but of humility, a rueful expression of our limitations. "Even if all possible scientific questions be answered, the problems of life have not been touched at all . . . and just this is the answer."[26] The *Tractatus* thus demonstrates in painful detail that our discourses cannot give us access to that for which we have the most urgent ethical need, and that to demand it from the realm of the sayable is a mistake.[27]

If the kind of answer one seeks is not forthcoming, should one bother at all with asking the question? This was a pressing concern not only for Wittgenstein but other twentieth-century philosophers such as Adorno, who asked whether "there exists an adequacy between the philosophic questions and the possibility of their being answered at all; whether the authentic results of the recent history of these problems is the essential unanswerability of the cardinal philosophic questions."[28] Adorno finds that providing adequate answers is the domain not of philosophy but of the sciences. Scientists carry out "research," which "assumes the reduction of the question to the given and known elements where nothing would seem to matter except the answer."[29] These answers complement and uphold the questions to which they respond. It is this kind of discourse that Wittgenstein holds responsible for blocking enigma and wonder: one in which the question and the answer are both equally available. In this way, the riddle is opposed to enigma; indeed, Hegel held a similar view on the subject, describing riddles as "absolutely solved" in his lecture on aesthetics.[30] A riddle can rob us of the experience of enigma by offering a cheap imitation of it.[31] Wittgenstein seems to wish that mystery could be expressed; this longing is betrayed by his privileging of wonder[32] and his investment in religious and aesthetic experience that he believed could have no expression in a discourse of questions and answers,[33] which seemed at the time to be philosophy's primary mode. One could adapt for Wittgenstein Kafka's famous assessment of hope:[34] there is mystery, an infinite amount of mystery, but not for us.

Wittgenstein's work may be understood as the search for an exit from this discursive structure while acknowledging that the transcendent can never be "shown" except by these means and by the implied limitations of these means. Early on Wittgenstein sets out to mark the limits between the realm of speech and the transcendent realm of silence. Having achieved this, he takes up another philosophical task: "the synopsis of trivialities."[35] (This appears to be another way to respect the decency of the shut door.) There is a commitment to the ordinary as trivial, but it is worth nothing that "triviality itself, and our responses to it, can dramatize a 'chronic sense that our lives are in mortal question.'"[36] The new orientation for philosophy is captured in the motto "Don't think, but look!"[37] How do we keep analysis from getting in the way of seeing things as they are?[38] For Wittgenstein, neither farsightedness nor shortsightedness will do: one must be able to look exactly at what is in plain sight. The epigraph to the *Investigations* ("It is generally the nature of progress to look greater than it really is") articulates the importance of vision, scale, and proportion for proper thinking. Access to the ordinary too, then, is a matter of focus and scale. James C. Klagge draws attention to Wittgenstein's role in World War I as a forward observer tasked with directing artillery fire to specific targets. The cover of Klagge's book no less than its contents highlights the visual aspect of Wittgenstein's military and philosophical endeavors, and a continuity between these domains in terms of the importance of correct vision, of not "missing" the intended goal.[39]

What happens when we fail to "see the world rightly"[40] is powerfully conveyed in the short stories of Edgar Allan Poe, another pertinent interlocutor for Wittgenstein, whose love of the *Detective Story Magazine* is well documented and reflects, I would argue, an abiding interest in effective modes of investigation and analysis.[41] The protagonist of Poe's story "The Sphinx" is a philosopher who recognizes that what appears to be a monstrous beast (because of its proximity in the fanciful narrator's field of vision) is simply a garden-variety moth. His virtue lies in being able to see things exactly as they are.[42] This is a rare trait among philosophers, it would seem. (The idea, however, is not new: consider the dictum *nil sapientiae odiosius acumine nimio*, "there is nothing more odious to wisdom than an excess of cleverness.")[43] A philosopher who fails to see this not only has poor vision, as Wittgenstein seems to suggest, but also bad posture, as Stanley Cavell claims in this striking passage, describing the typical philosopher as one who begins periodically to move through comfortable rooms and along sunny, unobstructed sidewalks as if they were fields of ice, or paths along a precipice—flailing through an unremarkable apartment, hunching along the sides of buildings—and who professes surprise that we let this interfere with maintaining our end of a conversation with him. The metaphysician conceives of himself as thinking about the essence of human language, while he strikes Wittgenstein as intellectually flailing and hunching.[44]

It is not just philosophers who are guilty of bad seeing. In Poe's story "The Purloined Letter," the Parisian police are unable to find a valuable letter that has gone missing because their search is too thorough and goes on indefinitely; they fail even though—indeed because—they employ "eyes," "probes," "gimlets," and "microscopes,"[45] whereas M. Dupin, surrounded often by shadows and "curling eddies of smoke,"[46] recovers the stolen missive. When Dupin (wearing green spectacles) visits the pilfering minister (known as the thief from the very beginning), it is not easy for him to locate the letter, even though it is sitting out in the open. This is because it has been placed in a different envelope,[47]

> radically different from the one which the Prefect had read us so minute a description. Here the seal was large and black, with the D—— cipher; there it was small and red, with the ducal arms of the S—— family. Here, the address, to the minster, was diminutive and feminine; there the superscription, to a certain royal personage, was marked bold and decided; the size alone formed a point of correspondence. But, then, the radicalness of these differences, which was excessive; the dirt; the soiled and torn condition of the paper. . . a design to delude the beholder into the worthlessness of the document.[48]

Here concealment consists not in relocating the letter to some undiscoverable place (which, as the story suggests, could not possibly exist under the police's gaze) but in changing its outward appearance and leaving it exactly where it is.

The situations and circumstances described in both stories call for modes of reading (or looking) that in each case adapt to respond to the unique demands of the text (or object) in question, allowing it to transform and refigure the reader/critic in its presence. This is Dupin's technique: "When I wish to find out how wise, or how stupid, or how good, or how wicked is any one, or what are his thoughts at the moment, I fashion the expression of my face, as accurately as possible, in accordance with the expression of his, and then wait to see what thoughts or sentiments arise in my mind or heart, as if to match or correspond with the expression."[49] What is described here is a mode of hospitality toward the object of study that does not give over to it completely. If it is enigma we are dealing with, we need to find a way to think about it without rendering it mundane, without robbing it of its mystique and therefore misunderstanding it completely, without "exhibiting, denuding, undressing, unveiling: the familiar acrobatics of the metaphor of truth."[50] Disciplines that arrogate to themselves the task of establishing truth tend to be uncomfortable with the fanciful and fictional (which must be chastised and humbled), and even with the figurative in language as such. In "White Mythology" Jacques Derrida takes a critical stance against the desire to eradicate metaphor from philosophy so that only literal, unambiguous, and true statements remain, which amounts only to the suppression of the metaphorical constitution of language itself.[51] Derrida excoriates these "dreams of nakedness" that characterize psychoanalytic reading in general,[52] and in Jacques Lacan's reading of "The Purloined Letter" in particular. Lacan in his seminar on Poe's story insists on bringing it into "broad daylight" even as he recognizes that "nothing of the drama could be grasped, neither seen or heard, without, dare we say, the *twilighting* which the narration, in each scene, casts on the point of view that one of the actors had while performing it."[53] In doing so, Lacan repeats the established expository posture of philosophy that is inhospitable and unfriendly toward enigma.

By contrast, friendliness toward enigma—inspired by Wittgenstein via Poe—might seem opposed to the notion of hidden depths and a hermeneutics of suspicion;[54] it might evoke practices adjacent to surface reading,[55] or perhaps "close but not deep" reading.[56] There is a general sense that Wittgenstein's most salient offerings to literary studies are tools and arguments for the postcritical/posttheoretical turn. I do not share this view. On my reading, Wittgenstein does not deny what we might understand as "depth." That is, he does not deny that there is a "closed door";[57] he does insist, however, that the door is not for us to open and, further, that "there is no point in talking about it, unless of course you want [people] to admire the room from the outside!"[58] This is different from saying that nothing is concealed. Consider the following remarks written during the composition of the *Tractatus*:

> I know that this world exists.
> That I am placed in it like my eye in its visual field.
> That something about it is problematic, which we call its meaning.
> That this meaning does not lie in it but *outside it* . . .
> The meaning of life, i.e. the meaning of the world, we can call God.[59]

Wittgenstein's (perhaps more familiar) formula of meaning as use in the *Investigations* might be read as an expression of the inaccessibility (and simultaneous inexorability) of meaning as "God." This latter meaning is expressed, and can be gleaned only, through the existence of this world as it is. I have attempted to show that this position is best understood through textual resources one might call "suspicious," "theoretical," or "continental": for instance, Levinas's distinction between enigma and phenomena, Hegel's distinction between enigma and riddle, or Poe's insight about analysis getting in its own way. These sources and traditions make possible a certain understanding of Wittgenstein's thought, without which his notion of "grammar" loses its particular force and ethical charge. The configuration Wittgenstein articulates between language and meaning (on two sides of an unsurpassable limit)[60] simultaneously renders the ordinary (the world as it is) meaningless and makes it the domain of the philosopher's work. It is the domain where forms of life shine through as mute traces of metaphysical meaning. And the absolute is imagined not just as ethereal heaven but also as bedrock,[61] like the eye that enables vision but cannot itself be seen visually. If we would like to think of as "ordinary" the conditions of possibility of our lives, for these are the grounds and foundations of our experience— fundamental, basic, and yet unremarked on—then this ordinary realm too is imbued with a new significance ("theology as grammar").[62] Wittgenstein sometimes refers to this foundation as natural history: "What we are supplying are really remarks on the *natural history* of human beings; *not curiosities*, however, but facts that no one has doubted, which have escaped notice because they are always before our eyes."[63]

Wittgenstein's writing on natural history and his references to nature (in particular to animals such as the duck rabbit, boxed beetle, bottled fly, talking lion, angry orangutan, expectant dog, intent cat, inferring squirrel, toothless goose, and more) have attracted a great deal of critical attention, some of which goes down the route of animal rights and environmental ethics. Wittgenstein's writing plausibly lends itself to such departures.[64] However, "life" in the later Wittgenstein and concepts such as natural history have less to do with nature (which he says he may as well "invent" for the purposes of writing philosophy),[65] and more to do with the limits of thinking, which, as we have seen, was a question of importance for him even in the *Tractatus*. In that early work, he attempts to demonstrate thought within its logical limits and expects his readers to infer the profundity of those limits. In his later work he describes not logical but practical limits as the bedrock that turns the spade.[66] If it is life that we seek to explain, language reveals that final explanations will not be found in theories but in the grammar of life: in how we live when we are not paying attention. This explicit turn to the pragmatic in Wittgenstein's later thought is illustrated in questions such as "Why do I not satisfy myself that I have two feet when I want to get up from a chair? There is no why. I simply don't. This is how I act."[67]

Wittgenstein's turn to grammar and forms of life is important not only because it eliminates the error that arises when we look for answers in more abstract realms but also because it reflects moral values that Wittgenstein held dear: intellectual honesty and humility. Discerning the marked influence of Saint Augustine on the *Investigations*, Ray Monk writes: "[Wittgenstein] often remarked that the problem of writing good philosophy and of thinking about philosophical problems was one of the will more than of the intellect—the will to resist the temptation to misunderstand, the will to resist superficiality. What gets in the way of genuine understanding is often not one's lack of intelligence but the presence of one's pride."[68] That

Wittgenstein valued the qualities of humility, gentleness, and temperance[69] is reflected in his reaction to the sight of the moon rising at the top of a hill two years before his death in 1951: "'If I had planned it, I should never have made the sun at all. See! How beautiful! The sun is too bright and too hot.' Later he said, 'And if there were only the moon, there would be no reading and writing.'"[70] Much earlier in his life, before he had written the *Tractatus*, Wittgenstein had an argument with his adviser, Bertrand Russell, about taking self-imposed exile in Norway. Russell recalls that he pushed back against Wittgenstein's decision: "I said it would be dark, & he said he hated daylight. I said it would be lonely, & he said he prostituted his mind talking to intelligent people. I said he was mad & he said God preserve him from sanity. (God certainly will.)"[71] Wittgenstein's remarks on the sun and his "hatred" of daylight recall Dupin's principled rejection of illumination[72]—and his use of green spectacles. In the hot light of the sun—as of logic—everything is exposed and nothing is understood. Riddles have answers only in the philosophy of noontime, and, like Sancho Panza, we might as well be told the solution before the problem and be done with it.[73]

While some have read Wittgenstein's later work as a farewell to philosophy, what he wishes to end is perhaps somewhat narrower: reading and writing (and this too may have been said in jest). Wittgenstein was tormented by the prospect, and process, of composing and publishing philosophy books, and his mind was often on books that were not books: for instance, "a book on Ethics which really was a book on Ethics" that "would, with an explosion, destroy all the other books in the world"[74]—in Eli Friedlander's words, "the apocalyptic book."[75] In his lectures on aesthetics, Wittgenstein described a book with chapters on "parts of speech . . . the verbs 'seeing,' 'feeling,' etc. Verbs describing personal experience. . . . You would have another chapter on numerals . . . a chapter on 'all,' 'any,' 'some,' etc. . . . a chapter on 'you,' 'I,' etc."[76] Among his publications, lost until recently, was a dictionary for elementary-school children. These are not commonplace philosophy books, to say nothing of the singularity of the two major works published during his lifetime, the *Tractatus* and the *Investigations*. Wittgenstein can thus be seen as involved in an urgent search for philosophy beyond a narrow conception of reading and writing, beyond the disciplinary sedimentations that became synonymous with the pursuit itself, for a philosophy beyond philosophy.

Wittgenstein's preference for moonlight is primarily intellectual: it is part of *the* mise-en-scène of good analysis. It is a question of the temperature of philosophy. While much of his writing may have had something of a febrile quality, Wittgenstein's ideal was "a certain coolness."[77] In anything hotter than moonlight, we see too much, and at the same time, not enough. The arctic glare of logic[78] reduces enigmas to mere riddles; but enigma has better chances of survival in more temperate climes. §6.5 of the *Tractatus* should not prevent us from seeing riddles where they appear—that is, everywhere in Wittgenstein's corpus. Wittgenstein's investment in ordinary language should not keep us from confronting the strangeness of his works and their yearning for transcendence. As Philip R. Shields writes: "Wittgenstein strives to look at everything as though it were a miracle."[79] Reveling in the moonlight is not a renunciation of philosophy or of thought. Rather, in the moonlight, we find a way of doing philosophy that gives us an alternative to its total renunciation. While Cavell finds a philosophical lineage as ancient as Plato in Wittgenstein's break with philosophy,[80] Alain Badiou places Wittgenstein in a smaller group, in the company of Friedrich Nietzsche and Lacan, writing that "anti-philosophy is always what, at its very extremes, states the new duty of philosophy, or its new possibility in the figure of a new duty."[81]

"Wittgenstein's full stop," as D. Z. Phillips puts it, has an undeniable significance for logical analysis and for the study of ethics, but also plays its role in the drama of our daily life with others.[82] We have seen that concealment is not an obstacle to understanding but the very thing that makes it possible: the moonlight, wafts of smoke, shadows, and green spectacles somehow allow us to see just enough. At the same time, unconcealment is a mode of mystery's self-preservation. What does this mean for our shared forms of life? When Wittgenstein says that we should put a lock on a door if we do not want anyone to enter it, he says it in the context of sharing one's philosophical work with a loved one:

> The book must automatically separate those who understand it from those who do not. Even the foreword is written just for those who understand the book.

Telling someone something he does not understand is pointless, even if you add that he will not be able to understand it. (That so often happens with someone you love.)

If you have a room which you do not want certain people to get into, put a lock on it for which they do not have the key. But there is no point in talking about it, unless of course you want them to admire the room from the outside![83]

If Wittgenstein was invested in the appearance of enigma in philosophy, he was also interested in the mysteries that are people: other minds. Scenes of exposure interest him not only in philosophy but also in everyday life shared with others. (Indeed, we might consider the two pursuits hermeneutically conjoined; in a striking essay Tiffany Atkinson suggests that "we might call 'reading'" the "two-way 'exposure'" that marks moments of embarrassment.)[84] Wittgenstein's insights about the right temperature and intensity of analysis seem relevant to everyday encounters in our closest communities. We do not seem to fully know the people we are close to, let alone strangers, and that not-knowing seems to be at the heart of our shared forms of life. Love is no guarantee of understanding, and in fact it seems necessary to keep some doors shut in the interest of love. The idea that love means baring oneself is in constant tension with a desire to conceal oneself out of shame, "because we don't want anyone else to look inside us, since it's not a pretty sight in there."[85] Almost with a tone of indignation, Wittgenstein asks:

Why shouldn't a man suddenly become much more mistrustful towards others? Why not much more withdrawn? Or devoid of love? Don't people get like this even in the ordinary course of events?— Where, in such cases, is the line between will and ability? Is it that I will not open my heart to anyone anymore, or that I cannot? If so much can lose its savor, why not everything? If people are wary even in ordinary life why shouldn't they—perhaps suddenly— become much more wary? And much more inaccessible?[86]

It is precisely in quotidian circumstances that such inaccessibility and remoteness plays out a high drama. This passage suggests that the natural condition of the heart is to be closed, and that its opening and closing is not mechanical, or even organic, but entirely unexpected, painful, and mysterious even to oneself: "Why shouldn't a man *suddenly* become much more mistrustful towards others?"[87] We do not understand these sudden events, nor what stimulus will suddenly unlock and expose us, "though [we] have closed [ourselves] as fingers."[88]

What bearing does such personal closing and opening have on the publicness of language, of which Wittgenstein is seen as a proponent? Cavell detects a note of fantasy in Wittgenstein's descriptions of private language,[89] a yearning for a privacy of the soul made impossible by language.[90] The fact that we share language did not stop Wittgenstein from feeling like "an alien in this world."[91] Nor does shared language make it any easier to love one's neighbor. While privacy in language may be a fantasy, so too is transparency in language. The enigma of language tries to pass itself off as mundane and unremarkable, like the stolen letter in Poe's story. To what higher status could any enigma aspire than to be completely unconcealed; to show everything, and hide nothing?[92] This is another way in which Wittgenstein's attention to the ordinary does not preclude a profound investment in enigma. Why else pay such close attention to the words of others? Wittgenstein attends carefully to them, painstakingly considering why a person says a certain thing, when, and in what context. What do they mean by it? The words of others are given the same attention as enigma; one listens to others as if at closed doors.

Wittgenstein's comments on riddles in the *Tractatus* are a comment on the possibility of the appearance of enigma in a given philosophical approach or mode. That riddles (with questions and answers) are distinguished from enigma—of which the only clue is the seeming transparency of language, and more specifically, logical language—is another hint that more than one kind of philosophical practice is possible. Although Wittgenstein claimed not to have read much philosophy, and his citational practice reflects a relative dearth of philosophical "texts" as objects, his work can be seen to have profound hermeneutic concerns and consequences. If love, or self-exposure, is "man's greatest happiness," why does a public language make its realization so difficult?[93] How do we touch the veil of language in a way that allows the enigma to stay hidden behind it? These concerns seem to have driven the change in style from the *Tractatus* to the *Investigations*. The transition has been thought of in many ways, and here I propose another: as the move from the impossibility of riddles in logic to the great riddle of the ordinary—what exists only when you do not look at it too closely?[94] Not looking too closely, but just far enough, is an ideal captured in Wittgenstein's rejection in 1930 of the figure of the ladder, "for the place I really have to get to is a place I must already be at now. Anything that I might reach by climbing a ladder does not interest me."[95] Wittgenstein's rejection of the ladder is a sign of his commitment to the ordinary, both as the only possible kind of experience (if the transcendent is to remain transcendent) and as posing the greatest and most compelling hermeneutic and interpretative challenges. The closures and disclosures that make our existence possible, as emotional and thinking beings, can be examined only under a soft illumination.

EESHA KUMAR is a PhD candidate in comparative literature at New York University. She is writing a dissertation on enumerative thinking, studying lists and kinds through a range of eclectic sources: Sanskrit poetics, experimental fictions, theories of caste, and Western philosophy.

Acknowledgments

My thanks to Annabel Barry and Joel Auerbach, with assistance from Duke University Press, for their sharp editorial interventions. For feedback on previous iterations of this essay—and warm encouragement—I am grateful to Wesley Cornwell, Olivia Stowell, Tarushi Sonthalia, Andrea Gadberry, and Hent de Vries.

Notes

1. Following Diamond, "Throwing Away the Ladder."
2. Wittgenstein, *Tractatus Logico-Philosophicus*, trans. Ogden, §6.54.
3. For an overview of the debate, see Bronzo, "Resolute Reading and Its Critics."

4. Stokhof, "Quest for Purity," 279–80.
5. Wittgenstein, *Tractatus Logico-Philosophicus*, trans. Ogden, §6.5.
6. See, e.g., Bryant, *Dictionary of Riddles*, 4.
7. University of Iowa *Tractatus* Map; Wittgenstein, *Tractatus Logico-Philosophicus*, ed. Bazzocchi.
8. Moi, *Revolution of the Ordinary*, 178.
9. In my view, Moi's treatment does not do justice to the difficulties of reading even *Philosophical Investigations*. For instance, she bases her claim that "nothing is hidden" for Wittgenstein on §435, in which there is a veritable (though not uncharacteristic) mélange of voices that are difficult to pull apart and assign either to Wittgenstein or to an imagined antagonistic interlocutor, where one does not know for certain whether quotations (e.g., from Saint Augustine in §436) are being used as supportive scaffolding or being held up as examples of poor philosophical thinking. At the very least, such instances pose interpretative problems worthy of acknowledgment and careful consideration. For more on the "voices" in the *Investigations*, see Higgins, "Wittgenstein's New Way of Talking to Himself."
10. Moi, *Revolution of the Ordinary*, 1.
11. See Gibson and Huemer, *Literary Wittgenstein*.
12. Perloff, *Wittgenstein's Ladder*, 17, 22, xiv.
13. Yousef, *Aesthetic Commonplace*, 2, 8–9.
14. Wittgenstein, "Preface," *Tractatus Logico-Philosophicus*, trans. Ogden, 27.
15. Monk, *Wittgenstein*, 178.
16. Monk, *Wittgenstein*, 150–51.
17. Badiou, *Wittgenstein's Anti-philosophy*, 169.
18. Wittgenstein, *Philosophical Investigations*, §XI.
19. Wittgenstein, *Philosophical Investigations*, §§350–51. See also Diamond, "What Time Is It on the Sun?"
20. Wittgenstein, *Philosophical Investigations*, §X, §268, §382.
21. Levinas, "Enigma and Phenomenon," 74.
22. Quoted in Waismann, *Wittgenstein and the Vienna Circle*, 68.
23. Of course, Wittgenstein had a very different attitude toward the metaphysical—the fact of existence was for him a primary source of wonder—than Levinas, whose career was dedicated to overturning metaphysics as first philosophy. For Levinas, moreover, the mystical must remain invisible, whereas for Wittgenstein, it must be "shown," even if it is not, and cannot be, said.

24. Levinas, "Enigma and Phenomenon," 74.
25. Wittgenstein, *Tractatus Logico-Philosophicus*, trans. Ogden, §6.53.
26. Wittgenstein, *Tractatus Logico-Philosophicus*, trans. Ogden, §6.52.
27. In this sentiment Wittgenstein echoes Kant, who, in perhaps the only joke in *The Critique of Pure Reason*, says that to ask an unreasonable question is "embarrassing, the ridiculous sight (as the ancients said) of one person milking a billy-goat while the other holds a sieve underneath" (*Critique of Pure Reason*, 197).
28. Adorno, "Actuality of Philosophy," 124.
29. Adorno, "Actuality of Philosophy," 126.
30. Hegel, *Aesthetics*, 398. See also Taylor, "Riddle," 139.
31. The absurdity of our answers to truly significant questions is illustrated in an episode of Douglas Adams's 1969 novel *The Hitchhiker's Guide to the Galaxy*. In it a computer is built to calculate the meaning of "Life, the Universe, and Everything." It is named Deep Thought, and it is "so amazingly intelligent that even before its data banks had been connected up, it had started from *I think therefore I am* and got as far as deducting the existence of rice pudding and income tax before anyone managed to turn it off" (*Ultimate Hitchhiker's Guide*, 111). At the end of its analysis, it has a simple answer—42—which is met with disappointment and bewilderment. But logic, or the realm of the sayable, can only give such answers, and it is our mistake to put questions to it that it is fundamentally incapable of answering. When Deep Thought is asked if this is all it has to show for seven and a half million years' work, it insists that it checked the answer thoroughly and that there is no error on its part: the problem is that the hyperintelligent race that created it had never actually known the question (121).
32. See Wittgenstein, *Lecture on Ethics*.
33. Some have argued that if philosophers are to engage in the game of questions and answers at all, their answers must be such that they obliterate their questions, because "philosophy never actually held a stake in the knowledge field anyway" (Stokhof, "Quest for Purity," 284). Philosophy for Adorno is this kind of riddle solving, where the "function of riddle solving is to light up the riddle-*Gestalt* like lightning and to negate it" ("Actuality of Philosophy," 127). Even though this kind of radical negation seems a more appropriate philosophical response to a question, it upholds the structure of question and answer, problem and (non)solution, call and response.
34. "Oh, there is hope, an infinite amount of hope, just not for us." Quoted in Barnouw, *Weimar Intellectuals and the Threat of Modernity*, 187.

35. Wittgenstein, *Wittgenstein's Lectures*, 26.

36. Wood, "Why Praise Astaire?"

37. Wittgenstein, *Philosophical Investigations*, §61.

38. A question this raises for this special issue is the relationship of the ordinary to things as they are, or the status quo.

39. Klagge, *Wittgenstein's Artillery*. This book provides an account of Wittgenstein's turn (following his experience at the front) toward the poetic, the noncognitive, and appeals to temperament rather than to intellect. Regardless of the specific relationship (causal or otherwise) of this turn and Wittgenstein's experience as an artillery spotter, this book highlights precisely the aspects of Wittgenstein's thinking that interest me.

40. Wittgenstein, *Philosophical Investigations*, §6.54.

41. Monk, *Wittgenstein*, 355.

42. One might object, arguing that the change of aspect that transforms the Sphinx in the title—from a terrifying creature bearing the omen of death, into *insecta lepidoptera crepuscularia sphinx*—closely resembles the extermination of the miracle by science described in Wittgenstein's *Lecture on Ethics*. However, the first appearance of the Sphinx does not count as a true miracle according to Wittgenstein's own criteria in the *Lecture on Ethics*. For anything to evoke wonder in an absolute sense, we must be unable to imagine its opposite. For instance, because we cannot coherently imagine the world not existing (because if the world did not exist, we could not imagine it existing or not existing), wonder at the existence of the world is true, language-confounding wonder. The beast in Poe's story *can* be imagined as other than it is, and as soon as it is, it is revealed to be a harmless bug. The salient message in the story remains the importance of clear vision, even if the aim is to correctly identify a miracle. See Wittgenstein, *Lecture on Ethics*, 47–49.

43. This is, incidentally, the epigraph to another of Poe's short stories, "The Purloined Letter." Poe attributes the saying to Seneca, although it was more likely Petrarch's. Barbara Johnson thinks about the implications of this misattribution in "Frame of Reference."

44. Cavell, "Wittgensteinian Event," 14.

45. Poe, *Eighteen Best Stories*, 258.

46. Poe, *Eighteen Best Stories*, 244. It is noteworthy that the origin of the word *camouflage* is the French word *camouflet*, which in the seventeenth century referred to smoke blown in someone's face as a prank (*Dictionnaires Le Robert*, https://dictionnaire.lerobert.com/ [accessed August 1, 2021]).

47. Such concealment recalls Hegel's discussion of riddles. He says that the solution to any riddle must be sought by guessing at its "obscure and perplexed envelope." This is W. M. Bryant's more colorful translation (Hegel, *Philosophy of Art*, 38). T. M. Knox's translation is "this apparently confused disguise," which is also suggestive, for being at once apparent and confused (Hegel, *Aesthetics*, 1:398). It recalls the previous discussion of Levinas and Wittgenstein, and the necessity of saying without saying. Wittgenstein reminds us to "not forget that a poem even though it is composed in the language of information is not used in the language-game of giving information" (*Zettel*, 28e).

48. Poe, *Eighteen Best Stories*, 261.

49. Poe, *Eighteen Best Stories*, 254.

50. Derrida, "Purveyor of Truth," 175.

51. Derrida, "White Mythology."

52. Derrida, "Purveyor of Truth," 175.

53. Lacan, "Seminar on 'The Purloined Letter,'" 52, 29; emphasis added.

54. See Felski, *Limits of Critique*.

55. See Best and Marcus, "Surface Reading."

56. See Love, "Close but Not Deep."

57. Wittgenstein, *Culture and Value*, 7e–8e. Wittgenstein, an avid reader of Dostoevsky, mentioned to his friend O. K. Bouwsma that while he enjoyed *The Brothers Karamazov*, the novel that he really wanted to return to was *Crime and Punishment*. A lot of listening at closed doors takes place in the novel, and Wittgenstein seemed particularly struck by the fact that after all his extensive preparations for the eponymous crime, Raskolnikov forgets to lock the door (Bouwsma, *Wittgenstein*, 11). On the motif of doors, one is reminded also of Emily Dickinson's poem "As there are apartments in our own Minds that—we never enter without Apology—we should respect the seals of others—" (*Envelope Poems*, 90–91).

58. Wittgenstein, *Culture and Value*, 7e.

59. Monk, *Wittgenstein*, 140; emphasis added.

60. This brings Wittgenstein's view of language close, in my opinion, to Ferdinand de Saussure's—a possibility that Moi rejects outright (*Revolution of the Ordinary*, 113–28).

61. There are two ways, Wittgenstein suggests, in which "bedrock" may be glimpsed: "first, to keep in mind that things are as they are; second, to seek *illuminating comparisons* to get an understanding of how they are" (Monk, *Wittgenstein*, 51; emphasis added). This evokes the "associative

imagination" attributed by Hegel (*Aesthetics*, 398) and, more recently, Daniel Heller-Roazen (*Dark Tongues*, 136–43) to riddling. This would suggest that the mental and linguistic processes associated with riddling form part of Wittgenstein's method. A line of inquiry opens up here regarding the relationship of metaphor, metaphysical language, and riddling. I would argue that some of Wittgenstein's best-known propositions may be read as metaphors, or riddles in reverse (extrapolating from Heller-Roazen, *Dark Tongues*, 68). If predicative definitions and riddles mirror each other in the order of subject and predicate, metaphor can be experienced as a kind of riddle in which neither element is missing; a subject and a predicate are brought together, and the frisson arising from the missing basis of comparison can produce a cognition that makes the world "vivid" again. See Ricoeur, *Rule of Metaphor*; and Cohen, *Thinking of Others*. Also to be further explored is Wittgenstein's dislike of metaphysical language (*Philosophical Investigations*, §116) in light of the aforementioned recent literature on the force of the copula *is* in metaphor.

62. Wittgenstein, *Philosophical Investigations*, §373.

63. Wittgenstein, *Philosophical Investigations*, §415; emphasis added.

64. See, e.g., Levvis, "Why We Would Not Understand a Talking Lion."

65. Wittgenstein, *Philosophical Investigations*, pt. 2, xii.

66. Wittgenstein, *Philosophical Investigations*, §217. This bedrock is best conveyed in certain passages in *On Certainty*. In this text Wittgenstein says that we operate with a "comfortable certainty . . . something that lies beyond being unjustified or justified; as it were, as something *animal*" (*On Certainty*, §§358–59; emphasis added). In more colloquial terms, "The squirrel does not infer by induction that it is going to need stores next winter as well" (§287).

67. Wittgenstein, *On Certainty*, §148.

68. Monk, *Wittgenstein*, 366.

69. While we make such a claim, it is important to acknowledge Wittgenstein's famous bouts of anger and even physical violence toward his students when he was a schoolteacher. That he did not practice gentleness does not mean that it was not (or would not later in his life become) a value of great importance for him. In fact, the apologies he made a decade later for his heinous behavior (Monk, *Wittgenstein*, 370–72) may have had something to do with his great yearning to be other than he was.

70. Bouwsma, *Wittgenstein*, 12.

71. Monk, *Wittgenstein*, 91.

72. See Perloff's discussion of Jacques Bouveresse on the "spirit of radical poverty in philosophy" and Cavell on "philosophizing as spiritual struggle" in *Wittgenstein's Ladder*, 16–17.

73. Hegel, *Aesthetics*, 397.

74. Wittgenstein, *Lecture on Ethics*, 46.

75. Friedlander, *Signs of Sense*, 13.

76. Wittgenstein, *Lectures and Conversations*, 1.

77. Wittgenstein, *Culture and Value*, 2e. Faced with this clash of temperatures, one is reminded of a wonderfully strange remark in Wittgenstein's notes: "the delightful way the various parts of the human body differ in temperature" (11e).

78. Wittgenstein, *Philosophical Investigations*, §107.

79. Shields, *Logic and Sin*, 111.

80. Cavell, "Wittgensteinian Event," 24.

81. Badiou, "Who Is Nietzsche?," 10.

82. Phillips, "Wittgenstein's Full Stop."

83. Wittgenstein, *Culture and Value*, 7e.

84. Atkinson, "Black and White and Re(a)d All Over," 117. Note the reference to a folk riddle in the title of this essay on the poetics of embarrassment.

85. Wittgenstein, *Culture and Value*, 46e.

86. Wittgenstein, *Culture and Value*, 54e. In "The Avoidance of Love" Cavell reflects on this "line between will and ability," for self-exposure and for being seen; he suggests that to have another person truly see us may be unbearable. Cordelia is dangerous because she acknowledges Lear's bottomless need for love and exposes his inability to receive it. As Cavell puts it: "We care whether love is or is not altogether forbidden to man, whether we may not altogether be incapable of it, of admitting it into our world. We wonder whether we may always go mad between the equal efforts and terrors at once of rejecting and accepting love. The soul is torn between them, the body feels torn . . . and the solution to this insoluble condition is to wish for the tearing apart of the world" ("Avoidance of Love," 300). Compare this figure of tearing in Cavell with this remark by Wittgenstein: "The linings of my heart keep sticking together and to open it I should each time have to tear them apart" (*Culture and Value*, 57e).

87. Wittgenstein, *Culture and Value*, 54e; emphasis added.

88. Cummings, "somewhere I have never travelled, gladly beyond," 65. As much as we may resent our involuntary disclosures, we may equally

resent the exposures of others to us; like Ivan in *The Brothers Kar-amazov*, who acerbically suggests that beggars "should ask for alms through the newspapers," because we cannot bear to confront their need (Dostoevsky, *The Brothers Karamazov*, 237).

89. Cavell, *Claim of Reason*, 344.

90. That this "privacy" was an abiding interest of Wittgenstein's may be supported by an essay of Cora Diamond's that finds in metaphors of logical space, accomplishments of logical analysis, and treatment of quantifiers a private language argument in the *Tractatus* ("Does Bismarck Have a Beetle in His Box?").

91. Monk, *Wittgenstein*, 516.

92. This idea is expressed in Hent de Vries's reading of Walter Benjamin's "Rastelli Narrates": "Tout montrer, ne rien cacher, voilà qui est plus miraculeux dans tout les cas que ce que la magie (ancienne ou moderne) pourrait espérer" (To show everything, hide nothing, is more miraculous in every case than magic [ancient or modern] could hope for) ("Excursus II," 91).

93. Wittgenstein, *Culture and Value*, 77e.

94. A paraphrase from Wood, "Why Praise Astaire?"

95. Wittgenstein, *Culture and Value*, 7e. The last lines of Yeats's poem "The Circus Animals' Desertion" might as well have been written for Wittgenstein (and Cavell): "Now that my ladder's gone / I must lie down where all the ladders start / In the foul rag and bone shop of the heart" (*Collected Poems*, 347–48).

References

Adams, Douglas. *The Ultimate Hitchhiker's Guide to the Galaxy*. New York: Ballantine, 2002.

Adorno, Theodor W. "The Actuality of Philosophy." *Telos*, no. 31 (1977): 120–33.

Atkinson, Tiffany. "Black and White and Re(a)d All Over: The Poetics of Embarrassment." In *The Writer in the Academy: Creative Interfrictions*, edited by Richard Marggraf Turley, 113–31. London: Boydell and Brewer, 2011.

Badiou, Alain. "Who Is Nietzsche?" Translated by Alberto Toscano. *PLI: The Warwick Journal of Philosophy* 11 (2001): 1–11.

Badiou, Alain. *Wittgenstein's Anti-philosophy*. New York: Verso, 2011.

Barnouw, Dagmar. *Weimar Intellectuals and the Threat of Modernity*. Bloomington: Indiana University Press, 1988.

Best, Stephen, and Sharon Marcus. "Surface Reading: An Introduction."
Representations, no. 108 (2009): 1–21.

Bouwsma, O. K. *Wittgenstein: Conversations, 1949–1951.* Indianapolis,
IN: Hackett, 1986.

Bronzo, Silver. "The Resolute Reading and Its Critics: An Introduction to
the Literature." *Wittgenstein-Studien* 3, no. 1 (2012): 45–80.

Bryant, Mark. *Dictionary of Riddles.* London: Routledge, 1990.

Cavell, Stanley. "The Avoidance of Love: A Reading of King Lear." In *Must
We Mean What We Say?*, 267–353. Cambridge: Cambridge University
Press, 1976.

Cavell, Stanley. *The Claim of Reason: Wittgenstein, Skepticism, Morality,
and Tragedy.* New York: Oxford University Press, 1979.

Cavell, Stanley. "The Wittgensteinian Event." In *Reading Cavell*, edited
by Alice Crary and Sanford Shieh, 8–25. London: Taylor and Francis
Group, 2006.

Cohen, Ted. *Thinking of Others: On the Talent for Metaphor.* Princeton,
NJ: Princeton University Press, 2008.

Cummings, E. E. "somewhere I have never travelled, gladly beyond." In *Selected Poems*, edited by Richard S. Kennedy, 65. New York: Liveright,
1994.

Derrida, Jacques. "The Purveyor of Truth." Translated by Alan Bass. In
The Purloined Poe: Lacan, Derrida, and Psychoanalytic Reading,
edited by John P. Muller and William J. Richardson, 173–212. Baltimore: Johns Hopkins University Press, 1988.

Derrida, Jacques. "White Mythology: Metaphor in the Text of Philosophy." Translated by F. C. T. Moore. *New Literary History* 6, no. 1
(1974): 5–74.

de Vries, Hent. *Le miracle au coeur de l'ordinaire.* Paris: Encre Marine,
2019.

Diamond, Cora. "Does Bismarck Have a Beetle in His Box? The Private Language Argument in the *Tractatus*." In *The New Wittgenstein*,
edited by Alice Crary and Rupert Read, 262–92. London: Routledge,
2000.

Diamond, Cora. "Throwing Away the Ladder: How to Read the *Tractatus*." *Philosophy*, no. 243 (1988): 5–27.

Diamond, Cora. "What Time Is It on the Sun? An Interview with Cora Diamond." *Harvard Review of Philosophy* 8 (2000): 69–81.

Dickinson, Emily. *Envelope Poems*, with transcriptions by Marta L. Werner
and Jen Bervin. New York: Christine Bergin/New Directions, 2016.

Dostoevsky, Fyodor. *The Brothers Karamazov*. Translated by Richard Pevear and Larissa Volokhonsky. New York: Everyman's Library, 1992.

Felski, Rita. *The Limits of Critique*. Chicago: University of Chicago Press, 2015.

Friedlander, Eli. *Signs of Sense: Reading Wittgenstein's "Tractatus."* Cambridge, MA: Harvard University Press, 2014.

Gibson, John, and Wolfgang Huemer. *The Literary Wittgenstein*. London: Routledge, 2004.

Hegel, G. W. F. *Aesthetics: Lectures on Fine Art*. Translated by T. M. Knox. Vol. 1. Oxford: Clarendon, 1988.

Hegel, G. W. F. *The Philosophy of Art: Being the Second Part of Hegel's "Aesthetik."* Translated by W. M. Bryant. New York, 1879.

Heller-Roazen, Daniel. *Dark Tongues: The Art of Riddlers and Rogues*. New York: Zone, 2013.

Higgins, C. J. "Wittgenstein's New Way of Talking to Himself." *Philosophical Investigations* 46, no. 1 (2023): 22–49.

Johnson, Barbara. "The Frame of Reference: Poe, Lacan, Derrida." In *The Purloined Poe: Lacan, Derrida, and Psychoanalytic Reading*, edited by John P. Muller and William J. Richardson, 213–52. Baltimore: Johns Hopkins University Press, 1988.

Kant, Immanuel. *The Critique of Pure Reason*. Translated by Paul Guyer and Allen Wood. Cambridge: Cambridge University Press, 1998.

Klagge, James C. *Wittgenstein's Artillery: Philosophy as Poetry*. Cambridge, MA: MIT Press, 2021.

Lacan, Jacques. "Seminar on 'The Purloined Letter.'" Translated by Jeffrey Mehlman. In *The Purloined Poe: Lacan, Derrida, and Psychoanalytic Reading*, edited by John P. Muller and William J. Richardson, 28–54. Baltimore: Johns Hopkins University Press, 1988.

Levinas, Emmanuel. "Enigma and Phenomenon." In *Basic Philosophical Writings*, edited by Adriaan T. Peperzak, Simon Critchley, and Robert Bernasconi, 65–77. Bloomington: Indiana University Press, 1996.

Levvis, Gary. "Why We Would Not Understand a Talking Lion." *Between the Species* 8, no. 3 (1992): 156–62.

Love, Heather. "Close but Not Deep: Literary Ethics and the Descriptive Turn." *New Literary History* 41, no. 2 (2010): 371–91.

Moi, Toril. *Revolution of the Ordinary: Literary Studies after Wittgenstein*. Chicago: University of Chicago Press, 2017.

Monk, Ray. *Wittgenstein: The Duty of Genius*. London: Vintage, 1991.

Perloff, Marjorie. *Wittgenstein's Ladder: Poetic Language and the Strangeness of the Ordinary*. Chicago: University of Chicago Press, 1996.

Phillips, D. Z. "Wittgenstein's Full Stop." In *Wittgenstein and Religion*, 79–102. Houndmills: Palgrave Macmillan, 1993.

Poe, Edgar Allan. *Eighteen Best Stories by Edgar Allan Poe*. Edited by Vincent Prince and Chandler Brossard. New York: Dell, 1965.

Ricoeur, Paul. *The Rule of Metaphor: The Creation of Meaning in Language*. Translated by Robert Czerny with Kathleen McLaughlin and John Costello. London: Routledge, 2003.

Shields, Philip R. *Logic and Sin in the Writings of Ludwig Wittgenstein*. Chicago: University of Chicago Press, 1997.

Stokhof, Martin. "The Quest for Purity: Another Look at the New Wittgenstein." *Croatian Journal of Philosophy* 33, no. 3 (2011): 275–94.

Taylor, Archer. "The Riddle." *California Folklore Quarterly* 2, no. 2 (1943): 129–47.

University of Iowa *Tractatus* Map. http://tractatus.lib.uiowa.edu/ (accessed August 16, 2021).

Waismann, Friedrich. *Wittgenstein and the Vienna Circle: Conversations*. New York: Barnes and Noble, 1979.

Wittgenstein, Ludwig. *Culture and Value*. Edited by G. H. von Wright. Translated by Peter Winch. Chicago: University of Chicago Press, 1980.

Wittgenstein, Ludwig. *Lecture on Ethics*. Edited by Eduardo Zamuner, Ermelinda Valentina Di Lascio, and D. K. Levy. Chichester: Wiley-Blackwell, 2014.

Wittgenstein, Ludwig. *Lectures and Conversations on Aesthetics, Psychology, and Religious Belief*. Oxford: Blackwell, 1966.

Wittgenstein, Ludwig. *On Certainty*. Edited by G. E. M. Anscombe and G. H. von Wright, translated by Denis Paul and G. E. M. Anscombe. Oxford: Blackwell, 1969.

Wittgenstein, Ludwig. *Philosophical Investigations*. Translated by G. E. M. Anscombe, P. M. S. Hacker and Joachim Schulte. Chichester: Wiley Blackwell, 2009.

Wittgenstein, Ludwig. *Tractatus Logico-Philosophicus*. Translated by C. K. Ogden. London: Kegan Paul, Trench, 1933.

Wittgenstein, Ludwig. *Tractatus Logico-Philosophicus: Centenary Edition*. Edited by Luciano Bazzocchi. London: Anthem, 2021.

Wittgenstein, Ludwig. *Wittgenstein's Lectures: Cambridge, 1930–1932*. Edited by Desmond Lee. Oxford: Blackwell, 1979.

Wittgenstein, Ludwig. *Zettel*. Edited by G. E. M. Anscombe and G. H. von Wright. Berkeley: University of California Press, 1967.

Wood, Michael. "Why Praise Astaire?" *London Review of Books*, October 20, 2005. https://www.lrb.co.uk/the-paper/v27/n20/michael-wood/why -praise-astaire.

Yeats, W. B. *The Collected Poems of W. B. Yeats.* Edited by Richard J. Finneran. New York: Simon and Schuster, 1996.

Yousef, Nancy. *The Aesthetic Commonplace: Wordsworth, Eliot, Wittgenstein, and the Language of Every Day.* Oxford: Oxford University Press, 2022.

The Rumors Are True

Gossip in the Films of F. W. Murnau

NICHOLAS BAER

> Platonic truth, even when *doxa* is not mentioned, is always
> understood as the very opposite of opinion. The spectacle of
> Socrates submitting his own *doxa* to the irresponsible opinions of the
> Athenians, and being outvoted by a majority, made Plato despise
> opinions and yearn for absolute standards.
>
> Hannah Arendt, "Philosophy and Politics"

Rumor had it that Socrates was impious toward the Olympian deities. In Plato's telling, Socrates addressed the malicious rumor in his speech before the Athenian tribunal in 399 BCE: "Those who spread that rumor, gentlemen, are my dangerous accusers, for their hearers believe that those who study these things do not even believe in the gods."[1] While Socrates tried to mobilize logos in self-defense, he was ultimately helpless against the onslaught of hearsay. A baseless rumor thus led to the death of the very philosopher who had questioned the beliefs of his interlocutors, helping them find the truth in their opinions. The case of Socrates indicates that rumors overpower logos, with *doxa* (belief, opinion) maintaining the upper

QUI PARLE   Vol. 33, No. 1, June 2024
DOI 10.1215/10418385-11125484   © 2024 Editorial Board, *Qui Parle*

hand over episteme (knowledge). As this essay demonstrates, the films of Friedrich Wilhelm Murnau rethink and complicate this Platonic opposition, according rumors an epistemic value.

A particularly dubious and disreputable form of *doxa*, rumors are an unverified yet uncannily potent form of truth claim—authorless yet forceful, trifling yet consequential, fickle yet enduring, unfounded yet steadfast.[2] Consider, for instance, how the character of Knock is introduced in Murnau's *Nosferatu* (1922): "There was an estate agent named Knock, about whom all sorts of rumors circulated. The only thing for certain was that he paid his people well." In this intertitle, the multifarious rumors lack an assignable source or even ascertainable content. The rumors' anonymous, quasi-autonomous agency is signaled syntactically, as the indeterminate speech acts themselves become the subject of the subordinate clause. Conveying Knock's mysterious ambiguity, the rumors circulate impersonally and intangibly, possessing a spectral currency that is here juxtaposed with the more certain and calculable currency of financial exchange.

However immaterial, rumors can gain substantial traction, spreading quickly and becoming virtually impossible to combat. It was on this basis that Martin Heidegger disparaged hearsay in his magnum opus, *Being and Time* (*Sein und Zeit*, 1927). In the section "Idle Talk" ("Das Gerede"), Heidegger wrote:

> What is spoken about as such spreads in wider circles and takes on an authoritative character. Things are so because one says so. Idle talk is constituted in this gossiping and passing the word along, a process by which its initial lack of grounds to stand on increases to complete groundlessness. . . . Idle talk, which everyone can snatch up, not only divests us of the task of genuine understanding, but develops an indifferent intelligibility for which nothing is closed off any longer.[3]

Heidegger posits a link between the broadening orbit and authoritativeness of idle talk and its total increase in groundlessness. While closing off the potential for genuine understanding (*Verstehen*), idle talk opens the way for an average, all-encompassing intelligibility (*Verständlichkeit*). Lacking a primary relation to that which is spoken about, idle talk proceeds through mere gossiping and passing the word along (*Nach- und Weiterreden*). Far from constituting a public sphere of discourse, everyday forms of communication and interpretation thus mark a surrender to the common realm of approximation and superficiality.

Where *Being and Time* dismissed *Gerede* as trivial, inauthentic discourse, recent scholarship has offered a more capacious, differentiated view.[4] In contemporary accounts, gossip concerns an absent party and establishes a relation among three types of actors (sender, object, receiver) and acts (attribution, communication, perception).[5] Think of Murnau's *The Burning Soil* (*Der brennende Acker*, 1922), in which Graf Rudenburg's second wife, Helga, forbids his daughter, Gerda, from continuing a courtship with his secretary, Johannes: "As your father's wife, I forbid you from exposing yourself further to the talk [*Gerede*] of the people with Johannes!" While directly appealing to patriarchal authority, Helga's command suggests a broad, complex circuit of human interconnectivity. Involving issues of intimacy and exposure, transgression and prohibition, gossip is here positioned at the nexus of knowledge transfer, social mores, and the strategic management of reputation.

Building on recent scholarship on rumors and gossip, this essay will examine the role of *Gerede* in Murnau's films as well as in later writings about his life and career. I will argue that while Murnau perpetuates long-standing figurations of gossip as a frivolous or even malicious activity, he also grants unverified information a truth value. Where Heidegger claimed that idle talk is based on "groundlessness" and "indifferent intelligibility," I will show that rumors in Murnau's films are often well-founded and also essential to a nuanced understanding of his work. My essay thus sheds light on an underexamined aspect of Murnau's oeuvre and addresses broader questions about the status of speculative, uncertain, or contested knowledge. A study of *Gerede* does not entail a concealment of authentic discourse but illuminates Murnau's episteme of *doxa*, or philosophy of rumors, as part of a dialectic of destabilized knowledge.

Reputation Management

Often delegitimized as idle women's talk, gossip has long been a gendered descriptor. Deriving from the Old English *godsibb* (godparent, sponsor), "gossip" came to designate a companion in childbirth, a close female friend, and finally anyone engaging in familiar, trifling talk or groundless, even slanderous rumor. (In German, the onomatopoetic word *Klatsch* was similarly ascribed to women as a defamatory form of speech, as evidenced by the derivative *Klatsche* [whip, flyswatter, woman], designations such as *Klatschtante* and *Klatschbase*, and colloquial phrases [e.g., *schmutzige Wäsche waschen, jemanden durchhecheln, jemanden am Zeug flicken*] that reference traditional types of collectively performed women's work.)[6] Tracing the semantic history of gossip back to the early modern period, Silvia Federici argues that it shifted from a term of affection and solidarity to one of ridicule and discord. For Federici, the increasingly derogatory connotations of gossip contributed to the demonization of women and the devaluation of their labor.[7]

Murnau's *The Last Laugh* (*Der letzte Mann*, 1924) reproduces enduring associations of women with idle chatter. The day after his niece's wedding, the hotel porter heads to work as the women in his stairway and courtyard scrub, dust, and dry their household items, recalling the etymological genealogy of *Klatsch*.[8] The groom's aunt surprises the porter with soup at his hotel, only to find him now working as a washroom attendant. As the aunt rushes home and breathlessly shares the news with the porter's niece, the camera hovers outside their apartment door, much like the neighbor who eavesdrops on their conversation. The niece tries to contain the information in a gesture of reputation management, yet the neighbor is already gleefully spreading the word to other tenants in the stairway. The piece of gossip sets off a chain reaction, animating the women and provoking schadenfreude at the expense of the porter's humiliating, emasculating demotion (fig. 1).

In this sequence, Murnau employs mobile-camera techniques to trace the rapid relay of gossip among women. As the transmission of information increases in distance and volume—from inside to outside, and from whisper to shout—the camera swishes across the buildings and floors of the tenements. At the close of the sequence, Murnau cuts from a static closeup of one tenant's face as she shouts the news from her balcony to a tracking shot into another woman's ear across the courtyard. The auditory dissemination of gossip thus

Fig. 1.   The aural dissemination of gossip in *The Last Laugh*.

becomes an occasion for Karl Freund's pioneering technique of the "unchained camera [*entfesselte Kamera*]," such that the movement of the camera enacts the travel of sound through space. Celebrated for its innovative cinematography and almost complete lack of intertitles, Murnau's film translates the aural phenomenon of gossip into an imagistic, nonverbal language: silent cinema as *stille Post*.

In "The Components of the Image," a chapter of *Cinema 2* (1985), Gilles Deleuze examines how the transition to sound changed the status of the speech act in film. Where speech acts were conveyed via intertitles in the silent era—with read text separated from the seen image—they became directly heard in sound films. Lending a new auditory dimension to the image, the "talkie" recovered the unique characteristics of discourse and made visible the realm of human interaction: "If it is true that the talking cinema is an interactionist sociology in action, or rather the other way round, if it is true that interactionism is a talking cinema, it will come as no surprise that rumour has been a cinematographically privileged object: Ford's *The Whole Town's Talking*, Mankiewicz's *People Will Talk*, and already Lang's *M*."[9] For Deleuze, the spread of rumor is thus a key concern of sound films that explore the relay of speech acts onscreen.

Predicated on the advent of synchronized sound, Deleuze's claims are complicated by *The Last Laugh*. For already in Murnau's silent film, rumor is a "cinematographically privileged object," linking people and places through cinematic circulation. Dynamizing the camera and relinquishing intertitles, Murnau developed a distinctly filmic language to visualize, thematize, and participate in the production and propagation of indeterminate speech acts.[10] If Murnau thereby offers what Deleuze later called an "interactionist sociology in action," he also diverges from a proto-Heideggerian account in which the widening orbit of *Gerede* leads "from an initial lack of grounds . . . to complete groundlessness." While reinforcing negatively gendered figurations of *Klatsch*, Murnau offers a scenario in which the transmission of gossip among women entails not total groundlessness but rather a tacit form of displacement; masculine shame becomes the source of feminine jouissance, and the act of defamation is itself defamed.

Anger Management

Gossip is pivotal to what Eve Kosofsky Sedgwick theorized as the "epistemology of the closet," helping discern "what *kinds of people* there are to be found in one's world."[11] Yet efforts to establish moving images as legitimate objects of historical study have often foreclosed rumors and gossip as potential sources of knowledge. In *The Liveliest Art* (1957), Arthur Knight sought "to forgo much of the chatty gossip about personalities or the behind-the-camera maneuverings that so often pass for film history."[12] Such suspicion of unsubstantiated information was radicalized by the "historical turn" in cinema studies in the 1980s. Where New Film History aspired to what Thomas Elsaesser characterized as "scientific or empirical standards of exactitude and knowledge," queer cinema and media scholarship has looked to rumors and gossip as means of countering the historical erasure of nonnormative identities and meanings.[13]

Reserved, secretive, and discreet, Murnau left his homosexuality a matter of unconfirmed speculation. In *Hollywood Babylon* (1959), Kenneth Anger included sordid, even scandalous insinuations about Murnau and the circumstances of his death in a freak car accident:

> Few around the Fox lot had not heard that director F. W. Murnau favored gays when it came to casting. Murnau's death in 1931 inspired a flood tide of speculation. Murnau had hired as valet a handsome fourteen-year-old Filipino boy named Garcia Stevenson. The boy was at the wheel of the Packard when the fatal accident occurred. The Hollywood *méchantes langues* reported that Murnau was going down on Garcia when the car leaped off the road.[14]

Anger thus offered a salacious metarumor—a rumor about what was rumored in Hollywood—that involved not only homosexuality but also a fatal act of pederasty (recalling Socrates's own assumed relationships with boys). Reproducing Anger's account in more culturally respectable terms, Lotte H. Eisner invoked ancient Greek figurations of Thanatos "as a handsome young man, with the sombre and enigmatic beauty which the young Filipino who drove Murnau to his death no doubt possessed." While emphasizing the sacredness of private life, Eisner posited that Murnau's "natural predispositions" were just as crucial a factor in his film art as in his untimely passing.[15]

In a spirited defense of *Hollywood Babylon* as a work of film historiography, Mark Lynn Anderson critiques ongoing efforts to correct Anger's factual errors and undocumented claims. Exemplary in this regard is Les Hammer's *F. W. Murnau: For the Record* (2010), billed as "the book that shatters the myth surrounding the accidental death of the silent film director" and "restores [his] illustrious name and reputation."[16] For Anderson, projects to refute Anger's account involve an annihilation of queer historical affect and meaning: "It is this de-queering of the film historical past that I see widely indulged by various projects of film history that seek to set the record straight through appeals to archival research and factual rigor."[17] In attempting to dispel the rumors of the past via authoritative evidence, researchers partake in disciplinary policing and normalization, negating the often indeterminate presence of queerness in film history.

Traces of Murnau's own queerness have been elusive, particularly as his brother and later estate keeper, Robert Plumpe, suppressed and denied the filmmaker's "homosexual tendencies."[18] Although scholarship has long explored the nonnormative figurations of gender and sexual identity in Murnau's films, the exhibition and publication of his private photographs have lent new insight into his own modes of desire and visual pleasure.[19] In the collection, one finds often nude images of Hans Jahnke in the surroundings of Berlin as well as of an unidentified young man in and around Murnau's villa in Los Angeles, sometimes staged according to models in paintings and sculptures (e.g., the *Spinario* or *Boy with Thorn*). The heterosexual love stories of Murnau's films gain more explicit homoerotic dimensions when one notes the queer gaze with which he depicted *Sunrise* (1927) star George O'Brien (fig. 2) or unknown South Sea Islanders during the making of *Tabu* (1931).

In their illuminating introduction to the volume of Murnau's photographs, Guido Altendorf, Werner Sudendorf, and Wolfgang Theis address the persistent rumors around the director:

> The fact that the rumors about Murnau, his films, and his life refuse to die down is also a good thing. Every time it is claimed that a lost Murnau film has been rediscovered . . . , old research is refreshed and new leads are pursued. . . . Almost every engagement with Murnau's life and films leads, if not to new documents, then at least to new clarifications.[20]

While granting a positive quality to rumors as an impulse for continued research into Murnau's biography and oeuvre, Altendorf, Sudendorf, and Theis uphold a traditional, value-laden set of dichotomies between loss and recovery, conjecture and empirical clarity, dubious and legitimate truth claims. Yet rumors and gossip can also be a crucial resource for the production and dissemination of queer

Fig. 2.   F. W. Murnau's queer gaze on *Sunrise* star
George O'Brien. Billy Rose Theatre Division,
New York Public Library Digital Collections.

historical knowledge that often eludes these conventional dichotomies, remaining speculative, unstable, and irreducibly ambiguous.
In my analysis, Murnau's films themselves adopt such a fluid, queer
epistemology, according unverified rumors a paradoxical truth
value and thereby complicating the Platonic opposition between
episteme and *doxa*.

Crisis Management

While rumors and gossip have been vital for feminist and queer historical scholarship, it might appear foolhardy to remain invested in
their intellectual utility and critical promise at the present juncture. A
key tool of resistance for the oppressed and marginalized—or what
James C. Scott called a "weapon of the weak"—the destabilization of
knowledge has become a core operation of contemporary digital media.[21] If cyberspace once promised a new enlightened public sphere,
it now ushers in misinformation, fake news, and conspiracy theories
that pervade newsfeeds and reverberate in algorithmically confined
echo chambers. The "post-truth" situation has thus underscored

the ambivalence and political promiscuity of rumors, legends, and other forms of *doxa*. Rarely was the dangerous potential of unverified information more apparent than during the coronavirus pandemic, which saw the viral proliferation of rumors—among them, the metarumor that the pandemic itself was merely a rumor.

Theorizing rumors in relation to the pandemic, Mladen Dolar notes their shared structural traits, including a mysterious origin and rapid, intangible transmission. Dolar addresses the blurred and contested boundary between scientific knowledge and unfounded opinion, or episteme and *doxa*:

> It's a very symptomatic situation where the "real" pandemic is paralleled with the pandemic of rumors; the latter cannot be quite disentangled from the former. The elusive dividing line of "scientific knowledge, protective measures etc. vs. rumors" is at the same time the locus where social antagonisms are played out, magnified by the terrific speed of spreading both information and toxic rumors, the inextricable mix of the two, through social media.[22]

Dolar observes the intertwined viral capacities of the pandemic, rumors, and social media platforms. While rumors have long implicated networks of communication and interconnectivity, digital technologies intensify their effects through an unprecedented increase in the number of social partners and interactions as well as in the speed, scale, and permanence of information transfer.[23] At the same time, Dolar identifies the historical precedent of *A Journal of the Plague Year* (1722), Daniel Defoe's account of the Great Plague of London of 1665, in which the spread of rumors precedes, accompanies, and even functions like the epidemic.

Another precedent, I would suggest, is Murnau's *Nosferatu*, about a plague that afflicts the fictional German town of Wisborg in 1838. As mentioned above, Knock is introduced in terms of the circulation of multifarious, indeterminate rumors, and he becomes the subject of intensified scrutiny and speculation when the pandemic seizes Wisborg. Nine years before "a city searches for a murderer" in Lang's *M* (1931), "the fear-ridden city was searching for a victim: it was Knock," as an intertitle states. Following Knock's escape from an asylum, an elderly woman spreads word to three young men (played,

Fig. 3.   The viral spread of rumors in *Nosferatu*.

among others, by Murnau and his lover, Walter Spies—if the rumors
are true): "People saw him! He ran out of the house! He strangled
the guard . . . " A further woman echoes the statement to another:
"He strangled him . . . the vampire!" Here, as in Defoe's book,
the plague and rumors become interlinked in their mechanism of
contagion (fig. 3).

Yet the rumors about Knock in Murnau's film are comparatively benign. In Lang's *M*, news of the child murderer travels across
disparate people and places, resulting in mass hysteria and mob

violence against an innocent man. Analyzing the sequence, Deleuze writes:

> It is one and the same indeterminate speech-act (rumour) which circulates and spreads, making visible the live interactions between independent characters and separate places. And the more autonomous the speech-act becomes as it goes beyond determinate characters, the more the field of visual perception that it opens up is presented as problematic, positioned on a problematic point at the limit of tangled lines of interaction.[24]

Like in a game of telephone, information loses truth value over the course of its transmission in *M*, causing faulty perception by the crowd. While the climactic chase of Knock in *Nosferatu* similarly leads to a (literal) straw man—prefiguring the vicious scapegoating and misguided movements of the coronavirus pandemic—the violent mob is not acting on the basis of false or unfounded suspicion. Rather than culminating in "complete groundlessness," as per Heidegger, the "gossiping and passing the word along" in *Nosferatu* serves the function of transferring knowledge among the people of Wisborg in a situational context of ambiguity and acute threat.

Defending himself before the Athenian tribunal in 399 BCE, Socrates sought in vain to refute unjust allegations: "There have been many who have accused me to you for many years now, and none of their accusations are true."[25] Adopting a different rhetorical gesture, Murnau's films accord rumors an epistemic value: Knock does help bring about the plague in Wisborg; the hotel porter in *The Last Laugh* is indeed demoted to washroom attendant; and whatever the exact circumstances of Murnau's own death, there is certainly a truth to his queer sexuality. Taking up the sharp opposition between episteme and *doxa*, Murnau's films rethink and complicate a distinction that subtends the history of philosophy. At the same time, his work resonates in the contemporary media and political environment, where the Platonic yearning for absolute standards of truth has given way to the dialectic of destabilized knowledge.

NICHOLAS BAER is assistant professor of German at the University of California, Berkeley, with affiliations in Film and Media, Critical Theory, and Jewish Studies. He is author of *Historical Turns: Weimar Cinema and the Crisis of Historicism* (2024) and coeditor of *The Promise of Cinema: German Film Theory, 1907–1933* (2016), *Unwatchable* (2019), and *Technics: Media in the Digital Age* (2024).

Acknowledgments

I would like to thank Julian Hanich, Maggie Hennefeld, Kristina Köhler, Michael Wedel, and the editorial board members of *Qui Parle* for invaluable comments on versions of this text. This essay builds on a special issue of *NECSUS_European Journal of Media Studies* on #Rumors that Hennefeld and I coedited in spring 2022.

Notes

1. Plato, "Apology," 19.
2. Dolar, "On Rumours, Gossip, and Related Matters."
3. Heidegger, *Being and Time*, 158.
4. Spacks, *Gossip*; Dunbar, *Grooming*; Adkins, *Gossip, Epistemology, and Power*. On the differences between rumors and gossip, see DiFonzo and Bordia, "Rumor, Gossip, and Urban Legends."
5. Giardini and Wittek, "Introduction," 1.
6. Althans, "'Halte dich fern von den klatschenden Weibern . . .'"
7. Federici, *Witches, Witch-Hunting, and Women*, 35–43.
8. On the ambiguous family relations in *The Last Laugh*, see Goergen, "Nichte oder Tochter?"
9. Deleuze, *Cinema 2*, 227.
10. See also Deleuze, *Cinema 2*, 321–22n9: "It will be asked whether cinema can achieve phenomena of interaction with its own means. But this can only be done in silent films which give up intertitles, and which proceed by aberrant movements. We saw this in Vertov's *Man with a Movie Camera*, where the gap acts as differential of movements. Or equally in *The Last Laugh*, it is the 'unleashed' camera which makes certain interactions visible."
11. Sedgwick, *Epistemology of the Closet*, 23.
12. Knight, *Liveliest Art*, 5.

13. Elsaesser, "New Film History," 247. See Crimp, "Right On, Girl-friend!"; Butt, *Between You and Me*; Anderson, *Twilight of the Idols*; and Siegel, "Secret Lives of Images."

14. Anger, *Hollywood Babylon*, 172.

15. Eisner, *Murnau*, 222.

16. Amazon, blurb.

17. Anderson, "Anger Management," 73.

18. Eisner, *Murnau*, 222.

19. Altendorf, Sudendorf, and Theis, *Friedrich Wilhelm Murnau*. On fig-urations of gender and sexual identity in Murnau, see Bergstrom, "Sexuality at a Loss"; Waugh, "Murnau"; and Wood, "F. W. Murnau."

20. Altendorf, Sudendorf, and Theis, "Vom Tod und Nachleben," 13: "Dass die Gerüchte um Murnau, seine Filme und sein Leben nicht ver-stummen wollen, hat auch sein Gutes. Jedes Mal, wenn behauptet wird, ein verlorener Murnau-Film sei wiedergefunden worden . . . , werden alte Recherchen aufgefrischt und neue Spuren verfolgt. . . . Nahezu jede Be-schäftigung mit dem Leben und den Filmen Murnaus führt, wenn nicht zu neuen Dokumenten, so doch zu neuen Präzisierungen."

21. Scott, *Weapons of the Weak*. See also Alexandra Juhasz's comments in Baer and Hennefeld, "#Rumors," 204.

22. Baer and Hennefeld, "#Rumors," 199.

23. Horodowich, "Gossip"; Solove, *Future of Reputation*; Andriopoulos, "Rumor and Media."

24. Deleuze, *Cinema 2*, 228.

25. Plato, "Apology," 19.

References

Adkins, Karen. *Gossip, Epistemology, and Power: Knowledge Under-ground*. Cham: Palgrave Macmillan, 2017.

Altendorf, Guido, Werner Sudendorf, and Wolfgang Theis, eds. *Friedrich Wilhelm Murnau: Die privaten Fotografien, 1926–1931—Berlin, Amer-ika, Südsee*. Munich: Schirmer/Mosel, 2013.

Altendorf, Guido, Werner Sudendorf, and Wolfgang Theis. "Vom Tod und Nachleben Friedrich Wilhelm Murnaus." In Altendorf, Sudendorf, and Theis, *Friedrich Wilhelm Murnau*, 9–16.

Althans, Birgit. "'Halte dich fern von den klatschenden Weibern . . .': Zur Phänomenologie des Klatsches." *Feministische Studien* 4, no. 2 (1985): 46–53.

Amazon. Blurb for *F. W. Murnau: For the Record*, by Les Hammer. https://www.amazon.com/F-W-Murnau-Hammer/dp/1618631829 (accessed March 6, 2024).

Anderson, Mark Lynn. "Anger Management; or, The Dream of a Falsifiable Film-Historical Past." *NECSUS*, Spring 2022, 67–87. https://necsus-ejms.org/anger-management-or-the-dream-of-a-falsifiable-film-historical-past/.

Anderson, Mark Lynn. *Twilight of the Idols: Hollywood and the Human Sciences in 1920s America*. Berkeley: University of California Press, 2011.

Andriopoulos, Stefan. "Rumor and Media: On Circulations and Credence (via Kant and Marx)." *Grey Room*, no. 93 (2023): 6–31.

Anger, Kenneth. *Hollywood Babylon*. London: Arrow, 1986.

Baer, Nicholas, and Maggie Hennefeld. "#Rumors: A Roundtable Discussion with Mladen Dolar, Richard Dyer, Alexandra Juhasz, Tavia Nyong'o, Marc Siegel, and Patricia Turner." *NECSUS*, Spring 2022, 194–210. https://necsus-ejms.org/rumors-a-roundtable-discussion-with-mladen-dolar-richard-dyer-alexandra-juhasz-tavia-nyongo-marc-siegel-and-patricia-turner/.

Bergstrom, Janet. "Sexuality at a Loss: The Films of F. W. Murnau." *Poetics Today* 6, nos. 1–2 (1985): 185–203.

Butt, Gavin. *Between You and Me: Queer Disclosures in the New York Art World, 1948–1963*. Durham, NC: Duke University Press, 2005.

Crimp, Douglas. "Right On, Girlfriend!" *Social Text*, no. 33 (1992): 2–18.

Deleuze, Gilles. *Cinema 2: The Time-Image*. Translated by Hugh Tomlinson and Robert Galeta. Minneapolis: University of Minnesota Press, 1989.

DiFonzo, Nicholas, and Prashant Bordia. "Rumor, Gossip, and Urban Legends." *Diogenes* 54, no. 1 (2007): 19–35.

Dolar, Mladen. "On Rumours, Gossip, and Related Matters." In *Objective Fictions: Philosophy, Psychoanalysis, Marxism*, edited by Adrian Johnston, Boštjan Nedoh, and Alenka Zupančič, 144–64. Edinburgh: Edinburgh University Press, 2021.

Dunbar, Robin. *Grooming, Gossip, and the Evolution of Language*. Cambridge, MA: Harvard University Press, 1996.

Eisner, Lotte H. *Murnau*. London: Secker and Warburg, 1973.

Elsaesser, Thomas. "The New Film History." *Sight and Sound* 55, no. 4 (1986): 246–51.

Federici, Silvia. *Witches, Witch-Hunting, and Women*. Oakland, CA: PM, 2018.

Giardini, Francesca, and Rafael Wittek. "Introduction: Gossip and Reputation—a Multidisciplinary Research Program." In *The Oxford Handbook of Gossip and Reputation*, edited by Francesca Giardini and Rafael Wittek, 1–20. New York: Oxford University Press, 2019.

Goergen, Jeanpaul. "Nichte oder Tochter? Die Familie des Portiers in *Der letzte Mann* (1924)." *Filmblatt*, no. 18 (2002): 50–55.

Hammer, Les. *F. W. Murnau: For the Record*. Morgan Hill: Bookstand, 2010.

Heidegger, Martin. *Being and Time*. Translated by Joan Stambaugh. Albany: State University of New York Press, 1996.

Horodowich, Elizabeth. "Gossip." In *Information: Keywords*, edited by Michele Kennerly, Samuel Frederick, and Jonathan E. Abel, 89–99. New York: Columbia University Press, 2021.

Knight, Arthur. *The Liveliest Art: A Panoramic History of the Movies*. New York: New American Library, 1957.

Plato. "Apology." In *Complete Works*, edited by John M. Cooper, translated by G. M. A. Grube, 17–36. Indianapolis, IN: Hackett, 1997.

Scott, James C. *Weapons of the Weak: Everyday Forms of Peasant Resistance*. New Haven, CT: Yale University Press, 1985.

Sedgwick, Eve Kosofsky. *Epistemology of the Closet*. Berkeley: University of California Press, 1990.

Siegel, Marc. "The Secret Lives of Images." In *The State of Post-cinema: Tracing the Moving Image in the Age of Digital Dissemination*, edited by Malte Hagener, Vinzenz Hediger, and Alena Strohmaier, 195–209. London: Palgrave Macmillan, 2016.

Solove, Daniel J. *The Future of Reputation: Gossip, Rumor, and Privacy on the Internet*. New Haven, CT: Yale University Press, 2007.

Spacks, Patricia Meyer. *Gossip*. New York: Knopf, 1985.

Waugh, Thomas. "Murnau: The Films behind the Man." In *The Fruit Machine: Twenty Years of Writings on Queer Cinema*, 74–85. Durham, NC: Duke University Press, 2000.

Wood, Robin. "F. W. Murnau." *Film Comment* 12, no. 3 (1976): 4–19.

Dead Tired

IANNA HAWKINS OWEN

I just got very, very tired.
  Fantasia Barrino

She just said she was tired. Tired to death.
  Octavia E. Butler, *Wild Seed*

On September 19, 1977, while developing the protagonist of her *Pat-ternist* novel *Wild Seed*, Octavia E. Butler journaled, "It must take [Anyanwu] a long, painful time to give up"—and it does.[1] Yet, in the novel's final form, published in 1980, "giving up" is not adequate to describe what Anyanwu desires or ceases to desire, plans or relinquishes. Instead, through the "long time" afforded by Anyanwu's supernatural life, Butler offers us a nuanced exploration of self-destruction and suicidal contemplation. Rather than absorbing enslaved suicide into collective narratives of resistance or defeat, *Wild Seed* invites us to hesitate before embracing its supposed virtues or failings by showing us the slow disarticulation of one Black woman from her design as resilient. Butler's granular attention to transforma-tion and residue calls to mind Vanessa Agard-Jones's theorization of

QUI PARLE   Vol. 33, No. 1, June 2024
DOI 10.1215/10418385-11125495   © 2024 Editorial Board, *Qui Parle*

diaspora through sand in "What the Sands Remember"; she reveals that we do not expect sand to hold one concrete and unchanging form but rely instead on its continual breaking down.[2] To be recognized for the capacity to come undone without judgment—it sounds nice.

The forms (and formlessness) of exhausted and desireless deaths explored in this essay do not fit easily into the scripts prepared for them. Instead, I argue that claiming those who die by suicide and ventriloquizing their motivations for collective purposes may twice obscure—twice fail—the figure taking such action.[3] Unburdened with presumed collectivity, this essay makes space for alternative readings of Black women's racialized and gendered tiredness. I suggest that Anyanwu's intention to die allows us to glimpse and explore the possibility of "giving up" or opting out of diaspora—not as an expression of condemnation or retaliation but as a declining, a reclining, and, sometimes, a dying.

In a 2005 essay on postcolonial writing, Bed Prasad Giri turned to the term *ordinary* to describe the remarkableness of diaspora's ambiguous relationship to newer socialities and political projects and to caution users of the notion of diaspora against taking it on as a "master trope of nonhegemonic forms of belonging and political resistance."[4] That same year Jacqueline Nassy Brown's work on Black Liverpudlians also insisted that the keyword makes no promises: "Diaspora must never be made synonymous with the project of unity—nor with origins, authenticity, difference, roots, routes, or hybridity. These terms just give voice to the discrepant desires and discontents of counter/*parts*."[5] Ordinariness deflates the headiness, or grounds the dizziness, of believing that language can resolve our aloneness. In "'And to Survive'" Christina Sharpe responds to a discussion of *In the Wake* and offers this clarification: "I tried to name and to perform 'the still-living desires for more than what we presently have' by attending to what I called an ordinary note of care. . . . I call it an ordinary note because it takes as weather, as atmosphere, the conditions of black life and death." Key here is the recognition that ordinary notes are moments and acts of connection that "are an interruption, not an end."[6] In this regard the ordinary is the intimate intraracial response to white supremacist violence's edgeless diffusion, and it is also temporary.

In *Wild Seed* ordinariness makes itself felt through supernatural Blackness. Anyanwu is immortal; her plan for suicide occurs many centuries deep into her lifetime under the domination of another character. Like the Black women in our own world, the immortal Anyanwu is imagined to be so strong as to never experience ordinary affects like tiredness and exhaustion. Yet this exceptional and projected quality is ultimately pierced by having *enough* time. Racial hierarchies have produced "giving up" as unimaginable for her; however, Anyanwu's immortal durability puts her in touch with the very ordinariness of it. Finally, this essay asks whether we can care for the dead, those who were too tired of living, without insisting on their renewal of their labor for the alive and their causes. Can we who remain give up our desires of the dead and listen more quietly to those who gave up desire itself? Or, to dare invert Saidiya Hartman's question while keeping its tone, can we bear to answer the dead tired when they ask us, "*Can I die?*"[7]

Giving Up

Around 1975 Octavia E. Butler began to brainstorm *Wild Seed*'s protagonist (then called Emma, later renamed Anyanwu). In her character creation notes, Butler speculates, "She might be sold into slavery. Or, her village might be attacked . . . ," and continues to list the anticipated progression of the novel and its options: "Emma's Ebo [*sic*] time as prologue, or as [chapter] one flowing into (Jumping to) the middle passage. The strange land, the auction, the plantation or city, north or south."[8] This sketch depicts Anyanwu's original conception as a slave in early America who comes to understand her shape-shifting powers, escapes from enslavement, and suffers re-enslavement to the figure readers come to know as Doro.[9]

In the published novel, Anyanwu is an established shape-shifting healer guided by commitments to kinship and care, and Doro is an ancient spirit-like being capable of unmatched body possession and psychokinetic abilities. Doro believes that the strength and control of Anyanwu's powers are essential to achieving his eugenicist vision of producing a magical race. After the two meet in eighteenth-century West Africa, Doro alternately threatens Anyanwu's mortal descendants and entices her with promises to marry her and give her immortal children through his race-building scheme. They voyage to his New World settlements, but, faced with Doro's broken promises and his killings (demonstrations of dominance and involuntary feeding), Anyanwu escapes. When Doro finds her again, she resubmits to him. But after Doro directly and indirectly kills members of her new community, Anyanwu plans to birth one last child and then end her life by refraining from healing herself. On the eve of her planned suicide, Doro confesses his loneliness and submits himself to Anyanwu for the first and only time. She decides to live and renegotiates her community's living conditions, while she continues to participate in the breeding project.

Despite Anyanwu's deviation from her plan to die by suicide at the novel's end, suicide is treated with more sustained attention in *Wild Seed* than in the rest of the *Patternist* series. The narrative chronology places *Wild Seed* (1980) as the first book in the series, followed by *Mind of My Mind* (1977), *Clay's Ark* (1984), and *Patternmaster* (1976). Because *Mind* was published three years earlier than *Wild Seed*, readers might already be aware that Emma (Anyanwu's Western name in this chronologically later novel) eventually dies of suicide at the close of *Mind*.[10] *Wild Seed* is, then, two partial stories of failure: Doro's eugenics and Anyanwu's emancipation. In a 1977 letter to her friend Maggie, Butler wrote:

> I have to figure out [some way] for my two immortal characters to have a complete story themselves—a story that can [exist] apart from MIND OF MY MIND. . . . The problem is, their goal is to build a new race around themselves, but they don't succeed until MIND OF MY MIND. So for [*Wild Seed*], they need—I need—to accomplish something else that will bring the novel to a satisfactory conclusion. I don't know where I picked up this working-backward style of mine. . . . Emma can only be partially successful. If she actually managed to stop Doro from breeding people, MIND OF MY MIND would never take place.[11]

The tactical move of embracing the inevitability of death while pointing to one's capacity to stake a claim in one's own death has a long history. Agential Black deaths have expressed political as well as personal responses to the specific pressures on Black lives. I agree with Terri L. Snyder when she writes of the necessity "to push beyond the model of resistance in order to grasp the complexities of suicide in slavery."[12] Indeed, this is also why I linger over *American Idol* winner Fantasia Barrino's explanation of her own experience with suicide in 2010: "I just got very, very tired."[13] Barrino's concise commentary on Black women's exhaustion, simultaneously plain, opaque, and ultimately ordinary, gets to the heart of this essay's concern. As an immortal character, Anyanwu serves a heuristic purpose concerning the afterlife of enslaved suicide: even her healing powers are not enough to reinforce or withstand the expectation of Black women's strength and resilience forever.

While working on this essay, I am filled with hesitation even as I steward a hope that its interventions will mean something to some survivor, somewhere. I think about C. I think about my teacher's sibling and about a colleague at my last job. I think of my friend's uncle and her ex-fiancé, who each died by suicide; of her cousin and both her parents' attempt of the same; and other partners who invoked this intention, including my ex in response to breaking up. I think about the consecutive suicides at my high school the year after I graduated, including the younger sibling of another friend. I think of two more friends who reached out and survived these thoughts. I think of my students who have explored these feelings in their work and who share the stories of their survival. I leave the prevention-strategy research in the far more capable hands of trained experts. My aim is much humbler—thinking, with the aid of speculative and neoslave narrative fiction, how to imagine the agency of those we've lost without celebrating them and without condemning them, but merely continuing to find ways to be present with their irreversible decisions, and with the pieces of us that follow them to wherever they've gone next.[14]

Wild Seed builds slowly toward Anyanwu's decision to take her life; the plan is developed long after her sexual and emotional servitude to Doro has become a habit. Even when their relationship appears loving, it is always already haunted by the specter of death. Doro engages in frequent body possession as a form of feeding to remain immortal and, at times, as a demonstration of his power and capacity to punish. Those he possesses die instantly; sometimes, the bodies are people Anyanwu used to know and care for. Anyanwu's submission is principally compelled by threats that apply pressure to her where she is most vulnerable: her capacity to be split open and still remain whole—which is to say, not merely her investment in maternity but also her capacity for endurance that stems from her immortality as well as from the intersection of her race and gender. Jennifer C. Nash describes Black womanhood as having "a relationship to time where loss organizes the ongoing conditions of lived experience. Loss was always there, and its felt manifestations are not a longing for a life where what was lost was present, but rather an attention to its constitutive presence."[15] Long before she meets Doro, Anyanwu's immortal life is woven from what remains of loving mortals: the mundane anticipation of loss, its endurance, and associated structures of feeling. Nash unfolds slow loss further, writing that it "ask[s] what [endurance and duration] feel like for Black women, and how Black women feel them."[16] The present essay is only one of many answers.

The structure of the novel complements Anyanwu's identification with her Black feminine form, as breasts bookend *Wild Seed*. Feeling out Anyanwu during their first encounter in her land, alternately threatening her and inviting her to join him, Doro concludes, "It was not until she began to grow breasts that he knew for certain he had won" (*WS*, 24). Here the breasts signal the characters' imminent sexual encounter, which will include Doro's enjoyment of her body, and also foreshadow the reproductive labor that will be extracted from Anyanwu for countless years to come. At the novel's end, following an emotional climax and after months of expecting her suicide, we learn, with a single line, that Anyanwu has *not* taken her life: "[Doro] slept, finally, exhausted, his head on her breast, and at sunrise when he awoke, that breast was still warm, still rising and falling gently with her breathing" (*WS*, 251). Again it is her breast in motion (first growing, now rising) that signals Doro's victory over Anyanwu's intention to opt out of her conditions. Rereading the line, we learn that Anyanwu's breast is warm *before* we learn that it is animated. For one punctuated breath, the reader may hope or fear that Anyanwu has only recently passed. Her body's warmth suggests life, but leaves space before the comma for the recession of life—for what's still warm to cool.

Reading Anyanwu's journey to this point and lingering with her speculative demise will reveal the limits of dominant frameworks to interpret enslaved suicide and to conceive of those who decline diaspora—those who fail, through their deaths, to get "in formation."[17] The ramifications produced by the confluence of these limitations impact the everyday lives of contemporary Black women and the tight affective spaces they are expected to fit in. Nash describes the circumscription of Black feminist representations to a binary logic of injury and recovery.[18] Nicole R. Fleetwood calls attention to "the repression of negative emotions and consensual practices that do not cohere in a progressive, transcendent, or uplifting personal, gender, and/or racial narrative."[19] Decades earlier, in the more private space of her hospital bed, Audre Lorde wrote, "There was a tremendous amount of love and support flowing into me from the women around me, and it felt like being bathed in a continuous tide of positive energies, even when sometimes I wanted a bit of negative silence to complement the pain inside of me."[20] Black women have so little room to deviate from ways to respond to their own experiences.

In addition to these departures, I'm drawn to ambivalence, and even less. I am interested in bodies that never recover, not just because they lack the necessary energy but because they are no longer interested in spending it. Butler's work invites alternative readings of suicide for the tired Black woman in the context of historic and contemporary framings applied to the enslaved—asking us to look beyond the binary lens of the rebel and the abject once more. Broaching these questions concerning enslaved suicide via Butler's critical fabulations acknowledges the persistent limitations of the formal archive, not only the pervasive gaps throughout but also the tendency of both well- and ill-meaning advocates to ventriloquize Black figures who lacked the means, rights, or desire to inscribe their own story.

Made Diasporic

The hold of the ship designated a zone of suspension and unmaking of someone into something else, as Hortense J. Spillers instructs.[21] More than the mere result of dispersal, less than a unifying politic, *diaspora* operates in unmaking's wake as a keyword that names the aspirational solidarity produced by the experience it also seeks to name. The violence of *being made* diasporic is multiple. The story that seems to end at the ship's railing does not; it continues to be told, and moved, and claimed. The resonances across Hartman's *Lose Your Mother*, Kevin Quashie's *Sovereignty of Quiet*, and Sarah Jane Cervenak's *Wandering* suggest that we are our most responsible to these stories when we learn to listen for them yet understand that there is only so much that is ours to find.

The frequency and description of suicide on slave ships were as grim as the "methods" employed to allegedly prevent it. Nets were erected on ship railings to catch those who jumped.[22] When weapons were within reach, others found the strength to slit their own throats. The bodies of suicides remaining aboard the ship or on the grounds of the plantation were mutilated to deter those who remained. Yet for insurance reasons, runaways were often preferred returned dead than alive. At times the pursuer and the fugitive were racing to see who would take their life first.[23] William D. Piersen estimates that "only a small minority of [enslaved Africans] willfully ended their lives. But since these suicides were part of one of the world's largest intercontinental migrations [*sic*], their numbers were probably into the hundreds of thousands over the three century span of the Atlantic slave trade."[24] The majority of reported suicide attempts on ship happened while still along the African coast while the majority on colonial American land happened within days of docking.[25]

Butler describes the atmospheric pull of suicidal ideation for Anyanwu, on board the slave ship:

> She pulled herself up onto the rail. "Anyanwu!" She did not quite hesitate. It was as though a mosquito had whined past her ear. A tiny distraction. "Anyanwu!" She would leap into the sea. Its waters would take her home, or they would swallow her. Either way, she would find peace. Her loneliness hurt her like some sickness of the body, some pain that her special ability could not find and heal. (*WS*, 58)

These are not Anyanwu's last suicidal thoughts, although only here does she entertain the possibility that ending her life might return her to West Africa. At times, she wonders why certain people don't take their lives or take them faster, and admires those in whom she perceives the "bravery" to see the act through to its completion (*WS*, 150, 211). Her New World husband Isaac's mother, for example, hangs herself to escape Doro's reach (*WS*, 123), not unlike Alice's final escape from Rufus in *Kindred*.[26] It is common knowledge among Doro's people that "the only sure way to escape him and cheat him out of the satisfaction of wearing your body" is suicide (*WS*, 97, 118–19, 122–23, 242–44). This mirrors Piersen's observation that enslavers "could catch most runaways, but were helpless to retrieve the dead."[27] Or, as Sharon P. Holland puts it, "the dead and their relations are perhaps the most lawless, unruly and potentially revolutionary inhabitants of any imagined territory."[28] In the case of self-destruction, Snyder cites Charles Ball, a former slave, who shared in 1837 that "suicide among slaves was 'regarded as a matter of dangerous example.'"[29] For this reason, Doro's method of suicide prevention is not so different from the enslavers of the historical record. By killing the enslaved before they can kill themselves, he is able to collect a last measure of usefulness and simultaneously intimidate others into submission by wearing the body as his own. Additionally, Doro profits from the dead body by breeding while he wears it; the enslaver was often able to profit from insurance policies or reimbursements from the colony for dead property.

Hartman famously noted, "There is not one extant autobiographical narrative of a female captive who survived the Middle Passage."[30] To write her own narrative more than one hundred years later during Anyanwu's writing career in *Mind of My Mind*, the captive figure must be supernatural. Moreover, to survive all the foreclosures of being Black and woman and slave, she must be superpowered (*WS*, 393). Hartman continued, "It would not be far-fetched to consider stories as a form of compensation or even as reparations, perhaps the only kind we will ever receive."[31] Against these intense desires and gaps, we can understand the impulse to situate enslaved suicide as a node in a larger tradition of collective resistance or symbolic escape, directing the abjected and terminal action of suicide to political use and to assertions of the dead's strength. Desirelessness, on the other hand, is difficult to defend and to identify with.

I adopt this term from Eunjung Kim, who writes, "The desireless figure can be understood as a mode of embodiment that reveals the ideological boundary of the human that is made legible through the nationalist and patriarchal language of desires."[32] Along with nationalist and patriarchal language, diasporan frameworks cast desirelessness into relief. As much as diaspora is about rupture, loss, and losing, it is also a commitment to connection, translation, circulation, coalition, and agitation at the boundaries of the human—to gain greater access to it.[33] Kim concludes her concerns with the question, "Is connecting through the absence of desire without having to register it as the presence of another normative desire possible?"[34] Our conceptions of diaspora are thoroughly enmeshed with the legibility of group constitution; the frameworks of resistance, return, and even abjection can be strategically useful to efforts at political organizing, community building, cultural expression, and so on. In contrast, recognizing individual exhaustion, ambivalence, and desirelessness, or at least discerning their turn away from group formation, produces incomprehensibility and eludes use by another. Yet if they cause any agitation to the circumscription of Blackness from the human, we must consider that they may chafe at a different side of its boundary.

Made Apparent

Return, resistance, and abjection are the dominant frameworks of interpretations for enslaved suicide. Alan Rice describes the spiritual return we observed at the start of Anyanwu's journey as a "utopian act of homecoming."[35] To this frame, Rice attributes happiness, joy, and pleasure to the disposition of those taking their lives and their witnesses. Snyder finds description in 1693 of enslaved suicide as aiming for transmigration and reunification.[36] Suicide as spiritual return will also be familiar to students of Gullah folklore, especially the story of Igbo Landing, which is alternately cast as a literal flight home or as a figurative flight through collective suicide by drowning.[37]

   The moral suasion interpretations of enslaved suicide enjoyed some sway in the 1830s and 1840s; the strategy emphasized the feminized victimhood of enslaved suicides and appealed to "evangelical readers' self-image as these afflicted victims' last best hope."[38] Abolitionists like William Lloyd Garrison invested in the circulation of "tearful" reports of enslaved suicide with the understanding that "fatalistic and utterly unthreatening" victims would gain more sympathetic support for the cause.[39] The abolitionist schism of 1840 saw a recommitment to moral suasion as well as the added tactic of fictionalized moral suasion seen in work like Stowe's 1852 novel, *Uncle Tom's Cabin*.[40] In *The Power to Die* Snyder observes and expands on these gendered trends in the coverage and discussion of enslaved suicide. Enslaved men were typically constructed as "heroically" weaponizing suicide as a form of "honorable" resistance to the conditions of enslavement, whereas women's suicidal acts were constructed as "passive," "indirect," or "unintentional"—or they were depicted as longing for death without acting on the desire, as shown in *Twelve Years a Slave, Incidents in the Life of a Slave Girl*, and *The Narrative of the Life of Mary Prince*.[41] Enslavers and the larger slavery system were blamed for Black women's (less frequently observed) suicide.[42]

The rebellious interpretation, which I will linger over, is one that codes physical resistance to subordination and provocations leading to death, along with self-directed violence in refusal of enslavement, as suicidal acts.[43] Rice characterizes the political aim of suicide as obvious: "It hardly needs to be said that suicide in itself struck a blow against the very institution of slavery, removing the productive body from its abuse in the system."[44] In the late eighteenth century and resurging after the abolitionist movement's fissure in 1840, Black and white antislavery activists and militants published stories of enslaved suicide as variously an expression of virtue, manhood, self-determination, and revolutionary action, and even called for enslaved suicide to be practiced as a targeted attack on or dispossession of the enslavement system.[45] For example, an enslaved man who drowned himself when robbed of his manumission in 1843 was sent off thus by *The Liberator*: "George has tasted liberty!!!"[46] In *We Shall Be No More* Richard Bell notes that the interpretations assigned by abolitionists to enslaved suicides were often strictly bounded by gender. Suicidal action by the enslaved was constructed as an avenue to assert manhood and claim (though not access) its associated privileges, while "black leaders rarely voiced enthusiasm for the idea that slave women had the courage and

virtue to mount the same . . . an assumption shared by many within the abolition movement—that black women lacked the capacity
for self-determination."[47]

Paul Gilroy and Stephen Best identify the resistance and revolutionary suicidal actions of the enslaved as early suggestions of diasporic political and philosophical consciousness. Drawing on historical accounts like that of Frederick Douglass's infamous fight with
Covey, Gilroy argues that the unfree's conceptualization of freedom
signals a diasporan ethical divergence from Western value systems
when he writes, "The repeated choice of death rather than bondage articulates a principle of negativity that is opposed to the formal
logic of rational calculation characteristic of modern western thinking and expressed in the Hegelian slave's preference for bondage
rather than death."[48] When the enslaved fail or refuse to adhere to
the dialectic's supposedly stabilizing relation, the "master" may remain secure in his title over those others who have not died, but the
suicidal actor is no longer a "slave," having opted out, so to speak, by
removing herself from relation. In "Come and Gone" Best theorizes
collective negation as "a philosophical project of self-divestiture, a
project that often involves the failure to make an appearance."[49] Reading the visual artist Mark Bradford's abstractionist work with tactile
removal, as well as the archival residue of mass Black suicides, Best
identifies each as expressions of negative political power and argues
that "self-annihilation presents a primary figure for diaspora."[50]
His work demonstrates that self-negation and queer negative socia-
bility unseat the prevailing narrative of positive, panethnic unity, and
long-suffering dedication to social change and self-possession in the
Black radical tradition—in other words, he decouples diasporic resistance from a teleology of improvement.

While the "self" of self-divestiture and self-annihilation is open to
both singular and plural interpretation, Best's citations home in on a
"shared sense of obligation to preserve the collective" shown in
scenes of mass suicide and destruction in the face of possible enslavement or reenslavement.[51] In mid-nineteenth to early twentieth-century
examples of such suicides or maroon community razings, he observes
"actualization through self-abnegation rather than against it."[52] Best
theorizes the creative capacity of collective suicide. That is, suicide's

enactment doesn't merely preserve the group to protect it from being conquered; it is also changed by such action—establishing a new form of relationality through shared obligation even as it removes all from relation. His work raises the possibility of further negations by the selves that comprise the mass action of self-abnegation. Departures from shared obligation could look like resistance, look like diaspora, look like the dead.

Seeing this, I feel my concern for dead tiredness thicken as the necessity of speculative and neoslave narrative fiction continues to grow. I celebrate with its scholars the pivotal role of critical fabulation in seeing beyond formal archives often marked by an inability to notice or imagine a Black woman as an agent in her own life. Beyond the limited examples that have survived, their desirelessness of others inflames my own desire to know: what kinds of death-bound agency and motivation belonged to the enslaved Black woman that will remain forever foreclosed to us? I join hands with Butler; we care for that tight space of willed surrender, of being dead tired, of opting out of endurance. Following the above interpretations, I consider the place of the solo and self-directed enslaved suicide that is not organizable or organized—*dis*organized, even. Anyanwu seems to engage in an individual act of Best's "logic of immurement," "entombing" herself without the context of group effort,[53] or in Butler's words, "shutting off" (*WS*, 246). Though they accept her suicide, Anyanwu's new family has no plans to participate in it. How can we ethically describe the practice of self-negation if we hold at bay any desire for collective deployment in the discursive mode? Might not some stories be occluded by configuring diaspora theory around the notion of a group will? Or, is diaspora still diaspora for the alone?

When Anyanwu first learns that Doro has arranged for her to marry his son Isaac (instead of himself) for breeding purposes, she disconnects her fallopian tubes. Feeling shocked, angry, and trapped, she briefly courts death through this inward defiance, and she announces that her altered organs will, like the suicides before her, prevent Doro from wringing more from her body. However, she ultimately submits to marriage with Isaac, accepting that submission in the short term might eventually allow her to recover Doro's humanity and her own. Isaac points out to Anyanwu that immortality makes her far more valuable to Doro than even he knows; her value is the only thing that stands between Doro and total loss of human feeling. Isaac goes on: "I'm afraid the time will come when he won't feel anything. If it does—there's no end to the harm he could do. I'm glad I won't have to live to see it. . . . You [Anyanwu], though, could live to see it—or live to prevent it" (*WS*, 120–21). This is compatible with Mark Reinhardt's reflection on pre–Civil War national narratives about motherhood (Anyanwu's primary identification) "as singularly capable of redeeming others."[54] However, by her own estimation, Anyanwu fails in the end to preserve the human feeling in Doro, and so fails more broadly in her typecast gendered duties.

At the close of the book Anyanwu turns her attention on herself, discovering and planning to address her own exhaustion. Doro sees her suicidal decision as a selfish act. After Anyanwu gives birth one last time and names new authorities in her place, Doro confronts her: "'Tell me what's wrong?' 'I've tried,' she responds. 'Then try again!'" (*WS*, 249). Anyanwu expresses her exhaustion with habituated living and submission through the alternative, nonverbal register of the planned suicidal act. She is tired, and she has no desire to talk about the future. Neoslave narratives such as *Wild Seed* explore suggestive interiors of the archive, consistent with Gilroy's observation that "the extreme patterns of communication defined by the institution of plantation slavery dictate that we recognize the antidiscursive and extralinguistic ramifications of power at work in shaping communicative acts."[55] Recognizing the limits of understanding, suicide declines further relation. The enslaver may continue to be a master, but of whom? Not her.

Anyanwu's plan, her "being-toward-death" maintained over the length of her final pregnancy, brings to mind Patrick Anderson's *So Much Wasted*, which outlines a politics of morbidity, described as "the embodied, interventional embrace of mortality and disappearance not as destructive, but as radically productive stagings of subject formations in which subjectivity and objecthood, presence and absence, life and death intertwine." Indeed, Anderson continues, "death is at the center of self-starvation's capacity to forge a subject whose existence is endangered by the very practice through which she or he produces power."[56] Anyanwu's commitment to oblivion gains her a negotiating power that she was not necessarily bargaining for (though a compromise is worked out at the novel's end). But I remain focused on her orientation toward oblivion, not its aftermath.

A New Position

In a scene that foreshadows Anyanwu's mortal decision, Doro asks to try something new, which he likens to the pleasure of "lovemaking" but "even more" (WS, 230–34). The act he proposes is a partial feasting on or partial possession of Anyanwu. Doro has been training to spiritually enter someone's body without completely taking over or devouring the soul. Between standard-issue humans, "even more" would merely sound like a request to try a new sexual position. For these immortals, however, it means "another kind of awareness" where Anyanwu experiences a vulnerability she has never allowed herself before: her own tiredness when faced with the visceral and spiritual reality of her death (WS, 234).

This new experience initially feels like falling in a manner that Anyanwu compares to a child's nightmare, but on her second go, the falling sensation gives way to something slower and more comfortable. A light in the darkness grows greater until "in a sense now, she [is] blind" but unharmed (WS, 232). Doro's presence is a "touch [ing] of her spirit" that reveals his hunger, his restraint, and his loneliness. "The loneliness form[s] a kinship between them" that transforms the experience yet again: both parties reach toward, blend into, each other (WS, 233). Yet when Anyanwu's consent to this experience ends, Doro's restraint has also reached its end. She reflects solemnly on his promise and betrayal of her safety, and finally accepts the inevitability of his loss of human feeling and inability to value others' lives. Both characters realize that Doro is spiritually consuming Anyanwu, and she is not resisting. "He was killing her, little by little, digesting her," to which Anyanwu resigns herself: "Well then, so be it" (WS, 234). The optimism born of pleasure slides into the too-bright light of lessons repeated often enough to finally be learned.

With acceptance comes permission to be tired. In the dialogue "Sex without Optimism," Lee Edelman and Lauren Berlant "see sex as a site for experiencing this intensified encounter with what disorganizes accustomed ways of being."[57] That said, the supposed sex in this scene is not just *la petite mort* but actual death, as Doro enters her body with both his physical form and his spiritual hunger, attempting to hold himself in that sweet spot before total consumption and displacement of his partner. Anyanwu had been so accustomed to surviving that she recounts several incidents when her instinctual reactions resulted in the accidental murders of weak and unwitting attackers (*WS*, 6, 22, 55, 70). She later describes living as a "habit" she has grown used to (*WS*, 123, 179). For the first time in her life of over three hundred years, Anyanwu experiences something truly new, distinct from her "accustomed ways of being" at the potential cost of her life: surrender—not sexual but mortal. Concurrently, she realizes that her situation in America and as one of "Doro's people" is intractable. Her efforts had not transformed Doro's relationship to the value of human life—for him, life consists only of "breeding and killing" (*WS*, 234). Their relationship, for so long defined by the passion of fucking and fighting and running and seeking, will now be entirely different.

The construction of Anyanwu's gender is central to the narrative, as is Doro's misogynist treatment of Anyanwu (his infantilization of her, his dismissal of her concerns, and his mulling over how to "tame" and "breed" her through manipulation [*WS*, 13–14, 20, 87]). To get Anyanwu to board his colony-bound vessel, he applies pressure to her maternal identity by threatening her existing children and by playing on her grief as an immortal mother to mortal children (*WS*, 15, 23, 116–17). He assesses that producing new children will tether her to the community of bondage that awaits her in his American colony (*WS*, 27–28, 87, 123). At the beginning of the novel, the strength of the shape-shifter's identification with "womanhood" is underscored by her frequent reflection on her investment in motherhood and caretaking, and by her enjoyment of shifting into a feminine form in sex acts. Butler designs Anyanwu's relationships with womanhood and motherhood as constants, no matter what shape she takes. For the readers of *Wild Seed*, Anyanwu's name stands in for the hendiatris of Black and woman and slave. We meet Anyanwu before she is enslaved; after arriving in Doro's colonies, she attempts to import and preserve these gendered investments despite the compromises she suffers or submits to, despite the hazards of holding to these convictions. Anyanwu understands what Doro recognized when he first met her: that her attachment to past and potential motherhood serve to "prolong her slavery" (WS, 132). At the same time, I recall Holland's concise summary: "It is not so much that captive peoples are not allowed gendered subjectivity but that these relationships mean nothing under a legal system that sanctions the treatment of humans as property."[58]

Anyanwu's total submission to Doro conditionally commutes the death sentences of her loved ones and herself (WS, 122–23, 179). This is consistent with Abdul R. JanMohamed's observation that under slavery, "the implication is . . . to live, the slave had to acquiesce in every way to his master; by asserting himself in any significant way against the master, he courted death."[59] During her habituation to these conditions, Anyanwu notices a change in her relationship to her subjectivity, which comes to a head in the "new position." Unlike the interchangeability of enslaved mortals, it is Anyanwu's rare shape-shifting ability and immortality that puts her in touch with the ordinariness of exhaustion. One privilege of surviving the passage of time is the capacity to grow weary of our habits, and even abandon them. In her partially digested state, Anyanwu, who has "formed a habit of submission" to Doro and to life itself, realizes she is ready to relinquish her habit (WS, 123). Rather than defiance, it is the revelation of her own tiredness with this paradigm that leads to her decision to die by suicide. Her preparations last nine months of a final pregnancy. Unlike the early moment at the ship's railing, Anyanwu no longer harbors intentions of returning to the continent or anywhere else. While previously she rebelled by escaping and hiding out in other animal and racial forms, now she stays put—now she puts up no resistance. She doesn't elicit death through indirection or confrontation but rather develops a plan, and though it causes others sadness, Anyanwu seems untroubled at last.

Of habituating the enslaved to enslavement, JanMohamed writes that "it is precisely life's attachment to itself that produces its value, a value that can be appropriated by the threat of termination or, to put it differently, by the threat to unbind life's categorical imperative to bind."[60] In the new position, spiritually undressed and half eaten in

Doro's otherworldly mouth, Anyanwu feels the absence of struggle, judgment, and fear; she notices the presence of desirelessness, tiredness, and a new capacity to let go. It must be said that Anyanwu's turn toward suicide is made possible *by* "loving" connection—her willingness to *feel* trust and intimacy *with* Doro, however temporary. Butler's notes in 1977 say plainly that "the Novel's goal is to teach Emma [Anyanwu] that the price in human suffering and to her own peace of mind is too high. Emma turns away from the covenant goal [the race building project]—breaks the covenant and eventually decides to die."[61] Yet, in the final text, the lesson for the protagonist doesn't arrive in the repetitive reminders of subordination that habituate Anyanwu to her status. Rather, it is reprieve—being held by Doro rather than holding back; surrendering desire itself—that ultimately reveals to Anyanwu her own "habit of living" that facilitates her recognition of exhaustion and even desirelessness in place of, or at the end of, endurance (*WS*, 179).

Earlier Anyanwu hypothesized that life requires the boundary of death to be legible and believed that her and Doro's heretofore untested capacity to die signifies their estrangement from the category of human. For the immortal Anyanwu, it is her excessive life—as flesh—rather than bare life that shaped her submission to Doro and produced the very exhaustion she is capable of symbolizing for contemporary Black women.[62]

Endings

Anyanwu's plan for suicide, a release from repair, is understood by Doro as a refusal to repair him. It's no surprise he thinks the song is about him. Kimberly Juanita Brown describes the trope of the strong Black woman in another way: "How does one survive slavery's flesh-and-blood defeating processes? The answer: use black women's bodies as the shield against which all atrocities can be siphoned, all exploitations contained."[63] Though it's clear to all involved that Anyanwu is not entirely intact by the novel's end, her confessions of desirelessness are eclipsed by the desires of others. This is similarly observed for a more widely known character, Baby Suggs of *Beloved*. What seems most unsettling about these two figures is that they refuse the legibility offered by resistance or negative affect; Baby is described as having "indifference lodged where sadness should have been."[64] Both recognize and subvert the conscription to give and give without taking something for themselves. Something ordinary will do. Baby claimed color. Anyanwu claimed her name (*WS*, 105–6).

Brutal as the material is, Black studies is no stranger to the tender ending. Hartman's departure from oral and archival history traditions to examine the sediment of the slave-fort floor in *Lose Your Mother* shows us that in some cases what remains is neither virtue nor surrender but only something pulverized beyond recognition. With so little left of the captured, it's hard to see the residue of blood and shit and skin defiantly—although we sometimes do. Or, we gather it as their defeat and hold it close to the chest as fuel to propel us beyond despair to something we can eventually call resistance.[65] We train our ears on the songs of girls and our eyes on the jump rope, rather than the composition of the ground it grazes. We look for color. We keep our names.

Again, I'm not making a case against resistance, nor am I celebrating defeat; rather, following Kara Keeling's construction, I'm trying to "look for" and "look after" Black women's tiredness.[66] When enslaved suicide ceases to be thought of as a collective and preservational action, when we can no longer recruit the dead to represent one of our many collective desires, we have few tools left to make sense of suicide. Writing about failure and disappointment and depression as stepping stones toward new visions, writing about the necessity of sublimating negative affects into survival strategies, although inspiring, has the effect of highlighting in those who die by suicide all the work they did not do, their failure to "properly" experience pain and grief and tiredness. *Why didn't they see what we all see from the other side of hurt? That the way out is through?* Perhaps because "through" and "out" are not the only paths, and survival is a set of terms that are not always available, accessible, or desirable. We must also be prepared to recognize that, sometimes, "read retroactively [suicide] is not only a leap toward death but also away from the death some are already living," as Eric A. Stanley writes.[67] If resistance and defeat can look exactly the same at a distance, what more have we missed? Did the slave jump for (a feeling misrepresented as) joy, or jump because someone said so, or jump overboard because "a woman should have something of her own" (*WS*, 105)? I think once more of the brief moment in *Wild Seed* that allows the reader to imagine that Anyanwu has only recently passed. No longer tired, one way or another.

....

IANNA HAWKINS OWEN is assistant professor of English and African American and Black diaspora studies at Boston University and will join the faculty of the University of California, Berkeley, in the fall of 2024. His first book, provisionally titled *Ordinary Failure: Diaspora's Limits and Longings*, is forthcoming; this essay represents its third chapter.

Acknowledgments

All Black genders deserve rest and a world that works to make the conditions of Black rest possible. This essay was inspired by a conversation with Fuifuilupe Niumeitolu after the death of our graduate-school colleague, C. I remember walking up the steps between the lions of the New York Public Library when C, with humor, released me from some of the things I thought I wanted from the PhD. I remember walking through the grass between the campanile and the Bancroft Library on the day we learned that she had died, and I remember the transformative and unsettlingly peaceful impact of Fuifui's words on my unready ears. I also feel deep gratitude for the feedback of Darieck Scott, Michael Cohen, Juana María Rodríguez, Adam F. Israel, Moya Bailey, Joseph Rezek, and Ananth Shastri; for conversations with Kathryn Benjamin Golden, Leigh Raiford, Lindsey Herbert, and Joseph Hirsh. My thanks also to the Huntington Library for stewarding Octavia E. Butler's papers and the Mellon Mays Undergraduate Fellowship and the Social Science Research Council for making my earliest archival travel possible. Finally, I am incredibly grateful to Annabel Barry and the editorial board of *Qui Parle* for their exceptional generosity and encouragement to complete this essay.

Notes

1. OEB #3217, "Commonplace Book (Large)," 1977–1982, Volume 1: July 6, 1977–May 5, 1978; page dated September 14, 1977. All OEB items are housed in the Octavia E. Butler Collection, Huntington Library Manuscript Collections, Pasadena, CA.

2. Agard-Jones, "What the Sands Remember."

3. This engagement with Butler is part of a larger project of addressing how the ordinariness of Black failure in public simultaneously wounds and keeps a promise to attend to the subjects whom the keyword *diaspora* hails. My book manuscript, *Ordinary Failure: Diaspora's Limits and Longings*, explores the ordinary intraracial failure of Black diasporic subjects. I see *failure* not as a term of judgment contrasted with success but as an opportunity to linger with the tender Black feelings it inspires.

4. Giri, "Diasporic Postcolonialism and Its Antinomies," 216, 220.

5. Brown, *Dropping Anchor, Setting Sail*, 128.

6. Sharpe, "'And to Survive,'" 173.

7. Hartman, *Wayward Lives, Beautiful Experiments*, 10.

8. OEB #2938, "Wild Seed: Novel: Early Notes," ca. 1975, undated page.

9. OEB #2944, "Wild Seed: Novel: Notes and Fragments," 1976, undated page.

10. Butler, *Mind of My Mind*, in *Seed to Harvest*, 452. *Seed to Harvest* is the anthology collecting all four *Patternist* novels, including *Wild Seed* (hereafter cited as *WS*). Notably, a fifth novel, *Survivor* (1978), was disavowed by Butler and excluded from the anthology.

11. OEB #3217, letter dated October 19, 1977.

12. Snyder, *Power to Die*, 7.

13. *Good Morning America*, "Fantasia."

14. The people named in this paragraph and in my heart encompass myriad racial, gender, sexual, class, age, religious, mad, and disabled groups. Though the present essay is focused on the suicidal thoughts and action of both fleshly and fictional Black women, high rates of suicide disproportionately affect several distinct and overlapping groups, including "veterans, people who live in rural areas, sexual and gender minorities, middle-aged adults, people of color, and tribal populations," according to Centers for Disease Control and Prevention, "Disparities in Suicide." A report released in 2023 by Johns Hopkins found that "Black youth have the fastest rising suicide rate among their peers of other races and ethnicities"; "between 2007 and 2020 the suicide rate among Black youth ages 10–17 increased by 144%"; and in 2021 "nearly 18% of Black high school students had made a suicide plan in the past year" (Johns Hopkins Center for Gun Violence Solutions, *Still Ringing the Alarm*, 4).

15. Nash, "Slow Loss," 2.

16. Nash, "Slow Loss," 3.

17. Beyoncé, "Formation," on *Lemonade*, Parkwood Entertainment and Columbia Records, 2016.

18. Nash, *Black Body in Ecstasy*.

19. Fleetwood, "Case of Rihanna," 423.

20. Lorde, *Cancer Journals*, locs. 456–57 of 1372, Kindle.

21. Spillers, "Mama's Baby, Papa's Maybe."

22. Bly, "Crossing the Lake of Fire," 181; Snyder, *Power to Die*, 42.

23. Watson, "Impulse toward Independence," 323.

24. Piersen, "White Cannibals, Black Martyrs," 154.

25. Piersen, "White Cannibals, Black Martyrs," 150–51.

26. Butler, *Kindred*, 248.

27. Piersen, "White Cannibals, Black Martyrs," 154.

28. Holland, *Raising the Dead*, 23.

29. Snyder, *Power to Die*, 99.

30. Hartman, "Venus in Two Acts," 3.

31. Hartman, "Venus in Two Acts," 4.

32. Kim, "Habituation of Desirelessness," 4–5.

33. Warren, "Appeals for (Mis)recognition"; Edwards, *Practice of Diaspora*; Gilroy, *Black Atlantic*; King, *Black Shoals*.

34. Kim, "Habituation of Desirelessness," 9.

35. Bly, "Crossing the Lake of Fire," 181; Rice, *Radical Narratives of the Black Atlantic*, 86; Piersen, "White Cannibals, Black Martyrs," 151.

36. Snyder, *Power to Die*, 36.

37. Works Project Administration, *Drums and Shadows*, 150; Walters, "'One of Dese Mornings,'" 19.

38. Bell, "Slave Suicide," 534.

39. Bell, *We Shall Be No More*, 246.

40. Bell, *We Shall Be No More*, 233.

41. Snyder, *Power to Die*, 124, 143, 148–50.

42. Bell, "Slave Suicide," 542.

43. Bell, "Suicide by Slaves," 491. See also Piersen, "White Cannibals, Black Martyrs," 150; and Bly, "Crossing the Lake of Fire," 182.

44. Rice, *Radical Narratives of the Black Atlantic*, 86.

45. Bell, *We Shall Be No More*, 201–46.

46. Quoted in Bell, *We Shall Be No More*, 242–43.

47. Bell, *We Shall Be No More*, 240.

48. Gilroy, *Black Atlantic*, 68, 56.

49. Best, "Come and Gone," 195.

50. Best, "Come and Gone," 195–98.
51. Quoted in Best, "Come and Gone," 195–96.
52. Best, "Come and Gone," 197.
53. Best, "Come and Gone," 202.
54. Reinhardt, "Who Speaks for Margaret Garner?," 94.
55. Gilroy, *Black Atlantic*, 57.
56. Anderson, *So Much Wasted*, 155–57, 330–31.
57. Edelman and Berlant, *Sex*, 11.
58. Holland, *Raising the Dead*, 46.
59. JanMohamed, *Death-Bound Subject*, 16.
60. JanMohamed, *Death-Bound Subject*, 75.
61. OEB #3217, page dated September 14, 1977.
62. Alexander Weheliye notes that Black feminist theories of the flesh com-
    plicate and "excavate" limited notions of bare life and civil death from
    their commitment to universal ideas of humanness (*Habeas Viscus*, 2).
    He then notes that "the flesh is not an abject zone of exclusion that
    culminates in death but an alternate instantiation of humanity that does
    not rest on the mirage of western Man as the mirror image of human life
    as such" (43). In other words, there is a parallel centrality, a reliance,
    rather than an exclusion, that characterizes "flesh" as a category more
    useful than "bare life" for understanding the condition of Blackness
    in the afterlife of slavery.
63. Brown, *Repeating Body*, locs. 2235–38 of 5579, Kindle.
64. Morrison, *Beloved*, 3–4.
65. In response to the minimization of wish and fantasy's capacities for
    use as resistance, Scott writes: "Surely, yes, such resistance [wishing]
    fails when the body/mind that enacts it is killed or beaten or tortured
    or starved into a cognizance of nothing other than bare survival—and
    these are common hallmarks of those of us embodied under the sign of
    blackness. But it is resistance nonetheless" (*Keeping It Unreal*, 35).
66. Keeling, "Looking for M—."
67. Stanley, *Atmospheres of Violence*, 97.

References

Agard-Jones, Vanessa. "What the Sands Remember." *GLQ* 18, nos. 2–3
    (2012): 325–46.
Anderson, Patrick. *So Much Wasted: Hunger, Performance, and the Mor-
    bidity of Resistance*. Durham, NC: Duke University Press, 2010.

Bell, Richard. "Slave Suicide, Abolition, and the Problem of Resistance." *Slavery and Abolition* 33, no. 4 (2012): 525–49.

Bell, Richard. "Suicide by Slaves." In vol. 2 of *Encyclopedia of Slave Resistance and Rebellion*, edited by Junius P. Rodriguez, 491–95. Westport, CT: Greenwood, 2007.

Bell, Richard. *We Shall Be No More: Suicide and Self-Government in the Newly United States.* Cambridge, MA: Harvard University Press, 2012.

Best, Stephen. "Come and Gone." *Small Axe* 19, no. 3 (2015): 186–204.

Bly, Antonio T. "Crossing the Lake of Fire: Slave Resistance during the Middle Passage, 1720–1842." *Journal of Negro History* 83, no. 3 (1998): 178–86.

Brown, Jacqueline Nassy. *Dropping Anchor, Setting Sail: Geographies of Race in Black Liverpool.* Princeton, NJ: Princeton University Press, 2005.

Brown, Kimberly Juanita. *The Repeating Body: Slavery's Visual Resonance in the Contemporary.* Durham, NC: Duke University Press, 2015. Kindle.

Butler, Octavia E. *Kindred.* Boston: Beacon, 2003.

Butler, Octavia E. *Seed to Harvest.* New York: Open Road Integrated Media, 2012. Kindle.

Centers for Disease Control and Prevention. "Disparities in Suicide." Last reviewed May 9, 2023. https://www.cdc.gov/suicide/facts/disparities -in-suicide.html.

Edelman, Lee, and Lauren Berlant. *Sex; or, The Unbearable.* Durham, NC: Duke University Press, 2014.

Edwards, Brent Hayes. *The Practice of Diaspora: Literature, Translation, and the Rise of Black Internationalism.* Cambridge, MA: Harvard University Press, 2003.

Fleetwood, Nicole R. "The Case of Rihanna: Erotic Violence and Black Female Desire." *African American Review* 45, no. 3 (2012): 419–35.

Gilroy, Paul. *The Black Atlantic: Modernity and Double Consciousness.* Cambridge, MA: Harvard University Press, 1993.

Giri, Bed Prasad. "Diasporic Postcolonialism and Its Antinomies." *Diaspora* 14, nos. 2–3 (2005): 215–35.

Good Morning America. "Fantasia—First Ever TV Interview since Her Recent Suicide Attempt! Live @ Good Morning America." YouTube, posted August 24, 2010, 8:53. https://www.youtube.com/watch?v= JA7WCBrrnEM.

Hartman, Saidiya. *Lose Your Mother: A Journey along the Atlantic Slave Route.* New York: Farrar, Straus and Giroux, 2007.

Hartman, Saidiya. "Venus in Two Acts." *Small Axe* 12, no. 2 (2008): 1–14.

Hartman, Saidiya. *Wayward Lives, Beautiful Experiments: Intimate Histories of Riotous Black Girls, Troublesome Women, and Queer Radicals.* New York: Norton, 2019.

Holland, Sharon P. *Raising the Dead: Readings in Death and (Black) Subjectivity.* Durham, NC: Duke University Press, 2000.

JanMohamed, Abdul R. *The Death-Bound Subject: Richard Wright's Archaeology of Death.* Durham, NC: Duke University Press, 2005.

Johns Hopkins Center for Gun Violence Solutions. *Still Ringing the Alarm: An Enduring Call to Action for Black Youth Suicide Prevention.* August 23, 2023. https://publichealth.jhu.edu/sites/default/files/2023-08/2023-august-still-ringing-alarm.pdf.

Keeling, Kara. "Looking for M—: Queer Temporality, Black Political Possibility, and Poetry from the Future." *GLQ* 15, no. 4 (2009): 565–82.

Kim, Eunjung. "The Habituation of Desirelessness: Anorexia and Asexuality." Paper presented to the National Women's Studies Association, Milwaukee, WI, November 14, 2015.

King, Tiffany Lethabo. *The Black Shoals: Offshore Formations of Black and Native Studies.* Durham, NC: Duke University Press, 2019.

Lorde, Audre. *The Cancer Journals: Special Edition.* San Francisco: Aunt Lute, 1997. Kindle.

Morrison, Toni. *Beloved.* New York: Vintage, 2004.

Nash, Jennifer C. *The Black Body in Ecstasy: Reading Race, Reading Pornography.* Durham, NC: Duke University Press, 2014.

Nash, Jennifer C. "Slow Loss: Black Feminism and Endurance." *Social Text,* no. 151 (2022): 1–20.

Piersen, William D. "White Cannibals, Black Martyrs: Fear, Depression, and Religious Faith as Causes of Suicide among New Slaves." *Journal of Negro History* 62, no. 2 (1977): 147–59.

Reinhardt, Mark. "Who Speaks for Margaret Garner? Slavery, Silence, and the Politics of Ventriloquism." *Critical Inquiry* 29, no. 1 (2002): 81–119.

Rice, Alan. *Radical Narratives of the Black Atlantic.* New York: Continuum, 2003.

Scott, Darieck. *Keeping It Unreal: Black Queer Fantasy and Superhero Comics.* Durham, NC: Duke University Press, 2022.

Sharpe, Christina. "'And to Survive.'" *Small Axe,* no. 57 (2018): 171–80.

Sharpe, Christina. *In the Wake: On Blackness and Being.* Durham, NC: Duke University Press, 2016.

Snyder, Terri L. *The Power to Die: Slavery and Suicide in British North America*. Chicago: University of Chicago Press, 2015.

Spillers, Hortense J. "Mama's Baby, Papa's Maybe: An American Grammar Book." In *Black, White, and In Color*, 203–29. Chicago: University of Chicago Press, 2013.

Stanley, Eric A. *Atmospheres of Violence: Structuring Antagonism and the Trans/Queer Ungovernable*. Durham, NC: Duke University Press, 2021.

Walters, Wendy W. "'One of Dese Mornings, Bright and Fair, / Take My Wings and Cleave De Air': The Legend of the Flying Africans and Diasporic Consciousness." *MELUS Journal* 22, no. 3 (1997): 3–29.

Warren, Kenneth. "Appeals for (Mis)recognition: Theorizing Diaspora." In *Cultures of United States Imperialism*, edited by Amy Kaplan and Donald E. Pease, 392–406. Durham, NC: Duke University Press, 1993.

Watson, Alan D. "Impulse toward Independence: Resistance and Rebellion among North Carolina Slaves, 1750–1775." *Journal of Negro History* 63, no. 4 (1978): 317–28.

Weheliye, Alexander. *Habeas Viscus: Racializing Assemblages, Biopolitics, and Black Feminist Theories of the Human*. Durham, NC: Duke University Press, 2014.

Works Project Administration. *Drums and Shadows: Survival Studies among the Georgia Coastal Negroes*. Savannah Unit, Georgia Writers' Project. Westport, CT: Greenwood, 1973.

Ordinary Expectation
Failure on the American Scene

SEAN MICHAEL MULLER

> They looked in vain to history for an explanation of themselves [and]
> found that they had no other place to search but within
> themselves. . . . Having failed to rivet the eyes of the world upon
> their city on the hill, they were left alone with America.
>> Perry Miller, *Errand into the Wilderness*

When someone learns that I'm an anthropologist studying addiction and deindustrialization in rural America, they start to talk about devastated landscapes and people "blasted," "ruined," or "wasted" by capital and chemicals. They'll share a story about life gutted by addiction or having seen—in front of their own eyes or in YouTube videos, documentary films, scripted television series, or sensationalist scholarship devoted to documenting America's poorer corners—a place they couldn't believe anyone would want to live.

I tell them about Washington County: situated between the eastern foothills of northern New York's Adirondack mountains and the western Vermont border, a landscape of rolling fields, dense forests, and small towns traversed by a road called "heroin highway," along

QUI PARLE   Vol. 33, No. 1, June 2024
DOI 10.1215/10418385-11125505   © 2024 Editorial Board, *Qui Parle*

which also moves fentanyl, heroin's deadlier and more prominent synthetic analogue.[1] This is an ordinary place where greenery covers up the failures of America and debris accumulating as evidence of the impossibility of its dreams fades into the background of progress. The image of a timeless white working class grounds the enduring expectations of what is ordinary here despite the economic, social, and political changes that have transformed its conditions of possibility.

Washington County became a deindustrial landscape during the 1970s globalization and financialization of capital.[2] Closing mills and factories were replaced by newly constructed prisons that only partly offset diminishing industrial and agricultural employment, leaving many people working in seasonal, tiring, and low-paying retail or service jobs supplemented by off-the-books income and unemployment insurance.[3] The natural assumption of upward social mobility and racial uniformity was sundered by a combination of economic decline and the influx of Caribbean and Central American immigrants arriving to work in the area's diminished timber, stone, shipping, agriculture, and tourism operations.

The official history of deindustrialization is one of natural economic "reindustrializing and restructuring," which David Harvey writes "cannot be accomplished without deindustrialization and devaluing first."[4] A geographically specific process of production depletes the resources available—the raw materials, the labor capacities, the limits of exploitation—and, therefore, to continue to grow in its normative accelerating and progressive mode, capital disinvests and departs.[5] The logic of competition justifies corporate decisions to close factories that no longer produce increasing profits—though, counter to this causal representation, these closures often occur at moments when profits are at all-time highs.[6] The process buries its costs—on environments, on communities, on bodies—in the epistemic murk of a rational order in which those experiencing its destructive effects are regarded as the temporarily wounded who will, ultimately, achieve better material circumstances as a result of their wounds and not as casualties.

Alternative economies exploit these conditions as the roads that are less frequently trafficked by shipments of lumber and stone become increasingly used to transport illicit chemicals. Material and affective economies conjoin with late-industrial America's empty spaces to produce a "ruined" subject in the interconnected figures of the addicted, infected, and criminal other occupying the depleted landscapes.[7] This is the weight of dispossession; it clings to our imagination and interpretation of the human casualties that accrue alongside the abandoned built environment—people whose lives, like the places where they're lived, are too often popularly and critically interpreted as the ruins of what used to be imaginable or possible. But ruin doesn't define everything here: partial "new economies" emerge from the nearly vacant, steeply devalued space produced by disinvestment. Postindustrial ecotourism and service economies thrive as the remains of the industrial past recede farther into memory, disappearing into the pastoral landscape. Ordinary dispossessions, addictions, and opportunities that appear alongside Washington County's emerging languid postindustrial future are unremarkable and exceptional at the same time.

The answer to the question of what "ordinary" means is evasive. It evokes self-evidence, banality, and naturalism while evading the material and affective infrastructures beneath these appearances. Tracing this subterranean architecture in *Ordinary Affects*, Kathleen Stewart writes that "the ordinary is a shifting assemblage of practices and practical knowledges, a scene of both liveness and exhaustion, a dream of escape or of the simple life."[8] This definition picks up the critical historical line drawn by Michel de Certeau's and Henri Lefebvre's studies of "everyday life" that focus on the practices and epistemologies making up an ever-fracturing whole.[9] These analyses of the everyday or—as this issue names it—the ordinary diagnose problems that cohere in the epistemic habits and anxieties that come to be understood as common sense.[10] Following Stewart's definition, however, I find another entry point into the ordinary in the image of the scene as the space and time where those habits and anxieties gather into tense articulations of expectations and have particular critical relevance and political resonance for an anthropology of America.

The complex web of exceptionalism, exclusion, dreams, and disappointments that makes up America is too massive to be made a coherent object of analysis. Because America is not just a geography or polity but a set of experiences and expectations, its problems cannot be apprehended meaningfully in totalizing terms. It is a map of overlapping material, affective, economic, and social geographies that contest the stability of one another's narratives. Advantage in one place grounds abjection in another, increasingly separated by less and less distance in worlds of late industrialism where a lingering industrial past continues to shape a supposedly already arriving postindustrial future.[11]

What Stewart once described as "an 'other' America" comes to live immediately next door to and is inseparable from the America of realized dreams.[12] These contradictory worlds press against each other in Washington County. Shaped by the damage of addiction and deindustrialization as well as the deferred forms of recovery offered—rehab and reinvestment cures that require individuals to continuously suffer in the name of a difficult-to-imagine, infinitely receding tomorrow—it is also home to service, tourism, and real-estate industries that capitalize on the resources of the land itself: the forests, rivers, and mountains of the Adirondack Park. Beauty and dispossession are the dual orders along heroin highway. Driven by people moving and using drugs, as well as police, tourists, and locals, the road both carries the promise of capital's teleological development and acts as an anxious vein of the toxic chemical economies sustaining the world left behind. There are two contradictory, overlapping senses of the late-industrial ordinary at work here: the ideal of a postindustrial pastoral alongside the lived reality of its intimate and interior spaces of material and affective aberrance embodied in the deindustrial rural.

The postindustrial pastoral evokes a world beyond deindustrial abandonment, industrial production, and the destructive effects of both. We imagine this world as an afterward where collapsing buildings are vacated and transformed into renovated homes, while plants and animals occupy the expectant remains around these salvaged investments. The deindustrial rural, on the other hand, exists in the real space between the industrial past and this idealized postindustrial future. It describes deindustrialization as an ongoing social and economic process that shapes the characteristic lack and excess of late-industrial life rather than as an isolated historical event. Ruination is a political designation that marks these sorts of spaces as uninhabitable, emptied out, and available for capitalist reappropriation masquerading as community-minded repair.

A scene is a fragment cut across these overlapping worlds that make up ordinary space and time. It is the product of landscapes, objects, and subjects, their relations and histories acted out in and through everyday life. In this sense, a scene is both an idealized stage on which actors rigorously perform their roles and a fractured field on which those roles are contested, denied, and realized. The set of problems my research addresses—addiction and dispossession in America's rural landscape—is apprehended here in three scenes where the ordinary and aberrant become indistinguishable as distinct structures of appearance. These are scenes where the natural history of dispossession both scaffolds and counterposes the dream understood as the ordinary expectation of American life, where the social and economic failures of the deindustrial present are inseparable from the possibility of a postindustrial future. Henry James described such particularly American scenes as compositions in which illumination and darkness were intrinsically connected to each other's visibility: uncertain compositions of light and shadow where "the general glare seemed to [be] at the end of something like a passage, in the shade of something like a court, and in the presence of something like a relic."[13] This essay works to disclose what Foucault called "the most common of secrets"—that a history is always also a history of what didn't or wasn't allowed to happen[14]—by attending to the ambivalence and contradictions that compose these single fragments in the flow of late American life.

Ordinary Landscape

The only way to get to Washington County is by car. You can take an Amtrak train or the Trailways bus to a few local stops between the state capital at Albany and the US-Canadian border, but once you're here, public transit is extremely limited and unreliable where it's available at all, and the distance between things is too far to walk or bike—especially in the winter months when temperatures rarely get above freezing. Walk along the roads here even a few thousand feet out of town and you become a curious object, a body made strange in a landscape composed mostly of the space between things.

Driving along heroin highway, language out of place breaks up the emptiness. On the side of a tall white commercial garage, dark green and black paint spells out "ethos=pathos=logos" in letters over seven feet tall. And at half the size and farther down the building's side: "Emotions are INSTINCTS." I first noticed the words in the spring of 2022; the contrast of dark paint on faded white aluminum siding caught my eye out the passenger-side window. The author crafted each letter with broad, even brushstrokes, taking care to make their message legible from the road. The next time I passed, I drove slowly, looking for other interruptions in the long stretches of roadside between small towns besides the familiar rhythm of houses, gas stations, auto mechanics, dairy barns, silos, and fields. The words are different from other missives covering the exposed granite faces of the roadcuts where the foothills have been blasted through to connect the distant towns up here: unevenly rendered swastikas, crosses flanked by dates two decades apart, and commitments held in cartoon hearts—crossed out and repainted in vibrant colors to replace the names of last year's love.

Completing these words required time, heavy cans of paint, multiple brushes, and a ladder to apply the second part of the text, which begins ten feet off the ground. The writer completed their work secure in the knowledge that anyone driving by wouldn't stop, because a body along the road here is an aberration—too poor for a car, too many drug-related arrests for a license, too out of sorts, chemically or otherwise. They must have been familiar with the vacant space at the side of the road seen only at the speed of passing through. Its capacity to be easily disregarded made it the perfect place to articulate a plea for legible presence in a space of disappearance.

Public education here doesn't expose students to Aristotle and literary theory; it prepares them for community college and entering what little postindustrial employment the area offers, mostly in the service and tourism industries. The words are out of place in this rural county, where the only option for formal education is an underfunded, standardized test-driven public system with double the state dropout rate, and in which half the students come from families struggling to survive the pressure of each month's bills. The sentiment—"ethos=pathos=logos, Emotions are INSTINCTS"—articulates a feeling that things here could be different.

These words use the space of emptiness to draw attention to its historical production and destructive effects on worlds living under the "burdens of 'nothingness.'"[15] Nothingness is an expectation that has historically been brought to bear on places at society's margins—and the apparent nothingness of northern New York has a dichotomous and conflicting identity as both valuable natural resource and haunting social failure. The edge of civilization is a space of potentiality and alterity both emptied and overrun with unruly energy, one of "those 'trashy' pockets of life across the American cultural landscape . . . where things are neither fully present nor absent but linger and echo in a simultaneous lack/excess."[16] The emptiness underpinning the ordinary rural landscape that passes for a postindustrial pastoral is inseparable from the human and material presence that populates and complicates that appearance, the "occup[ation of] an always already occupied place."[17] The "trashy"-ness of the rural, the mechanical and domestic debris that conjoins in the signature forms of deindustrial ruination—car parts on kitchen tables, furniture in front yards—is a structural character of its seeming emptiness. It signifies the complicated persistence and existence of lives flickering in and out of social belonging: illuminated as objects of public sympathy or consternation while being enveloped in the shadows at the margins of industrial consumption. Kept in the putatively liminal but practically permanent state of economic, social, and psychic instability through underemployment, undereducation, and overexposure to the material promise of an increasingly unachievable American dream, these places become visible as new frontiers for capital and invisible as sites where exceptional suffering is inscribed in ordinary life.

A defaced garage along a rural road brings the ordinary order of this America where, increasingly, "there are only winners and losers now," into a scene of critique.[18] Strange language calls attention to problems in a setting rarely regarded as worthy of attention because it is seen as the space between places. The towns along heroin highway are more readily recognizable as sites of abjection—empty main streets, vacant lots, the disparity and tension between well-cared-for homes and their seemingly abandoned or collapsing neighbors, which the anthropologist Catherine Fennell has called "going-homes," all register as ordinary in their own right.[19] These are places not yet caught up to the postindustrial promise, not yet subject to the impending reinvestment and revitalization that deindustrial devaluation necessarily precedes along capital's linear historical trajectory. This scene becomes a critical site because the line of the highway cuts across a landscape whose ordinary structure appears self-evident, the natural beauty of rural America whose pastoral imagination permeates the late-industrial scene.

Something out of joint with that structure reveals its ambivalent existence—the tensions and attachments composing its mutually dependent material, affective, economic, and social geographies where good lives are bound to "going" ones. Part of what makes this place the site where pastoral futures can be imagined is its emptiness; and that emptiness is the result of depleted conditions of possibility for the people already living here. The potential for economic and social rebirth is predicated on a wave of death expedited by disregard.

Ordinary Architecture

The deindustrial rural—stuck between an industrial utopian past and a promised postindustrial future—is a space shaped by what the anthropologist Michael M. J. Fisher has called "the meantime": "the gaps between visions and implementations [and] the differential gears of accelerations and decelerations."[20] This deindustrial meantime appears like a stubborn error troubling the realization of the postindustrial pastoral: a place where a historical moment has failed to recede and instead keeps reproducing the abject ordinary of late-industrial precarity.

Washington County, however, fails to fit into either the category of the totally devastated or the totally revitalized. Its built environment is full of contradictions, of histories that haunt but also promise. Restoration of the 160-year-old rural farmhouse is a dream, like the dream of an American good life, that lingers all around—realized in some places and rotting in others—but remains inaccessible to the people who occupy the landscape dotted with the "bones" of these potential rebirths.[21] To look critically at this built environment is to study "the wake of the future"[22]—the disparity between expectations and experience that describes ordinary appearance as a present living under the threat and promise of an idealized past.

Critical scholarship has demonstrated how the ongoing processes of deindustrialization continue to haunt the material and affective worlds that struggle to emerge into promised "new economies." Much of this work tracks how the built environment reflects and reinscribes this failure as the architecture of prosperity and stability turned into the architecture of sustained abandonment. The anthropology of North America has been at the forefront of this sort of scholarship over the last few decades, from Philippe Bourgois's influential work linking deindustrialization's social and economic devastation of an urban neighborhood and the resulting rise of alternate and illicit economies;[23] to Fennell's study of kinship, exclusion, and civics asking how a built space becomes an identity and how those identities—and the ties they form—are challenged as the space people occupy changes or fails to change around them;[24] to Walley's tracing of life surrounded and stalked by the past that describes how, as the industrial environment around her parents' house became increasingly devastated, they were forced to exist like ghosts in a world they once occupied as vital participants.[25]

Thinking with such scholarship, I argue that the architecture of the postindustrial pastoral is in direct and productive conflict with that of the deindustrial rural. In Whitehall, a small former industrial town split down the middle by a stretch of heroin highway that is also Main Street, these two material realities press against each other so closely as to confuse which encapsulates the ordinary appearance of the place. Whitehall lingers architecturally in the past, its streets a collection of late nineteenth- and early twentieth-century commercial buildings and former upper-middle-class family homes with gabled roofs and wraparound porches. The commercial properties sit mostly empty, while most houses exist somewhere along a spectrum of neglect—though there are exceptions: open businesses and well-kept homes haven't completely disappeared. Local archives contain documents cataloging the town's former grandeur, a history of the domestic, productive, and recreational infrastructure that haunts the place as an expectation of revitalization and its return to pastoral ideals.

Driving through town, you notice the speed with which the mostly empty parking lots and commercial properties surrounded by the woods on the outskirts of town give way to the empty ground-floor storefronts of old brick buildings on Main Street. Parallel to this central social and commercial artery flows its fluvial mirror, the barely trafficked Champlain Canal, which cuts town into its east and west sides. Looming over the east side of the canal and overlooking the rest of town is a massive stone mansion built by State Supreme Court judge Joseph Potter in 1874 on what was then the clear-cut top of a large hill named Skene Mountain. In the local historical society archives I found that its now regionally exceptional architecture was once common among the homes of Whitehall's prominent industrialists and government employees.[26] Though all the other homes were abandoned or neglected as cycles of economic boom and bust led to cycles of social disinvestment and despair, Skene Manor remains a solitary symbol of capital's promise, the American dream that it insists remains within reach hovering over a place eluded by that dream's possibility.

The architectural leftovers of the industrialist era exist alongside the architecture of a late-industrial present in this scene along heroin highway. The former compose the ordinary dream of a return to affluence—a frontier crossed from deindustrial rural abandonment to postindustrial pastoralism. The present, however, troubles this transition by populating this frontier with a world out of that ordinary: not-quite gone, though its presence is always treated as aberrant and temporary. The specters of rural addiction and persistent poverty traverse these disintegrating built environments: the castles cut up into many apartments, the rotting craftsmanship of an earlier, affluent era exist in parallel to the hastily constructed discount stores and mobile homes. These architectures of impermanence are designed to dehumanize those who inhabit them[27]—to keep them below the line of meaningful regard. Living surrounded by what is understood to be a moldering ruin of the past, an abject present, and exempt from any future, is to be perceived as inhabiting a pathological and teleological narrative. And the bodies match the homes: declining, rotting, dying, waiting to be rescued through a return that requires their erasure.[28] This is true of addiction and poverty, both conditions whose structural order preclude the possibility of escape, whether due to the lack of access to resources that ground opportunity—the ability to make one's time worth enough money to establish stable conditions of existence—or the promise of chronic relapse. The "trashy places" at the margins of America have a dual ordinariness: as the frontier of the postindustrial future waiting to be cleared of human and material debris, and as the landscape of deindustrial suffering mired in continuous material and affective abandonment. Two types of "trash" are at work here: a surface layer of trash covering an essential geography of American exceptionalism, and a deep stratigraphy of trash, excluded, all the way down, from the possibility of becoming otherwise, or belonging to a better future.

Ordinary Affects

I use the title of Stewart's analysis of the fleeting feelings, objects, and events whose connections and fractures congeal into the shape of life to ask, What is the ordinary experience of addiction? Disappointment as a fixed position: the feeling that the conditions of possibility are cut so close to your body that you're trapped in the tightly circumscribed world of disadvantage and despair of which you've always already been a marginal citizen.[29] It is the experience of writhing in place—of unsustainable speed and deathly slowness in a body fused to a depleted landscape.[30] In addiction, feelings and places are connected through chemicals and bodies. Anxiety makes a home in the psychic, social, and material architectures of dispossession. It becomes a nervous certainty that how one feels and where one is are natural conditions—that immobility is an essential quality of the addict's "infrastructure of feelings."[31]

In *Marxism and Literature* Raymond Williams describes "the structures of feeling" as the "affective elements of consciousness and relationships: not feeling against thought, but thought as felt and feeling as thought: practical consciousness of a present kind, in a living and interrelating continuity."[32] This concept continues to influence contemporary affect-oriented scholarship, though the move from "structure" to "infrastructure" reflects a meaningful conceptual shift. The structures Williams identified were monolithic, all-encompassing affective experiences of a national consciousness, generation, or population. The feelings he sought to describe were totalized: they shaped the possibilities and potentiality of large groups, they gave an emotional ground and horizon to historical events. The infrastructure of feelings described by scholars like Lauren Berlant, Ruth Wilson Gilmore, and Kathleen Stewart doesn't try to name the affective character on these grand scales; it is more focused on what Foucault called the "polyvalence" of the concept.[33] Feelings, in these authors' analyses, are both momentary arrangements and enduring constellations of the tension between people, objects, places, and histories—they can be flashes of rage, disgust, or adoration and thickly stratified resentments or commitments between individuals and groups. They reflect the conditions of possibility under which they can be felt and, otherwise, cannot be imagined. Economists and anthropologists both locate this infrastructure of addiction in the experience of loss of hope and the loss of means: despair and dispossession.[34] I want to trace the shape of these feelings: What does it mean to be desperate? What limitations and attachments does desperation make reasonable and imaginable? As someone who became, as Angela Garcia describes herself, "an anthropologist *because* of addiction," I struggle to know how and where to place myself in this work.[35] After more than a decade of self-destructive alcoholism and drug use and two years of sobriety, I returned to the area in rural New York where I had grown up and began driving heroin highway, which became the entry point for my theoretical inquiry and ethnographic field site. Descending into and emerging from my own despair made suffering as a way of ordinary life visible to me in a place I otherwise saw as simply emptied out by deindustrialization—a distant historical event that left behind ruins, poverty, and illness. I recognized the script that seemed to tell the future of these people and places so definitely: wasted lives in wasted space, junkies in fields of junk whose expectation of cure was always already inseparable from the inevitable return to disease and criminalization. Experience is not authority, but it is an open door onto a problem that appears all the more strange and disturbing for its familiarity. I approach the question of what it feels like to struggle with addiction by weaving the experiences of two of my early interlocutors with my own.

James described his struggle with alcoholism as an endless loop of anxiety, illness, and hopelessness.[36] Standing on an elevated subway station in outer Brooklyn, his body could not support itself against the withdrawals, making each tremble of the platform into an embodied shock. "I felt like I was dying all the time," he recounted, sitting in his car, parked along the East River, the heat turned up and the windows cracked to let in the cold air. Nick, another of my early interlocutors who struggled with alcohol and cocaine addiction, similarly described the feeling of "every day unfucked up [being] miserable, unbearable . . . so I would drink to excess, I'd take whatever drug I could get a hold of, just to get myself out of that place of feeling the same way for another day." The medical anthropologist Byron Good writes that illness narratives have a distinct sense of time, because they are always unfinished from the perspective of a sufferer who can speak only from inside an ongoing experience.[37] Because addiction is commonly, medically, and legally understood to be a chronic relapsing disease, its narrative has a strange extended[38] temporality—one in which the terminal point of a cure is an ever-receding horizon. James's and Nick's bodies pass time and pass through space, from moment to moment and place to place, all while struggling with the promise that tomorrow will be the same as today: a future devoid of the ability to imagine or take hold of resources to alter material circumstances or possibilities for different affective constellations.

My own experience of addiction was similar. The terror of facing everyday moments where bodily symptoms became inseparable from emotional disturbances filled me with the paralyzing feeling that nothing could change. Consuming chemicals brought relief from daily withdrawal by placing my trembling, writhing "bod[y] guilty of being out of sync" in the flow of life, "at the speed of an entire population."[39] Brought up to speed and out of paralysis, only to return to a state of despair. Momentarily free yet further alienated from the possibility of a future meaningfully different from the one I knew already: the long stretch of tomorrows mirrored by the one strung-out, anxious day I was already living. This feeling was ordinary as much as it contradicted the ordinary flow of unaddicted lives around me.

This ordinary experience is captured in the cycle of one scene: the lived experience of the loss of the future, an eternal return to a present moment that bears the weight of remembrance of things to come. It is the promise of impossibility. One scene that recurs, over and over, the precise details inscribed differently on different raced and gendered bodies, with the experience remaining the same: that of an unchanging temporal frame in which suffering and exclusion are the past, present, and future compressed into each moment. James, Nick, and I moved through the world of the meantime—in the gaps between appearance and imagination—with a certainty that whatever events we were a part of and whatever choices we made would fail to change the naturalized limits of our lives. Affective immobility shapes the possible narratives of addiction and recovery—itself a contested ideal and incoherent expectation defined as permanently and naturally precarious.[40]

This recurring scene of feelings, chemicals, environments, and bodies has a history where aberrance accumulates into an ordinary sensibility and sentiment that surrounds you in a geography of dehabilitation: a space—both real and imagined—that is at once emptied out of possibility and futurity while teeming with all kinds of life. As a site where addiction is emerging as both a public health and political crisis, the deindustrial rural is a stage on which this scene is played out again and again, with increasing frequency and urgency.

On the Late American Scene

"Each scene," Stewart writes, "is a tangent that performs the sensation that something is happening—something that needs attending to."[41] These fragmentary moments written, contemplated, and reexamined open the conceptual space to trace what happens in a world where ordinariness and aberration are in a constant tension that produces one's naturalization through the other's disappearance. A critical approach slows down the speed of life being lived to bring into focus the interdependent contradictions composing each scene.

Returning to the United States early in the twentieth century after decades of living abroad, Henry James embarked on a journalistic tour of his native country, later published as *The American Scene*. James found traveling in the land of his birth an experience defined by contradiction. No people on earth, he reasoned, were in a better position to live more comfortably in greater numbers than Americans, yet this possibility was the product of unsustainable intensity of production and moral corruption. Everywhere he arrived, he saw greatness encroached on by failure—affluence alongside abjection, the most cultured lives of the nation beset by the threats of low-class living. America was endangered by immigration, racial mixing, social tensions, rampant materialism, and greed.[42] "What strikes me," wrote James, "is the long list of the arrears of your undone; and so constantly, right and left, that your pretended message of civilization is but a colossal recipe for the *creation* of arrears, and of such as can but remain forever out of hand."[43] The "recipes" of endless expansion and extraction produced populations and landscapes "undone" in pace with the production of the dreamworlds of abundance and improvement. American exceptionalism produced a fractured geography of exceptions—people and places left out of the possibility of achieving the promise made and held on to all around them.

As late capitalism and late industrialism have become familiar terms describing the contemporary rural reality in Washington County, so I describe those same landscapes along heroin highway as a kind of late America: a place where the endurance of dreams depends on suffering somewhere to ground the possibility of its achievement elsewhere. The apparently ordinary cannot be separated from aberration and abjection. A postindustrial pastoralism absorbs the effects of rural deindustrialization into its appearance and creates a world where suffering recedes into the background, becoming overgrown until it falls out of sight and, eventually, out of mind. Because this connection is so naturally, seamlessly incorporated into the worlds of the people who live in and look toward rural America, it can best be apprehended by focusing on moments where aberrance—normally relegated to the shadows—appears clearly in the light of the ordinary order around it.

The scene is an analytic space in which to regard this everyday world through an at once isolated yet inseparably connected site where power weighs down in ways not readily apparent at the speed of passing through. It offers anthropology a field site in which to study the ordinary through "the most intense point of lives . . . where they clash with power, struggle with it, endeavor to utilize its forces or to escape its traps."[44]

....

SEAN MICHAEL MULLER is a PhD student in anthropology at Columbia University. His research focuses on addiction and deindustrialization in the United States. He is interested in tracing the affective and material connections between landscapes, politics, and expectations that shape late-industrial America.

Acknowledgments

My thanks to my colleagues Brendan John Brown and Christopher R. Thompson, who read drafts and shared insightful comments that helped shape what appears in print here, despite an extremely tight deadline. I am also grateful to Jason Pine for his exceptional generosity and mentorship. Finally, my deepest gratitude to Drew Villano, who consistently pushes me to describe reality rather than depend on the obfuscating power of academic language and whose writing ceaselessly inspires me.

Notes

1. According to weekly reports published by the US Department of Health and Human Services, deaths related to fentanyl and other synthetic opioids have increased over 1,000 percent since 2013, while the number of heroin-related deaths steadily decreased (Mattson et al., "Trends and Geographic Patterns").
2. Harvey, *Condition of Postmodernity.*
3. As local industrial production decreased, it also became difficult to live off the small-scale agricultural production practiced by Washington County's family farms. For a fascinating political analysis of the death of the American farm, see Dudley, *Debt and Dispossession.*
4. Harvey, *Condition of Postmodernity*, 296. Friedrich Nietzsche and Michel Foucault both use the term *official history* to mean a very specific construction of truth in the present moment. It is important to locate their use of the term historically and understand that their target in

condemning such "official" discourse was historians whose critical projects attempted to establish total truths of social progress. I use *official history* here to evoke a historical common sense around deindustrialization and addiction that is reproduced in dominant epistemic, economic, political, and biomedical frameworks. See Foucault, "Nietzsche, Genealogy, History."

5. Dudley, *End of the Line*; Walley, *Exit Zero*.

6. Walley, *Exit Zero*, 79.

7. This subject is often racialized when people speak about who brings drugs into an area. *Up from the city* and *south of the border* are metonyms that ascribe criminality to people whose race causes them to stand out against an overwhelmingly majority-white population. These assignments of blame based on race also displace the political—and narrative—ramifications of recognizing that most people who use and distribute drugs in the area are white and local.

8. Stewart, *Ordinary Affects*, 1.

9. Certeau, *Practice of Everyday Life*; Lefebvre, *Production of Space*.

10. Stoler, *Along the Archival Grain*.

11. Fortun, *Advocacy after Bhopal*.

12. Stewart, *Space on the Side of the Road*.

13. James, *American Scene*, 294.

14. Foucault, "Life of Infamous Men," 90.

15. Fennell, "Rethinking Vacancy," 419.

16. Stewart, *Space on the Side of the Road*, 41–67.

17. Stewart, *Space on the Side of the Road*, 58.

18. Stewart, *Ordinary Affects*, 93.

19. Fennell, "Rethinking Vacancy," 431–32.

20. Fischer, *Anthropology in the Meantime*, 4.

21. Aspirational real-estate listings in the area describe aging structures as having "good bones" (Geffner, "How to Tell If a House Has 'Good Bones'").

22. Fischer, *Anthropology in the Meantime*, 4.

23. Bourgois, *In Search of Respect*.

24. Fennell, *Last Project Standing*.

25. Walley, *Exit Zero*.

26. Historical Society of Whitehall, New York, "Castles, Manors, and Other Charming Residences."

27. Shapiro, "Attuning to the Chemosphere."

28. Ahmann, "Introduction"; Fennell, "Rethinking Vacancy"; Morris, "Shadow and Impress."

29. Garcia, *Pastoral Clinic*; Pine, *Alchemy of Meth*.

30. Pine, "Economy of Speed."

31. Gilmore, "Abolition Geography"; Berlant, *On the Inconvenience of Other People*.

32. Williams, *Marxism and Literature*, 132.

33. Foucault, *History of Sexuality*, 100. I include Stewart—though she doesn't use the term *infrastructure of feelings*—because her work on affect is essential to how I think with Berlant's and Gilmore's work.

34. Case and Deaton, *Deaths of Despair*; Garcia, *Pastoral Clinic*. Case and Deaton's argument adheres to the boundaries of strict quantitative analysis. However, that they give an affectively charged name to conclusions drawn from their data strikes me as relevant to a critical anthropological analysis of rural America.

35. Garcia, *Pastoral Clinic*, 32.

36. The names of my interlocutors have been changed, and the quotations here were compiled from multiple interviews.

37. Good, *Medicine, Rationality, and Experience*.

38. Or circular: addiction, as noted by other anthropologists who study it and by their interlocutors, is an extremely repetitive experience. See Bourgois and Schonberg, *Righteous Dopefiend*; Garcia, *Pastoral Clinic*; O'Neill, *Hunted*; Pine, *Alchemy of Meth*; and Zigon, *War on People*.

39. Virilio, *Speed and Politics*, 56.

40. Garcia, *Pastoral Clinic*.

41. Stewart, *Ordinary Affects*, 5.

42. James's xenophobic, racist, and generally hateful attitudes were enshrined by scientific convention and political protection in the America of the early twentieth century—a place as exclusionary as he finds it to be exceptional, though this analysis eludes him.

43. James, *American Scene*, 463.

44. Foucault, "Life of Infamous Men," 80.

References

Ahmann, Chloe. "Introduction." *Anthropological Quarterly* 95, no. 2 (2022): 241–75.

Berlant, Lauren. *On the Inconvenience of Other People*. Durham, NC: Duke University Press, 2022.

Bourgois, Philippe. *In Search of Respect: Selling Crack in El Barrio*. New York: Cambridge University Press, 1995.

Bourgois, Philippe, and Jeffrey Schonberg. *Righteous Dopefiend: Selling Crack in El Barrio*. Berkeley: University of California Press, 2009.

Case, Anne, and Angus Deaton. *Deaths of Despair and the Future of Capitalism*. Princeton, NJ: Princeton University Press, 2020.

Certeau, Michel de. *The Practice of Everyday Life*. Translated by Steven Rendall. Berkeley: University of California Press, 1984.

Dudley, Kathryn Marie. *Debt and Dispossession: Farm Loss in America's Heartland*. Chicago: University of Chicago Press, 2000.

Dudley, Kathryn Marie. *The End of the Line: Lost Jobs, New Lives in Postindustrial America*. Chicago: University of Chicago Press, 1994.

Fennell, Catherine. *Last Project Standing: Civics and Sympathy in Postwelfare Chicago*. Minneapolis: University of Minnesota Press, 2015.

Fennell, Catherine. "Rethinking Vacancy; or, Thinking with the Going Home." *Anthropological Quarterly* 95, no. 2 (2022): 417–36.

Fischer, Michael M. J. *Anthropology in the Meantime: Experimental Ethnography, Theory, and Method for the Twenty-First Century*. Durham, NC: Duke University Press, 2018.

Fortun, Kim. *Advocacy after Bhopal: Environmentalism, Disaster, New Global Orders*. Chicago: University of Chicago Press, 2001.

Foucault, Michel. *The History of Sexuality, Volume One: An Introduction*. Translated by Robert Hurley. New York: Pantheon, 1978.

Foucault, Michel. "The Life of Infamous Men." In *Power, Truth, Strategy*, edited by Meaghan Morris and Paul Patton, translated by Paul Foss and Meaghan Morris, 76–91. Sydney: Feral, 1979.

Foucault, Michel. "Nietzsche, Genealogy, History." In *Language, Countermemory, Practice: Selected Essays and Interviews*, edited by Donald F. Bouchard, translated by Donald F. Bouchard and Sherry Simon, 139–64. Ithaca, NY: Cornell University Press, 1977.

Garcia, Angela. *The Pastoral Clinic: Addiction and Dispossession along the Rio Grande*. Berkeley: University of California Press, 2010.

Geffner, Marcie. "How to Tell If a House Has 'Good Bones.'" Zillow.com, October 18, 2022. https://www.zillow.com/learn/house-has-good-bones/.

Gilmore, Ruth Wilson. "Abolition Geography and the Problem of Innocence." In *Futures of Black Radicalism*, edited by Gaye Theresa Johnson and Alex Lubin, 225–40. New York: Verso, 2017.

Good, Byron. *Medicine, Rationality, and Experience: An Anthropological Perspective*. New York: Cambridge University Press, 1994.

Harvey, David. *The Condition of Postmodernity: An Enquiry into the Origins of Cultural Change*. Cambridge, MA: Blackwell, 1989.

Historical Society of Whitehall, New York. "Castles, Manors, and Other Charming Residences." Compiled by Carol Senecal, 2015. https://files .acrobat.com/a/preview/ce8f1385-0925-4944-8443-07f98b076346 (accessed August 31, 2023).

James, Henry. *The American Scene*. London: London, Chapman and Hall, 1907.

Lefebvre, Henri. *The Production of Space*. Translated by Donald Nicholson-Smith. Cambridge, MA: Blackwell, 1991.

Mattson, Christine L., Lauren J. Tanz, Kelly Quinn, Mbabazi Kariisa, Priyam Patel, and Nicole L. Davis. "Trends and Geographic Patterns in Drug and Synthetic Opioid Overdose Deaths—United States, 2013–2019." *Morbidity and Mortality Weekly Report* 70, no. 6 (2021): 202–7.

Morris, Rosalind. "Shadow and Impress: Ethnography, Film, and the Task of Writing History in the Space of South Africa's Deindustrialization." *History and Theory: Studies in the Philosophy of History* 57, no. 4 (2018): 102–25.

O'Neill, Kevin Lewis. *Hunted: Predation and Pentecostalism in Guatemala*. Chicago: University of Chicago Press, 2019.

Pine, Jason. *The Alchemy of Meth: A Decomposition*. Minneapolis: University of Minnesota Press, 2019.

Pine, Jason. "Economy of Speed: The New Narco-capitalism." *Public Culture* 19, no. 2 (2007): 357–66.

Shapiro, Nicholas. "Attuning to the Chemosphere: Domestic Formaldehyde, Bodily Reasoning, and the Chemical Sublime." *Cultural Anthropology* 30, no. 3 (2015): 368–93.

Stewart, Kathleen. *Ordinary Affects*. Durham, NC: Duke University Press, 2007.

Stewart, Kathleen. *A Space on the Side of the Road: Cultural Poetics in an "Other" America*. Princeton, NJ: Princeton University Press, 1996.

Stoler, Ann Laura. *Along the Archival Grain: Epistemic Anxieties and Colonial Common Sense*. Princeton, NJ: Princeton University Press, 2009.

Virilio, Paul. *Speed and Politics*. Translated by Mark Polizzotti. Los Angeles: Semiotext(e), 2006.

Walley, Christine. *Exit Zero: Family and Class in Postindustrial Chicago*. Chicago: University of Chicago Press, 2013.

Williams, Raymond. *Marxism and Literature*. Oxford: Oxford University Press, 1977.

Zigon, Jarrett. *A War on People: Drug User Politics and a New Ethics of Community*. Berkeley: University of California Press, 2019.

Brown Gathering
Archive, Refuse, and Baduy Worldmaking

ADRIAN DE LEON

During the summer of 2021 a Los Angeles gallery affiliated with the University of Southern California showcased the works of Diane Williams, an installation artist who calls the Philippines and Southern California her homes. The exhibit was called *The Precarious Life of the Parol*, named after a Philippine ornamental lantern made of bamboo and paper and displayed in Filipinx households for the Christmas holidays. Attendees beheld an array of tapestries and sculptures, painstakingly crafted from wire, wood, plastic bags, empty cans, and other everyday trash objects. At lunch across from the gallery, I asked Williams why it was that, despite the titular reference, there did not exist a single traditional *parol* in her entire exhibit.

She noted that, initially, she had tried to research the Spanish colonial history of the parol and to trace a linear progression from its earliest forms to its present appearances in the diaspora. But she found little archival evidence, and the popular histories written about the parol were, according to her research, apocryphal at best. As for the materials from which she composed her sculptures, she remarked that her family began to hear about her artistic practice and, in

QUI PARLE   Vol. 33, No. 1, June 2024
DOI 10.1215/10418385-11125515   © 2024 Editorial Board, *Qui Parle*

response, revisited the items of their everyday lives and chose objects to send to her. From Seafood City grocery bags to empty cans of SPAM, these "physical cultural detritus" (as Williams calls them) came to signify the relationship between their collectors (her family members), the artist, and the exhibit to come.

"It's *baduy*, right?" she offered.

"Not in the pejorative, of course," I responded.[1]

We laughed at what felt like an inside joke. In Zinc Café, a posh semi-outdoor establishment, it seemed transgressive (and relieving) to be speaking so jovially about the power of discarded objects. *Baduy*, meaning "in poor taste" or "uncool" in Tagalog, at once indexes the Filipinx *ordinary*—the objects and practices of migrants' everyday life—and the racialization of Filipinx ordinariness vis-à-vis its *temporality*. To be specific, the nontrendiness of Williams's self-described baduy practice is not a comment on her craft but an aesthetic appraisal of a longer history of Filipinx racialization as being "backward" and "not yet civilized": markers of anachronism that have shaped the Filipinx subject during and "after" American colonialism.[2]

When I reflect on our conversations over the years, I am reminded of *rasquache*, the Chicano aesthetic of improvisational bricolage, in which artists "make do" with the ordinary materials and tools around them.[3] Through her work Williams herself becomes at once the curator of cultural detritus and the medium for her family's cathexis with the artistic work she constructs using their objects. As a weaver, she derives her aesthetics from feminist histories of craft, especially the craft of native women in her home island of Luzon. And, as a member of her family, she tests each suture against the weight of her familial archives, presenting detritus anew through tapestries and sculptures. For me, her work's insistence on its *collectivity* (that it is embedded in her family and her community, as well as a particular milieu of immigrant waste objects), as opposed to a figure of a solitary genius using rarefied materials, foregrounds a productive tension between racialized creators and the white disciplinary spaces in which they exhibit their art.

If, for Williams, *Parol* is baduy or rasquache, what might this exhibit say about the shared experiences of brown(ed) migrant artists as they encounter the Western artistic tradition, the American gallery, or the capitalist economy of artistic value? Or, conversely, what do the latter manifestations of colonial and institutional discipline attempt to do to brown(ed) artists, whose unruly practices encounter these spaces that seek to appraise or suppress them? And what does it mean specifically for Filipinx art, from a community that is now just finding its foothold within mainstream American popular culture, to invest not in "elevation" or "modernization" but in salvaging what is being lost to the aggressive displacements of late-capitalist modernity?[4] What does it mean today for Filipinx people to be stubbornly baduy?

❬ ❬ ❬

Parol is an exhibit assembled out of the constitutive messiness of Philippine history and the quotidian unruliness of immigrant life: the haphazardly found objects, the improvisational and contingent acts of collection, the uncool and baduy. This essay dwells not only on *Parol* and its creation but also on Williams's artistic and curatorial practice within the cultural milieu of Philippine immigrant life throughout the spaces of American imperialism across the Pacific. At the time of writing, Williams has done two shows that feature pieces from *Parol*. The first was the titular exhibit, which was her thesis at the USC Roski School of Art in Los Angeles. The second, at the College of the Canyons in Santa Clarita, California, took place shortly after, titled *The Mess of Empire*. While her previous shows have been described as "surreal visions of immigration,"[5] in which she primarily drew on Continental feminist thinkers like Simone de Beauvoir, *Parol* marks a departure in which she pivots to global South thinkers like Neferti X. M. Tadiar as her anchoring theorists. This shift away from the monstrous and ornate masks in her earlier exhibits has enabled her to center "found, discarded, salvaged materials" as the objects of meditation themselves.[6] Coupled with the fact that her exhibits coincided with the tail end of the COVID lockdown and the interstitial phase in which live gallery visits had not yet enjoyed the traffic of pre-pandemic years, it is telling that (save for this essay, which is the first scholarly work to date on Williams's work), *Parol* has not yet been substantially reviewed or featured in the critics' circuits.

According to her artist statement, Williams "weaves *physical cultural detritus* as metaphors for how the marginalized are often viewed as 'detritus of society' while monumentalizing these embodied objects" (emphasis added).[7] Let me follow the movement of Williams's "messy practice." If, as Dylan Rodriguez notes, the Filipinx racial condition cannot be articulated outside empire, and following Amy Kaplan, imperial culture is constituted through a fundamental anarchy—a failure of the cohesion of the nation-state—then for Williams, "mess" is not just an aesthetic but also a critical analytic and a world-making practice.[8]

I read Williams's "messy practice" as queer curation, which Gayatri Gopinath notes is an "intersubjective, interrelational obligation to engaging the past."[9] Furthermore, thinking with Martin F. Manalansan IV, when "clutter" is understood as a practice of queer immigrant homemaking, it also offers us a means through which we might understand the material and affective lives of diaspora under empire.[10] Thus messy archives and queer curation are not "careless" even if—in the prerogative of imperial normativity—they are "disorderly." It follows that gathering mess into aesthetic objects embedded within the history of Filipinx migration enables Williams to enact stewardship, relation, and care—and to reject colonial ordering.

The pieces that make up Williams's *Parol* guide us toward what I call *brown gathering*: quotidian practices of archiving that mobilize the kinship networks of minoritarian subjects as an affective and circulatory infrastructure of collecting, preserving, and (re)signifying the objects of brown life. Brown gathering simultaneously attests to the intimacies of state violence and the practices of minoritarian subjects. The objects that compose Williams's pieces, and the cultural contexts from which they are gathered, materialize what José Esteban Muñoz calls the "brown commons," a turbulent yet shared space of being together between human and nonhuman collectives, at the margins of capitalist and imperial violence, from which alternative forms of life might emerge.[11] Thinking with Muñoz, I suggest that brown gathering emerges when the queer ecology of the brown commons is under attack, when the minoritarian life within this organic-inorganic interface turns to craft to make sense of detritus.[12]

We can understand this when we refract these practices not through nonwhite alterity (as brownness is often configured) but rather through the contemporary condition of disposability and the creative practices of subjects made disposable—what Tadiar calls "remaindered life."[13] Brown gathering, as a world-making practice within the queer ecology of the brown commons, reckons with this disposability not as an undesirable and uncivilized state of being to overcome, but as the material to write histories and politics otherwise. Put differently, brown gathering, as a method of collective "thinking with," between different intellectual and aesthetic traditions to make sense of an inchoate diasporic experience, is both a curatorial and a citational practice—and the scaffolding of this essay.

As curatorial and aesthetic engagements with the material archives of brown kinship, the aesthetic works that (contingently) cohere through brown gathering do not cohere at all. What I mean is that, in the case of *Parol*, the pieces are a testament to the cluttered nature of accumulation under a racialized capitalism in the Philippines and the Filipinx diaspora. Sarita See elaborates on this through her study of American knowledge production and its inextricable relationship with the systematic and violent dispossession of Filipinx people. Put simply: the imperial collection (like the museum, gallery, library, archive, academy) encourages plunder through the supposed achievement of knowledge and progress.[14] One who performs brown gathering brings together what has been rampantly accumulated in/as the detritus of imperial globalization but disenchants the triumphalist narratives that might give justification to the mountain of debris.

Williams creates tapestries and sacred objects in *Parol* out of literal garbage, specifically the trash objects produced from diasporic Philippine life. Once gathered, these trash objects are formed into the visceral and material forms of reproductive labor and domestic worship: severed umbilical cords, fetal forms, woven rugs, (indigenized) Christian iconography. The pieces in *Parol* spill onto the floor, between exhibition and excrement, opening an aesthetic space of abject incommensurability that talks back to the telos of primitive accumulation.[15] Thus brown gathering is a practice that assembles refuse objects together not to enact their rehabilitation but to advance *refusals* of hegemonic regimes of aesthetic and racial value—in other words, to advance a collective politics of the unassimilable and ungovernable.[16]

I frame my investigation around three categories, which reflect Williams's object-based theorization: skeletal frames (wood and wire) to explore archives of excess and mess; plastics to speak about the temporality of diaspora; and discarded food containers (SPAM cans and sauce mixes) to theorize the politics of the brown body. Williams's practice centers these discarded materials, which are (to think with Max Liboiron) the objects that constitute the ongoing violence of land relations under capitalism, a process called *pollution*, which Liboiron also names *colonialism*.[17] These objects, like the brown subjects that signify them, are testaments to the ongoing plunder of empire and to what empire jettisons around the world.

Frames

In *Anting-Anting* (fig. 1), a modified parol star hangs in place, held together by a perpendicular half of a picture frame with a hook at the end. Unlike the circular symmetry of a traditional parol, this figure springs forth unevenly from the center. The shape of the parol reappears throughout the exhibit in its asymmetrical form but is further destabilized through its title: *anting-anting*, the name for a Tagalog amulet rooted in indigenous mythologies, syncretized with Spanish Catholic symbolism. Routing the parol through a Tagalog amulet and native spirituality destabilizes the form from its Spanish Catholic associations; likewise, routing the amulet through a Christmas ornament pulls the anting-anting out of an atavistic place of precoloniality, highlighting its persistence today among Filipinx communities as a syncretic spiritual object.[18]

But what draws my eye in this piece are the parastructures that "frame" the amulet. Below, a wooden frame bends out of shape as if making a futile attempt to contain the object within. Along the vertical axis, two slabs of concrete hold in place a dowel below the amulet and half a wooden frame supporting the dangling piece from above. Of note are the drips and pools of paint along the base. With

Fig. 1. *Anting-Anting*. Photo credit: Ryan Miller.

the exception of three dregs of white paint along the green Knorr seasoning pouch, none of the paint actually ends up back on the amulet. Was the wood a frame, a canvas, or a catch tray—or all at once? Without the coherence of the platonic amulet, or the parol form, or the two-dimensional canvas, or the civilizational teleology of History, *Anting-Anting* "makes do" with whatever scraps do not seem to fall away from the underlying structure. Rather than flattening the representation of this amulet, the sculpture asserts the amulet's excess, unbounded by the frame and failing to conform to what it tries to approximate, whether an anting-anting or a parol.

The Santo Niño Story (fig. 2) situates the parol within the colonial history of the Santo Niño de Cebu, a religious icon said to have been given in 1521 by the conquistador Ferdinand Magellan to Humabon, the Rajah of Cebu, who converted to Christianity. The original Santo Niño, now kept in its eponymous basilica, bears Habsburg-era regalia, and was considered to be miraculous when it was found by conquistadors as the only surviving Spanish object of first contact in the wake of Magellan's death at the hands of the chief Lapu-Lapu. Like the parol, the Santo Niño connotes a syncretic relationship

Fig. 2.   *The Santo Niño Story.* Photo credit: Artist.

between Filipinx Catholic material culture and Spanish colonialism. Yet, despite the dignified and stately countenance of the source material, I cannot ignore the shadows in the background of this particular piece, nor can I overlook the almost improvisatory (if sacrilegious) rendering of the icon. The Santo Niño, rather than standing upright on an altar, dangles loosely from above. This is a hanging of the icon, the shadow—gallows for the Santo Niño's mangled form—pointing to the violent colonial roots of a venerated object of Philippine life.[19]

In many of the pieces in *Parol*, materials—things—are literally falling away. Accounting for these forms and materials at the precipice of disintegration places Williams's work within the affective forms of "noncapitalist" strata that Tadiar elaborates on in her 2009 book, *Things Fall Away*. In a study of Philippine historical experience within literary and cultural productions in the 1990s, Tadiar attends to aesthetic practices through which literature enacts the "political seeds of an alternative future, which already exist in the form of devalued social modes of experience." Debris and rubble are particularly potent allegories for Tadiar as she makes her way through urban writers in Manila: "As part of the daily work of survival, urban experience in this sea of contradictions [of globalization] is how one relates to the dirt, the noise, the pollution, the excess matter of one's surroundings. More, it is how one lives *as* a particle of that dirt, noise, and pollution."[20] The pieces in *Parol* articulate Philippine mythologies that barely cling to form, drawing out the essential Filipinx nature of the objects at hand. Yet they also exist *within Los Angeles itself*, a city that, like Manila, is caught in the multiplicities of stratification, rubble, marginalization, and the spectacle of postmodernity.[21] In the context of globalization, Williams's practice foregrounds the experience of falling away, flaying, dripping; I posit that, in *Parol*, these are the motifs of Filipinx diasporic historical experience, between Luzon and Los Angeles. If the constitutive archive of queer diasporic life is mess, disciplining this clutter into coherent forms neither salvages this detritus into liberal subjects nor enables an atavistic return to a precolonial root of the parol. Rather, Williams conserves the omissions of historical knowledge and curates contemporary detritus *as the materials through which Filipinx subjects might constitute historical experience itself*, as absence, as mess. Brown gathering enables an act of care for discarded lives by way of care for their discarded objects, which emerge from the social life of Philippine subjecthood.

Williams's calling her source materials "physical cultural detritus" thus specifically names them not as raw materials but as *already discarded and refused*. While the final product might constitute a cultural production, the materials that cling to the form, to paraphrase Tadiar, are "things [that] fall away" despite their approximation at cohesive narratives and references to Philippine historical symbols. Williams's practices of weaving, assembling, and suturing point to the tentative and fleeting nature of such constructions. The forms and histories are grounded by each piece's title, as well as by the spectral presence of the parol lantern, often distilled into a repeating motif. What remains in each piece, then, is a hauntology of the parol and other historical forms of Philippine life distilled down to their skeletons: a manual loom for the tapestries, or exposed wood and wire for the sculptures.

Thus, without the veneer of a neatly cohesive object (and subject), brown gathering resists the reproduction of civilizational logics under the authoritative linear time of History. For colonial subjects like Filipinx people, this is the logic of racial uplift and tutelage; and for migrant subjects like Filipinx people, this is the logic of cultural assimilation and integration. Instead, as Williams's practice demonstrates, brown gathering denatures the telos of the nation-state by pointing to (and meditating on) its bloodied and cluttered remainders, or the violent costs of colonial uplift. Nor does brown gathering invite us into a sanitary and formal kind of aesthetic contemplation. In the context of the gallery, contemplative time is not an endpoint, but is instead an asymptote; brown gathering does not *actually* reach this, because the very archival materials (and archival ethics) constitutive of the art objects resist postsensory aesthetic pleasure and thus commodification. To think with the literary scholar David Lloyd, brown gathering eludes the Kantian mode of artistic contemplation (as the hegemonic regime of beholding art objects) that claims to transcend the "savage" world of the senses toward the "civilized" practice of locating universality in aesthetic forms.[22]

In *Parol* we are told the form (the parol) but can never see it cohere, whether in its (lack of) origins or in its renderings among the exhibit's pieces. What we see instead are the materials and craft practices of minoritarian art, as well as the traces of minoritarian eating and collecting. Therefore brown gathering makes visible the underpinnings of modern aesthetics: race.

What I mean is this: the sacred motifs in *Parol*, constructed out of the trash objects produced from diasporic Philippine life, do not seek to obscure the excess of a racialized ordinariness but rather place it front and center, compelling the viewer to attempt to seek out a form that refuses to come together. By centering unruly discarded objects within and beyond both the physical wooden frames and the interpretive frames of artistic and historical form, Williams foregrounds the political possibility of the baduy, or the racialization of migrant objects and practices in terms of their anachronism. In *Anting-Anting* and *The Santo Niño Story*, these are the empty soup-mix packets (especially *sinigang*, a tamarind-based brothy dish from the Philippines often associated with home cooking); the crocheted flowers knotted together with household rags; the seamstress's balls of yarn and other soft objects used as pincushions; and the wood and wire frames that allude to mythological forms. Their *care*ful assemblage, or their queer curation, showcases the unfiltered mess of commodities around which the everyday milieu of the Filipinx migrant exists; commodities which, despite their entropic quality, nonetheless provide the raw materials to articulate contingent and tentative modes of historical experience.

Plastics

In *Anting-Anting*, and indeed across all the pieces in *Parol*, Williams uses a variety of plastics to shape her works: acrylic, wrappers, resin, grocery bags. In the ceremonial life of Philippine holidays, this is a common phenomenon; in the archipelago, many households repurpose similar discarded objects into ornaments. (I myself, as a child in Manila, used plastic bottles and pebbles to create makeshift maracas for Christmas carols in the neighborhood, while my cousins made tambourinelike instruments with bottle caps nailed to a piece of wood.) The omnipresence of plastics in *Parol* suggests to me a disaggregation from monolithic understandings of plastics as petrochemical by-products that systemically defile pristine nature. When understood as objects subjected to the practice of brown gathering, plastics are not just pollutants; they also chart the intersections between Filipinx racialization under capitalism and historical and contemporary regimes of disposability.

Following Williams's aesthetics along the grain of her archival materials, I contextualize her work as a collector working within the refuse of history. Situating her art, from her materials to her craft, within the rubble of the neoliberal present, Williams turns to plastics to trace relations and counterhistories within regimes of disposability rather than to engage in a liberal disavowal of ongoing ruin (which we might call respectability politics). As plastics are objects that decay at rates far slower than anthropocentric lifetimes, Williams's uses of them in *Parol* compels onlookers to pause and slow down, to enter a different contemplative space against teleological History, but not as sanitized and desensitized observers of the work.[23] Rather, *Parol* invites other temporalities to enter: the gustatory body, the decaying object, the half-life, the tenuous, the ephemeral, the fleeting, the precipice. In other words, *Parol* calls on the onlooker to enter the racialized temporalities of waste.

When I first encountered *Curtain of Illegibility* (fig. 3) and *Roadside Memorial* (fig. 4), I nearly tripped over the artworks littering the area where a viewer might be expected to behold them, interrupting the spatial logic of aesthetic contemplation. The litter, which comprises the pieces themselves, literally *litters*—as surplus, as refuse, as unruliness that compels me to follow it upward to the works above. While both pieces are tapestries that seem to be constructed out of the same raw materials, *Curtain* is more of a sutured quilt (as well as, of course, a curtain), whereas *Roadside Memorial* appears to have been worked on a loom. They are at once artistic pieces and the scaffolding and infrastructure for other visual interventions: the parol motif, repeating until saturation; and a spray-painted X (fig. 4) that gestures to the unseen subject of the memorial, a dead body.

Thus, despite their similarities in form, these pieces diverge in their symbolic strategies. *Roadside Memorial* indexes a *trace*—an *absent presence*—of corporeal *remains*, crudely demarcated by the

Fig. 3. *Curtain of Illegibility.* Courtesy of UTA Artist Space.

woven inorganic garbage of Filipinx life. By contrast, *Curtain of Il-legibility* holds within its appellation an irony, in that it is rife with two quite legible (and visually loud) symbols: the semiotic satura-tion of the parol-like star, and the logo of the supermarket chain Sea-food City. Let us think through the latter. Like Jollibee and other

Fig. 4.   *Roadside Memorial*. Photo credit: Ryan Miller.

Filipinx-owned transnational companies, Seafood City turns a diasporic nationalism into a corporate one, turning migrants from workers to worker-customers. In migrant households, these grocery bags are accumulated in excess and often archived by happenstance, relegated to the cupboard underneath the kitchen sink; Williams herself notes that she received these plastic bags from family and friends who had surplus containers in their homes as well.[24] While re-creating migrant lifeways through the compilation of commodities and tastes familiar to Filipinx families is a necessary and pleasurable reproductive labor on which the propagation of ethnic culture depends, the corporate nationalism that makes American (including Asian American) corporations profitable does not account for the pollution it produces.

Though the bags' corporate origins are obscured, the preponderance of plastics in *Roadside Memorial* nonetheless suggests a relationship between petrochemical waste and necropolitical states. Williams twisted and flayed the various plastics until they could be woven more easily—yet still meticulously—in the manner of yarn. I understand *Roadside Memorial* to be situated within the regime of President Rodrigo Duterte and the necrostate established under his so-called war on drugs. The Duterte regime exemplifies the death drive of neoliberal capitalism in the global South, whereby unproductive and undesirable subjects are viewed by the sovereign as utterly nonrecyclable and inorganic, and thus deserving of being put to death.[25] In the Philippines, the urban poor are resignified as disposable subjects—Vicente Rafael understands them through Giorgio Agamben's notion of *bare life*—by other names: "drug personalities," "drug pushers."[26] Their interior lives, and anything that signifies them as marginally human, are flushed out, rendering them disposable subjects, the refuse unabsorbed into the liberal bourgeois order of the neoliberal nation.

I would like to return to Williams as a collector, as a brown gatherer, and the means through which she constructs an alternative temporality for contemporary diaspora. In her construction of the "collector as allegorist of the Anthropocene," the literary critic Elizabeth DeLoughrey might route *Parol* through the intersections of waste and negatively racialized migration.[27] Following her thought: whereas the anthropologist Mary Douglas declared that waste is "matter out of place," and the sociologist Zygmunt Bauman likewise called "wasted lives" the discarded subjects of a political body, I would posit that Filipinx diaspora, displaced by multiple imperialisms and corporate-military occupations and jettisoned around the world for the profit of the nation-state, is constitutively a discarded subject.[28] Of Caribbean writers and artists who allegorize the Anthropocene, DeLoughrey writes that they "[engage] the reader as participant by calling attention to our responsibility as witnesses to states of waste in the age of the Great Acceleration."[29] Thus a practice that gathers refuse is not just an aesthetic and poetic critique of the Anthropocene; it is also a critique of capital's relentless march to progress, a march which, to paraphrase Walter Benjamin's famous thesis, leaves behind rubble in its wake.[30]

Following DeLoughrey, I posit that Williams, with a practice rooted in Filipinx migration and archival methods, exemplifies this collector as allegorist. And the allegory she specifically constructs around environmental destruction is the temporal relationship between Filipinx diaspora and plastics. According to the geographer Liboiron, plastics "exist in geological time" and cannot be discarded within the accelerated times of capitalism, nor within the lifetimes of Western humanity. Likewise, plastics "defy containment" both within space (waste management and recycling) and within time: "[Plastics'] long temporality means their future effects are largely unknown, making uncertain the guarantee of settler futures."[31] If waste is matter out of place, and diaspora is made of discarded subjects, then how does one recount not only the history of discard, but also a *history of the condition of being disposable*?

Addressing the historicity and temporality of rubble is at the heart of Williams's use of plastics. In our interviews, she situated *Parol* within an intersection between the creative practices of remaindered lives and speculative practices in the face of absences in colonial archives.[32] In *Parol* Williams weaves plastics as if these materials—and the craft that she channels through her hands—were themselves the *fabula* (the raw materials of a narrative) of a history in absentia. As explained earlier, she could not find the clear origins of the parol, no matter how painstaking her research.[33] Parols appear out of place and shores up historical palimpsests out of time, combining Chinese influences (rice paper lanterns) and Spanish colonial spiritualities with native craft. In the figures above, plastics are woven (in the Ilokano language of northern and central Luzon, *inabel*) using looms, signified with the parol motif yet unresolved in that no origin story is ever offered. Following Liboiron, who charts their thinking on plastics through the feminist historian Michelle Murphy, there are ways of thinking about plastics otherwise, from what Murphy calls *alterlife*: "a politics of non-deferral . . . a challenge to reinvent, revive, and sustain decolonizing possibilities and persistences right now as we are, *forged in noninnocence*, learning from and in collaboration with past and present projects of residence and resurgence."[34] By placing the geological time of plastics in proximity with the dilated and improvisational temporality of native craft (weaving and sculpting), Williams theorizes tentative histories of Filipinx diaspora within the nonteleological time of an organic-inorganic interface, a brown space—the brown commons.

Thus in *Parol* Williams enacts *a refusal of any sort of rehabilitative project*, even as the third space opened by brown gathering might one day give way to the purchase and commodification of the works. A work like *Parol* is consequently positioned within a struggle between the livelihood of the artistic profession and the frictions born from a commitment to baduy objects that *remain devalued*. As scholars have shown, the global Filipinx subject has been and continues to be *racialized to care for the world*.[35] Whereas the racialization of care produced a Filipinx person who might be put to work, the idea that labor (including farm labor and domestic service) might recuperate the allegedly uncivilized and idiotic Filipinx people emerged during the late Spanish colonial period. Sony Coráñez Bolton probes the constitutive debilitation of the Filipinx native within the writings of Chinese and Spanish mestizos, who saw their native counterparts as unenlightened and in need of uplift.[36] The United States would take on this rhetoric through colonial education and ableist representations of their new imperial subjects. After formal Philippine independence in 1946, the postcolonial state continued to send workers overseas, with the program's numbers magnifying in the late twentieth century. However, at this point, migrant workers were to suspend their personal needs and, as heroes and martyrs, to suffer for the *overall rehabilitation of the Philippine nation*.[37] By the 2010s, under the Duterte regime's war on drugs, the unproductive lower strata would be deemed too far gone to rehabilitate; the domestic (and particularly, urban) poor were marked for disposal by extrajudicial killings.[38]

Alluding to the disposability of Filipinx life (through labor export and state violence) by way of the curation of disposed plastics, the baduy nature of *Curtain of Illegibility* and *Roadside Memorial* thus insists on the ways that matter *persists*, even as this matter is marked as anachronistic and out of fashion, and even as the political class of the island nation might seek to sweep this matter under the rug for the sake of progress. Matter persists through the temporality of plastic itself, whose decomposition takes place in the *longue durée* of geological and petrochemical time. This persistent matter, which literally interrupts the spatial and temporal character of aesthetic contemplation, opens up space and time for another kind of contemplation, which is *mourning*. In *Curtain of Illegibility*, it is the mourning of an untraceable historical past in the absence of a formal archive; and in *Roadside Memorial*, it is the mourning of lives lost to the death drive of the Philippine government. Paraphrasing DeLoughrey, Williams's use of plastics invites the onlooker to become a *witness*, not only to "states of waste" but also to those rendered as wasteful by a murderous state regime.

Viscera

What animates Williams's work, even as the pieces in *Parol* seem to fall away from cohesive form, is a search (however futile) for Philippine diasporic identity. Earlier, I suggested that *Parol* is an act of caring for the past, a queer curation of a messy migrant archive, a brown gathering. This practice also enables Williams to enact counterhistories of Philippine geopolitics and of the environmental destruction of the global South. In this section, I want to suggest that Williams becomes both curator of, and *medium for*, an intimate counterhistory of American imperialism and Philippine subjecthood, situated deeply within the *brown body*. Her works zoom in from the spatial to the embodied aspects of imperialism and lives otherwise.

Certainly, the acts of weaving and sculpting—and twisting wires, suturing cans, and other such practices—testify to the embodied handiwork of native craft. But I recognize, too, that *Parol* is a profoundly gustatory and visceral endeavor, and it must be emphasized that some of the most notable pieces of physical cultural detritus in these pieces are food wastes—specifically, food packaging.

From SPAM cans and takeout boxes to empty seasoning wrappers and grocery-store bags, Williams's materials create a gustatory terrain of the Filipinx body, assembled through the practice of brown gathering, which we have called various names: messy, plastic, iconoclastic, tentative, caring. Here, by means of a conclusion, I call Williams's practice *organic, visceral, ecological*—otherwise, *brown*.

The three pieces above are drawn from the full range of Williams's forms: a sculpture, a tapestry, and a curtain. Appended to—or, more accurately, dragging from—each artwork, food wastes tethered together by wire or yarn resemble eviscerated entrails. In *The Spam Story* (fig. 5), crushed cans trail from the bottom of the parol's frame, thinly held together to the bottom vertex of the star form. In *Weaving Colonial Consumption* (fig. 6), two cans of SPAM, still maintaining their rectangular shapes, are joined by a white-and-yellow takeout container covered in acrylic. And in *Batik and the Lasa of Control* (fig. 7), two food containers contain empty wrappers and labels. These food containers are tethered to other familiar motifs in *Parol*: the parol star frame (fig. 5), the loom (fig. 6), and the curtain (fig. 7). As I behold each of them, I find myself meditating on another absence: the food itself. SPAM is a ubiquitous item in the Filipinx diasporic diet whose traces haunt the construction of these artistic creations.

Together, these pieces sketch a visceral politics of creative labor under the condition of remaindered life. I take my cue from Kyla Wazana Tompkins through whose work I understand a queer-of-color feminist politics of socialized and racialized eating. In *Racial Indigestion* Tompkins notes that, in the nineteenth-century United States, eating emerged as a "trope and technology of racial formation" and the gustatory making of the modern American body politic.[39] I take her argument to extend to the imperial body politic as well.

Fig. 5. *The Spam Story.* Photo credit: Artist.

Fig. 6.   *Weaving Colonial Consumption*. Photo credit: Artist.

Fig. 7. *Batik and the Lasa of Control*. Photo credit: Ryan Miller.

For Tompkins, critical eating enables us to think through the continuities of the mouth and digestive tract between subjects rather than the commodified objects that constitute our foodstuffs. If we take eating as constitutive of racial formation, we foreground the sociality of the body, a gustatory element of "the touching without appropriating it to itself" on which the brown commons is built.[40] Laying food waste on the floor in the manner of guts, these works gesture to the fact that, despite the lushness and nutritional bounty of the Philippine archipelago, food security has been withheld from native people by the twin forces of militarism (SPAM cans, from food rations) and capitalism (all manner of branded packaging). And while the Filipinx diaspora constitutes its foodways through available materials in ethnic culinary infrastructures, corporations benefit from this gustatory nostalgia as a means to create markets. The messy archiving of migrant households takes place around the wastes of this corporate nationalism. Thus in *Parol* Filipinx embodiment is inseparable from the material violence of commodified nourishment and military provisioning.

SPAM, in particular, suggests a fundamental indigestibility of colonial consumption. The work of CHamoru poet Craig Santos Perez helps me situate the gustatory terrain of the militarized commodity in transpacific relation. In "SPAM's Carbon Footprint," Perez traces the entangled relationship between CHamoru diets and American settler militarism on Guam through the tinned meat. In this poem, Perez saturates the text with "SPAM®" by repeating it no fewer than thirty-nine times, suggesting that, like the American military and American capital, SPAM embeds itself ubiquitously into the bodies of the colonized.[41] Likewise, SPAM cans are ubiquitous in Williams's pieces, a trope that appears particularly along the spillage on the floor.

Commissioned by the US army quartermaster and produced by Hormel Foods in Minnesota, SPAM was provided as food aid in the post–World War II Pacific. Filipinx people, like CHamoru and Okinawan people, indigenize SPAM as cultural object and as common provision.[42] In SPAM, Pacific peoples under military occupation resignify a military foodstuff and foreground histories of imperialism otherwise submerged in the metropole. This resignification is so strong that other transnational companies, like McDonalds, have needed to "glocalize" their products and offer SPAM on the menu. Yet, as Perez notes, the Pacific dependence on SPAM also signals a fundamental food insecurity under military occupation, which reserves fresh produce and access to Indigenous provisioning for the exclusive (parasitic) use of the colonizer. He writes: "The end result [of Guam's affection for SPAM] can be found in the newspaper's obituary pages. In 2004, Public Health reported that heart disease was the leading cause of death on Guam, representing 33.7% of deaths."[43]

I highlight SPAM's unhealthiness not to moralize Pacific peoples' eating habits, but to point to the ways that Williams deploys SPAM in her work. The insider might note that "Filipinx people love SPAM." The questions, then, that unearth the uneasiness of ongoing imperialism force-fed into the brown body are *when and why* did they come to love SPAM in the first place? The key ingredient, according to Robert Ji-Song Ku, lies in SPAM's origins as a food preservation technique. In the United States, SPAM is paradoxically both a symbol of military technological ingenuity and, due to its cheapness and ubiquity during economic downturns, a marker of white trash, especially after the second half of the twentieth century began to shift the culinary cultural capital of middle-class whiteness toward the valorization of freshness. Concurrently, Hormel's signature product took on other cultural meanings in the transpacific military colonies of the United States, becoming comfort food and status marker in the Philippines, South Korea, Okinawa, Hawaiʻi, and Guam.[44] Williams reflects SPAM's transpacific ubiquity in *Parol*'s repeated use of the blue cans; the symbolic saturation of SPAM lays bare the ecological and gustatory costs of military imperialism in the Philippines. The repetition of Americanisms like SPAM in an exhibit whose hauntology is a Filipinx cultural artifact (the parol) gestures toward the inextricability of US colonialism from any excavation of Philippine family and cultural histories. In the Philippines, SPAM is *pasalubong*, a transnational gift from a return migrant to a beloved person at home who welcomes and receives (*salubong*) them, but in the United States, SPAM, and thus Filipinx American culinary culture, is baduy: uncool, anachronistic, low-class.

Another visceral form, which I will briefly dwell on, emerges from the tethered materials that drag along the ground. Approached differently, the entrails of food wastes resemble an umbilical cord. This trope also appears in various other pieces in *Parol*, such as *Curtain of Illegibility* and *Roadside Memorial*. The umbilical cord, for Williams, emerged from her engagements with Saidiya Hartman and Gaiutra Bahadur, for whom "umbilicality" serves as a means to theorize the enslaved and indentured (non)relationship with a homeland. "What these texts enabled me to be is stubborn with our histories—not stopping at what you can't find in the archives," Williams declares as we discuss texts like Hartman's *Lose Your Mother* and Bahadur's *Coolie Woman*.[45] "Just because the text isn't there, doesn't mean that we can't write our own stories. What do you do from there? Do you just stop? If historians say I have no history— is that it?"

In *Parol* she emphatically answers no.[46] Akin to the coolie labor mobilized for indentured servitude, Filipinx diaspora has access to some tangible idea of home, which is the archipelago. Yet, under the violence of multiple imperialisms, the idea of home has been usurped by the nation-state form of the Philippines today, subjected to authoritarian violence, imperial and military occupation, and the detritus of the global North on its shores. The umbilical relation is *patid* (severed), yet the labor to imagine that kinship (*kapatid*) remains, snaking across the floor, reaching out into the otherwise contemplative walking space of the beholder, asking to see, touch, and connect. Williams's invocation of transimperial histories of indenture (as opposed to *only* the Philippine subject under multiple imperialisms) suggests that, despite the broken tie to a home country, other intimacies can be imagined through shared experiences of colonial occupation and displacement. Thus, in the absence of a fixed origin point for the parol, the artist productively refashions these archival silences into a *relational politics*—beyond a visceral (genealogical, ancestral) relationship toward a kinship born from intimacy and close contact. Or, in Tagalog, from *kapatid* (a blood relationship) to *kaugnay*, from a shared sense of *ugnay*: a relation, a contact, a touch.

What can we make of this gustatory and visceral terrain of Williams's counterhistory of Philippine diaspora? Here I return at last to my initial delineation of brown gathering, as what mobilizes the kinship networks of minoritarian subjects as an affective and circulatory infrastructure of collecting, preserving, and (re)signifying the objects of brown life. A visceral politics of kinship reinvigorates these food wastes in their transit from underneath the kitchen sinks of Williams's family and friends to the dynamic potential of her studio and into the exhibition space as art objects. The beholder— the art enthusiast, the gallerygoer, the happenstantial reader of this essay—is also invited into this reconfiguration of kinship with both detritus and the communities that mobilized it. After all, before they ended up woven by the skillful hand of the artist, the Seafood City bags once contained cans of corned beef and SPAM, which, in turn, contained beloved morsels of meat fried and prepared for the breakfast table. In this way, *Parol* might constitute what Anita Mannur calls an *intimate eating public*: "critical third spaces . . . wherein food, forms of eating, and commensality become sites from which to resist imperialist policies, homophobia, practices of racial profiling, and articulations of white supremacy."[47] Drawing on Lauren Berlant's concept of minor intimacy, Mannur shows how both the act of eating and the sensory unruliness of brown(ed) cuisines challenge ideas of intimacy beyond the normative desires of neoliberal multiculturalism and nationhood.[48] Certainly, the kinship ties from which Williams (brown) gathers her materials might be a traditional family network (such as the immediate and extended families of her and her partner). But a gustatory critique in approaching *Parol* reveals how, like the queer curatorial quality of Williams's practice, these food-waste objects become artistic materials out of an initial act of care: nourishing one another. Not only are discarded objects reappraised in a gallery space as art; these objects are also selected after an initial act of queer curation, which is the act of (Filipinx) diasporic grocery shopping itself, the rummaging through plundered and enclosed ecologies on store shelves for ingredients to compose a sensory landscape that feels something like home.

(At least, home for the time being.)

If diaspora severs—or at least makes tenuous—the umbilical relationship of the displaced to their mother/land, the cathexis of brown

gathering enables diaspora to speculate on the reconstitution of a
body jettisoned from home. Under brown gathering, neither a return
migration to the home country nor an assimilation into the host
country's body politic may be valorized as a teleological endpoint
for the migrant subject. The artist, quite literally, makes do with the
detritus of globalization, until their assembled forms might flash
with a possible relational subjectivity, between human and more-
than-human materials, between displaced subjects across the global
South, and between refusals of manifold imperialisms, whether or
not they are named after formal nation-states. The industrial technologies of tastemaking and preservation, with the traces of organic
foodstuffs, enclosed by petrochemical and metallurgical containers,
find new life in the hands of an artist deeply invested in imagining
anew a postcolonial history discarded.

❆ ❆ ❆

There is an uneasy irony in both the subject and the location of Williams's show. Just a few blocks from the show is Downtown Los
Angeles's Skid Row district. Like the art gallery and the South Central private university that now owns it, the Arts District faces itself,
its storefronts huddling into a walkable neighborhood that tries to
steer its walking traffic toward the more affluent Little Tokyo. Security measures—neighborhood security, gated streets, police presence,
carded entrances—keep the traffic from the southwest away from
this postindustrial fortress. But despite the university and the neighborhood's attempts, the fort's walls are little more than a membrane,
alive and (selectively) porous to the vicissitudes of street life in Downtown Los Angeles. As artists in Los Angeles vie for gallery spots in the
well-frequented Arts District, many other people vie for the right to
spaces rapidly being privatized around them. What does it mean for
Parol to make this place home?

I imagine what a "return migration" might look like for the show,
should it ever circulate across the Pacific. In Manila, the artistic
(and financial, political, cultural) capital of the Philippines, it might
find an audience in the southern districts of Makati, Pasay City, and
Taguig (now home to the developer-led "Bonifacio Global City,"
or BGC), where art aficionados frequent its small and ambitious

galleries. As an interlocutor and admirer of Williams and her practice, I would love for this homecoming, this *balikbayan*, to be made
for her tapestries and sculptures. But, as in Los Angeles, those "arts
districts" became so after a rapid series of gentrification schemes
that razed working-class areas and makeshift slums between luxury
developments—my childhood neighborhood in Taguig included.

All of these quandaries of commodification and circulation, of
course, would depend on whether or not a Philippine (let alone an
American) buyer acquires Williams's art. Indeed, Williams acknowledges that the works in *Parol* will be hard, if not impossible, to sell
on the art market. While to me the pieces evoke a splendor that cap-
tures diasporic world making from the Philippines, she is more pragmatic. "No one wants to buy trash," she jokes, pointing to the cans
of SPAM and the plastic bags that, for all intents and purposes, are as
ubiquitous as immigrant Angeleno trash. In my mind, she could very
well have been talking about Filipinx art in the imperial American
market.

Nonetheless, *Parol* offers me emergent forms of being that refuse
(though do not escape altogether) the value regimes of commodified
art. What gives value to these objects is (among many things) Williams's practice, which enables her to act not only as a solitary artist
with a singular aesthetic vision but also as a careful gatherer of baduy objects, and as an intimate medium for the myriad diasporas of
disposable objects and dispensable lives.

Brown gathering advances a form of cultural and knowledge production that is radically situated within the brutal realities of contemporary neoliberal political economy. As a practice of diasporic
archiving and storytelling, brown gathering foregrounds other kinds
of materials and temporalities about which histories of colonialism
and capitalism might be told. Under Williams's stewardship, brown
gathering does not attempt to recuperate discards into respectable ~~objects~~ subjects but instead offers an alternative relationship
to refuse and the refused, to the in/organic, to minor histories, to
the margins.

And is that not what being baduy, being brown, being brown*ed*,
is—life disposed of and remaindered, life dispossessed and devalued,
life otherwise?

Fig. 8. *Embracing My Inner Baduy*. Photo credit: Ryan Miller.

ADRIAN DE LEON is a writer and public historian at New York University, where he is assistant professor of US history. His most recent books are *barangay: an offshore poem* (2021) and *Bundok: A Hinterland History of Filipino America* (2023). His next book, provisionally titled *Balikbayan: The Invention of the Filipino Homeland*, is forthcoming.

Acknowledgments

I would like to thank Naveen Minai, Neelofer Qadir, and two of the three early reviewers for their encouragement and shepherding. To the demeaning and ungenerous "Reviewer Zero," thank you for fueling the most unstoppable forces that drive my writing: my pettiness and spite. My thanks to Natchee Blu Barnd and Jason Magabo Perez for opening new gates and the *Qui Parle* editorial team for opening others. For the sedimentary work of theorization as I sat with the slow temporality of this piece, my endless gratitude to the following colleagues and students at the University of Southern California: Jonathan Leal, Ann Tran, Jason Vu, Marissa de Baca, Milie Majumder, Natsumi Ueda, Rojeen Harsini, Lillian Ngan. Special thanks to my research assistant, Alyssa Ng, for the editorial help, and to Diane Williams—it has been a privilege to cotheorize with you across materials and genres. Thank you for the generosity and engagement over the last few years; I hope that this essay can be a small but meaningful gesture of reciprocity.

Notes

1. Diane Williams, interview by author, Los Angeles, July 26, 2021.
2. On anachronism and the racialization of Filipinx people, see Kramer, *Blood of Government*; Tadiar, *Things Fall Away*; and Isaac, *Filipino Time*.
3. Ybarra-Frausto, "Rasquachismo."
4. Tagle, "Salvage Acts."
5. Brown, "Diane Williams' Surreal Visions of Immigration."
6. Dambrot, "Meet Artist Diane Williams."
7. Williams, "The Precarious Life of the Parol."
8. Rodriguez, *Suspended Apocalypse*; Kaplan, *Anarchy of Empire*.
9. Gopinath, *Unruly Visions*, 4.
10. Manalansan, "'Stuff' of Archives."
11. Muñoz, *Sense of Brown*, 4.
12. As my analysis foregrounds nonnormative and (often) undesired forms of minoritarian kinship under neoliberal multiculturalism (especially between brown subjects and the trash objects they use), I pivot my analysis around queer-of-color critique and multiple traditions within ethnic studies while foregrounding (but not separating out) Philippine/Filipinx experience. I am indebted not only to Muñoz but to thinkers like Gopinath, Manalansan, Anita Mannur, and their respective intellectual genealogies for allowing me to grasp at a particular brown aesthetic practice—not with a neoliberal normative articulation of brownness as the end goal but with care for the contingency of this practice and the works at hand and for the ephemeral (and remaindered) nature of both the materials and their community contexts.
13. Tadiar, "Decolonization"; Tadiar, *Things Fall Away*.
14. See, *Filipino Primitive*.
15. See, *Filipino Primitive*.
16. While I theorize brown gathering from the particular subjecthood of diasporic Filipinx people, there is a capacious potential for relationality inherent in this method. Like rasquache (Ybarra-Frausto, "Rasquachismo"; See, *Filipino Primitive*), this practice is a sensibility with which minoritarian artists approach (and tend to) the inchoate stuff of everyday life. Brown gathering is thus a practice of diasporic worldmaking embedded in the objects (including waste) of migrant life. It does

not presuppose the nation-state and its distributed alterities; instead, it strategically disarticulates and disidentifies from official forms of difference. Put another way, it prizes an aesthetics of counterassimilation, a racialized mode of making do wherein practitioners "make it work" through their labor and "make it make sense" through their craft (See, *Filipino Primitive*).

17. Liboiron, *Pollution Is Colonialism*.
18. For more on religious syncretism in the modern Philippines, see De la Cruz, *Mother Figured*.
19. Bautista, *Figuring Catholicism*.
20. Tadiar, *Things Fall Away*, 9, 226.
21. Davis, *City of Quartz*.
22. Lloyd, *Under Representation*, 75–80.
23. Lloyd, *Under Representation*; Mannur, *Intimate Eating*, 4.
24. Williams, interview by author, Los Angeles, April 15, 2022.
25. Rafael, *Sovereign Trickster*.
26. Rafael, *Sovereign Trickster*, 111.
27. DeLoughrey, *Allegories of the Anthropocene*, 100–101.
28. DeLoughrey, *Allegories of the Anthropocene*, 99–132; Douglas, *Purity and Danger*, 36; Bauman, *Wasted Lives*.
29. DeLoughrey, *Allegories of the Anthropocene*, 100.
30. Benjamin, "Theses on the Philosophy of History," 257–58.
31. Liboiron, *Pollution Is Colonialism*, 17.
32. Hartman, *Lose Your Mother*.
33. Williams, "The Precarious Life of the Parol."
34. Quoted in Liboiron, *Pollution Is Colonialism*, 22; emphasis added.
35. Choy, *Empire of Care*; Tadiar, *Things Fall Away*; Rodriguez, *Migrants for Export*; Suarez, *Work of Mothering*; Velasco, *Queering the Global Filipina Body*.
36. Coráñez Bolton, *Crip Colony*. To think alongside J. Logan Smilges, if brown gathering is to be an alternative mode of worldmaking under collective conditions of neoliberal-imperial duress, it is necessarily a queer practice. In their elaboration on the coconstitution of queerness and disability, Smilges urges scholars to push "for *queer*'s return to its original pathology, for a circling back to the people, spaces, discourses, and affects that once defined it," from the myriad gay activisms of the 1960s to the twin devastations of HIV/AIDS and neoliberal abandonment through the end of the twentieth century (*Queer Silence*, 9). The resultant state initiatives and activisms, which prized a speaking (activist) subject in the face of homophobia, reified a liberal personhood

that severed the relationship between queer and disabled in favor of a rehabilitated and respectable form of *queer*: a homonational subject. Smilges argues for a queer ethic rooted in care, not for the purposes of recuperating (one into) a legible, liberal person but to care for an/other even if they do not cohere at all.

37. Rafael, *White Love*; Tadiar, *Things Fall Away*.
38. Diaz, "Following *La Pieta*"; Rafael, *Sovereign Trickster*.
39. Tompkins, *Racial Indigestion*, 2.
40. Nancy, *Inoperative Community*, 34.
41. Perez, "SPAM's Carbon Footprint."
42. Fernandez and Alegre, *Sarap*.
43. Perez, "SPAM's Carbon Footprint."
44. Ku, *Dubious Gastronomy*, 190–223.
45. Williams, interview by author, Los Angeles, April 15, 2022; Hartman, *Lose Your Mother*; Bahadur, *Coolie Woman*.
46. Williams, interview by author, Los Angeles, April 15, 2022.
47. Mannur, *Intimate Eating*, 6.
48. Berlant, "Intimacy"; Mannur, *Intimate Eating*, 8.

References

Bahadur, Gaiutra. *Coolie Woman: An Odyssey of Indenture*. Chicago: University of Chicago Press, 2013.
Bauman, Zygmunt. *Wasted Lives: Modernity and Its Outcasts*. Malden, MA: Polity, 2004.
Bautista, Julius J. *Figuring Catholicism: An Ethnohistory of the Santo Niño of Cebu*. Quezon City: Ateneo de Manila University Press, 2010.
Benjamin, Walter. "Theses on the Philosophy of History." In *Illuminations: Essays and Reflections*, edited by Hannah Arendt, translated by Harry Zohn, 253–64. New York: Schocken, 2007.
Berlant, Lauren. "Intimacy: A Special Issue." *Critical Inquiry* 24, no. 2 (1998): 281–88.
Brown, Betty Ann. "Diane Williams' Surreal Visions of Immigration." *Artillery Magazine*, March 5, 2019. https://artillerymag.com/womananimal other/.
Choy, Catherine Ceniza. *Empire of Care: Nursing and Migration in Filipino America*. Berkeley: University of California Press, 2003.
Coráñez Bolton, Sony. *Crip Colony: Mestizaje, US Imperialism, and the Queer Politics of Disability in the Philippines*. Durham, NC: Duke University Press, 2023.

Dambrot, Shana Nys. "Meet Artist Diane Williams." *LA Weekly*, July 12, 2021.

Davis, Mike. *City of Quartz: Excavating the Future in Los Angeles*. London: Verso, 1990.

De la Cruz, Deirdre. *Mother Figured: Marian Apparitions and the Making of a Filipino Universal*. Chicago: University of Chicago Press, 2015.

DeLoughrey, Elizabeth. *Allegories of the Anthropocene*. Durham, NC: Duke University Press, 2019.

Diaz, Josen Masangkay. "Following *La Pieta*: Toward a Transpacific Feminist Historiography of Philippine Authoritarianism." *Signs: Journal of Women in Culture and Society* 44, no. 3 (2019): 693–716.

Douglas, Mary. *Purity and Danger: An Analysis of Concepts of Pollution and Taboo*. London: Routledge, 2002.

Fernandez, Doreen G., and Edilberto N. Alegre. *Sarap: Essays on Philippine Food*. Quezon City: Mr. and Mrs. Pub. Co., 1988.

Gopinath, Gayatri. *Unruly Visions: The Aesthetic Practices of Queer Diaspora*. Durham, NC: Duke University Press, 2018.

Hartman, Saidiya. *Lose Your Mother: A Journey along the Atlantic Slave Route*. New York: Macmillan, 2008.

Isaac, Allan Punzalan. *Filipino Time: Affective Worlds and Contracted Labor*. New York: Fordham University Press, 2021.

Kaplan, Amy. *The Anarchy of Empire in the Making of U.S. Culture*. Cambridge, MA: Harvard University Press, 2002.

Kramer, Paul. *The Blood of Government: Race, Empire, the United States, and the Philippines*. Chapel Hill: University of North Carolina Press, 2006.

Ku, Robert Ji-Song. *Dubious Gastronomy: The Cultural Politics of Eating Asian in the USA*. Honolulu: University of Hawai'i Press, 2014.

Liboiron, Max. *Pollution Is Colonialism*. Durham, NC: Duke University Press, 2021.

Lloyd, David. *Under Representation: The Racial Regime of Aesthetics*. New York: Fordham University Press, 2018.

Manalansan, Martin F., IV. "The 'Stuff' of Archives: Mess, Migration, and Queer Lives." *Radical History Review*, no. 120 (2014): 94–107.

Mannur, Anita. *Intimate Eating: Racialized Spaces and Radical Futures*. Durham, NC: Duke University Press, 2022.

Muñoz, José Esteban. *The Sense of Brown*. Durham, NC: Duke University Press, 2020.

Nancy, Jean-Luc. *The Inoperative Community*. Edited by Peter Connor. Translated by Peter Connor, Lisa Garbus, Michael Holland, and Simona Sawhney. Minneapolis: University of Minnesota Press, 1991.

Perez, Craig Santos. "SPAM's Carbon Footprint." *poets.org, 2010. https://poets.org/poem/spams-carbon-footprint.*

Rafael, Vicente. *The Sovereign Trickster: Death and Laughter in the Age of Duterte*. Durham, NC: Duke University Press, 2022.

Rafael, Vicente. *White Love and Other Events in Filipino History*. Durham, NC: Duke University Press, 2000.

Rodriguez, Dylan. *Suspended Apocalypse: White Supremacy, Genocide, and the Filipino Condition*. Minneapolis: University of Minnesota Press, 2009.

Rodriguez, Robyn Magalit. *Migrants for Export: How the Philippine State Brokers Labor to the World*. Minneapolis: University of Minnesota Press, 2010.

See, Sarita Echavez. *The Filipino Primitive: Accumulation and Resistance in the American Museum*. New York: New York University Press, 2017.

Smilges, J. Logan. *Queer Silence: On Disability and Rhetorical Absence*. Minneapolis: University of Minnesota Press, 2022.

Suarez, Harrod J. *The Work of Mothering: Globalization and the Filipino Diaspora*. Urbana: University of Illinois Press, 2017.

Tadiar, Neferti X. M. "Decolonization, 'Race,' and Remaindered Life under Empire." *Qui Parle* 23, no. 2 (2015): 135–60.

Tadiar, Neferti X. M. *Things Fall Away: Philippine Historical Experience and the Makings of Globalization*. Durham, NC: Duke University Press, 2009.

Tagle, Thea Quiray. "Salvage Acts: Asian/American Artists and the Uncovering of Slow Violence in the San Francisco Bay Area." *ACME: An International E-Journal for Critical Geographies* 18, no. 5 (2019): 1112–27.

Tompkins, Kyla Wazana. *Racial Indigestion: Eating Bodies in the Nineteenth Century*. New York: New York University Press, 2012.

Velasco, Gina. *Queering the Global Filipina Body: Contested Nationalisms in the Filipina/o Diaspora*. Urbana: University of Illinois Press, 2020.

Williams, Diane. "The Precarious Life of the Parol." https://dianewilliams artist.com/parol (accessed September 1, 2022).

Ybarra-Frausto, Tomás. "Rasquachismo: A Chicano Sensibility." In *Chicago Aesthetics: Rasquachismo*, 5–8. Exhibit catalog. Phoenix: Movimiento Artistico del Rio Salado, 1989.

The Pathos of Finitude

Ordinariness, Solitude, and Individuality in Nonphilosophy

THOMAS SUTHERLAND

"When [Michel] Foucault speaks of the 'death of Man' at the end of *The Order of Things*," remarks Béatrice Han-Pile, "he is not heralding some kind of mass extinction."[1] Indeed, Foucault is not predicting the end of the human being, the decline in use of the word *man* as a descriptor for human beings in general, or even the demise of the unitary, autonomous ego as the presumed center of all human experience; rather, in a very narrow sense, he is heralding the death of man's figuration as an *empirico-transcendental doublet*. This specular doublet, which for Foucault is a defining feature of post-Kantian philosophy and the human sciences, locates both knowledge and its conditions within a single ambivalent figure: "man" appears as an empirical entity able to grasp, within "himself," the conditions of his own knowledge; an amphibological being determined by natural laws but also able to elude these laws by reflecting on their conditions of possibility—a simultaneously *ordinary* and *extraordinary* being, bounded by yet able to go beyond his own finitude.

Foucault claims to dimly perceive the incipient reappearance of a long-lost unity of language, viewing this return as a sign that "man is

QUI PARLE   Vol. 33, No. 1, June 2024
DOI 10.1215/10418385-11125525   © 2024 Editorial Board, *Qui Parle*

in the process of perishing as the being of language continues to shine
ever brighter upon our horizon."[2] But this can be nothing more than
a wager, Foucault's refusal to supply any causal explanation for epistemic rupture meaning that he cannot verify that such a rupture is
taking place. He merely hopes that the possibility of posing such affir-
mations "may well open the way to a future thought," for "man is
neither the oldest nor the most persistent problem that has been
posed for human knowledge."[3]

By contrast, as François Laruelle sees it, man *is* in fact the oldest
and most persistent problem for human knowledge, or at least for
the Western intellectual tradition: "Philosophy has never known
the real subject, it has never known man."[4] Laruelle does not place
any bets on the death of man, arguing that the tendency to "celebrate
the death and overcoming, and then return, of man" is not peculiar
to the Foucauldian archaeology of knowledge but actually a recur-
rent philosophical trope (*ET*, 248). He wishes to instead dislodge
the *real* man (whom English speakers nowadays would probably
prefer to call the real person or individual), whom he identifies
with the abstract concept of "the One," from the sphere of human-
ism, anthropology, and philosophy, all of which fail to think man
in his [*sic*] essence.[5] Philosophy, Laruelle argues, "is a way of thinking
that reduces all phenomena to a combination of two mutually related parameters: Unity and Scission or Identity and Difference"
(*ET*, 249). The empirico-transcendental doublet is thus, for him,
not a uniquely post-Kantian figuration but merely one expression
of an invariant proclivity within the philosophical interpellation of
man. Instead of approaching man from the perspective of philosophy's preexisting rules, injunctions, and techniques, Laruelle wishes
to set out from man himself in his singular essence, establishing a
rigorous science that claims to be, from the outset, a priori sufficient to this singularity.

Whereas the philosopher "conscripts man into service for their
own very peculiar goals and values," Laruelle institutes a transcendental science that, he argues, enables one to think man in his essence,
on his own terms—and in doing so, to think, on the one hand, man
apart from the various appearances philosophy has projected on him
and the uses to which it has put him, and on the other, philosophy

from the perspective of man himself.[6] This is what Laruelle describes as a science of *ordinary man*. Finite, solitary, and entirely without qualities, drawing "an inalienable essence from himself," this so-called ordinary man denotes the radical immanence of the individual we all are, prior to our inevitable philosophical interpellation (*BM*, 7). Rather than looking to broaden philosophy's horizon, incorporating those aspects of daily life and conventional language it ignores or marginalizes, Laruelle tries to wrest ordinary lived experience from philosophy's grip in the hopes of finally severing the empirico-transcendental doublet with which philosophy has constricted it.

In this article I examine Laruelle's unusual conception of ordinariness in more depth, looking at how he seeks to undermine the aforementioned doublet through a purely transcendental science, defined by a resolute formalism and rejection of all empirical, figural, and representational content.[7] I argue that Laruelle's fondness for the concept of "man" (acting as a descriptor for "the One") and his attendant preoccupation with subjective finitude points toward an aspect of his project not straightforwardly explicable on its own terms: namely, his desire to guide the reader, whom he presumes to be already ensconced in the debates and jargon of academic philosophy and its surrounding milieus, toward a certain subject position. At the same time that Laruelle enjoins us to recognize a fundamentally "ordinary" core of ourselves—a passive, powerless subject who does not participate in the world furnished and represented by philosophy—he also formulates a nonphilosophy that is, in both its means and ends, seemingly at odds with such an interpretation, inducting its initiates into an ethos of continual inner labor and productivity, maintaining a "strong but tolerant indifference to philosophy" through ongoing work on and modification of its discursive materials (*BM*, 1). Ultimately, I suggest that, for all of nonphilosophy's sizable merits, it is more fruitful to view philosophy (within which we must include nonphilosophy, as a distinctive *détournement* of continental philosophy's conceptual and methodological riches) as constituting a discursive corpus that does not have some especial purchase on the real but interpellates audiences and draws distinctions, including that of ordinariness and its inverse, in variegated ways.

Ordinariness and Everydayness in Contemporary Thought

In the context of contemporary philosophy, mention of ordinariness and its vindication will probably conjure up thoughts of "ordinary language philosophy," which finds its roots in the later work of Ludwig Wittgenstein—who rejected the notion that philosophizing demands a manner of speaking distinct from the ordinary use of language—and was initially developed at Oxford in the postwar period, principally through the work of Gilbert Ryle and J. L. Austin. It might also remind one of Walter Benjamin's investigations into the objects and routines of bourgeois urban life, Martin Heidegger's emphasis on the everydayness of our existence, Henri Lefebvre's attempt to remedy philosophy's habitual devaluation of regular life, Jürgen Habermas's interest in the formal structures that constitute everyday communicative practices, or Michel de Certeau's heterological studies regarding the practice of daily life. In diverse ways, all these approaches look to rectify the perception that philosophy is unconcerned with or actively hostile to ordinary moments of human existence and ordinary ways of speaking, that it positions itself as in some way *extra*ordinary.

The work of Certeau—who dedicates to "the ordinary man" his best-known book, *The Practice of Everyday Life* (1974; translated 1984), in which he foregrounds the outwardly insignificant tactics individuals and groups use within determinate situations in defiance of abstract strategies of domination—would come to play a crucial role, alongside Roland Barthes's semiological readings of the minutiae of French daily life, in the development of the English-language cultural studies tradition (first in Great Britain, then in Australia, the United States, and elsewhere), as Raymond Williams's affirmation of an organic, and above all "ordinary" English working-class culture (a "popular" culture, in the traditional sense of the phrase) opposed to both bourgeois "high" culture and a deracinated "mass" culture, was gradually displaced by a more generalized affirmation of daily, minor acts of resistance, especially in the realm of media consumption.[8] This discipline's "concern with the experiential dimension of everyday life" and "understanding of culture as a site of contestation," as John Frow and Meaghan Morris expound, found its expression in an obsession with popular, everyday, and mundane forms of culture.[9]

Although the development of cultural studies clearly forms part of what Simon During describes as "the ongoing European philosophization of the humanities," relying heavily on the importation of ideas and frameworks from continental philosophers, this development did not play out on a strictly philosophic terrain, emerging primarily out of English literature departments.[10] In fact, cultural studies' preoccupation with the everyday often led to it being situated in diametric opposition to philosophy. "Whereas philosophy has traditionally aspired to discover perennial and transcendent truths," writes Rita Felski, "cultural studies emphasizes the social embeddedness of human activity and the importance of group identities formed around such categories as class, gender, race, sexuality, age, and ethnicity."[11] Far more than its philosophical forebears, cultural studies introduced a feminist dimension into analyses of the quotidian, stressing "the extraordinary ways in which we can use our ordinary selves," as Elspeth Probyn puts it, or doing justice "to variability and precariousness in the ways in which gender identities . . . are constructed in the practices of everyday life in which media consumption is subsumed," as Ien Ang likewise writes.[12] Crucially, emphasizes John Hartley, cultural studies' preoccupation with everyday life was intended to be *critical* in outlook, "a kind of intervention analysis, dedicated neither to the improvement of everyday activities themselves, nor to appreciation of cultural pursuits, but to critique of the society of which these activities were both symptom and stage."[13]

This very notion of "critique" is now largely taken for granted within universities, having become an instrumentalized posture by which the scholar justifies their own relevance in the face of budget cuts, institutional pressures, and a systematic devaluing of the humanities. The outlook Hartley gestures toward, however, whereby the practices of everyday life are neither endorsed nor condemned but viewed from a dispassionate, self-reflexive position as a result of which their conditions become appreciable, is not self-evident; on the contrary, it has a very particular history, grounded in the fraught relationship between philosophy and ordinariness. To better appreciate this history, we need to go back several centuries earlier to the concept of "critique" articulated by Immanuel Kant, whose analytic of finitude attempts to cleanly divide empirical knowledge from transcendental reflection, turning attention toward the formal *conditions* of cognition. The effect of this split is to divide "man" between two distinct forms of cognition: one ordinary, the other speculative.

Of course, presentation of human beings' cognition as divided in some fashion is a perennial feature of philosophy. But this division traditionally occurs along lines of truth and falsity, tearing humans between a sensible or worldly existence mired in ignorance and a higher knowledge to which only the philosopher can provide access. Kant, whose critique concentrates on the sources and boundaries of knowledge rather than the nature of the real in itself, relies instead on a distinction between ordinary (i.e., empirical) and transcendental cognition. This is in no way a distinction between truth and its obverse; rather, it separates the normal, everyday experience in which a posteriori knowledge (the kind we associate with the natural sciences) is acquired from a specialized mode of reflective thought with which the a priori conditions of this knowledge can be grasped. Importantly, the latter is a specifically philosophical stance, the historical absence of which has not hindered progress in other sciences. The "duty of philosophy," in Kant's estimation, "is to abolish the semblance arising from misinterpretation, even if many prized and beloved delusions have to be destroyed in the process," and this can take place only if one brings reason to bear on itself, independent of all experience, through this philosophical mode of comportment.[14]

Kant's self-styled disciple J. G. Fichte makes this latter point even clearer, arguing that one either "views the sensible world from the standpoint of ordinary consciousness, which one can also call the standpoint of natural science, or else one views it from the transcendental standpoint."[15] This distinction is not identical to the one Kant draws—for Fichte, the former standpoint views the world in terms of people and things possessing an independent existence, such that they would remain even in the subject's absence, while the latter views these same objects as constituted by the subject's consciousness—but it sustains the notion that the philosopher has a higher, speculative way of thinking at their disposal, allowing them to reflect on the conditions of ordinary consciousness. This standpoint does not enable them to transcend their everyday existence (and supplies no reason why they should want to do so) but imparts the means of grasping its condition. Between Kant and Fichte then, a peculiar sense of the ordinary is established, which will continue to echo throughout many later philosophers' work: namely, as not inherently untruthful but not properly philosophical either.

This post-Kantian distinction between ordinary and philosophical standpoints exemplifies the empirico-transcendental doublet described earlier: "man" is posited as a being capable of reflecting on his own ordinary experience and through this reflection able to gain insight into the (nonempirical) conditions of this experience that remain unthought within its confines, establishing the formal boundaries of all possible knowledge (for Kant) or locating the origins of such knowledge (for Fichte), and ultimately permitting him to realize a freedom unimpeded by empirical determination. Man is thus figured as an ambivalent, amphibological being, a *homo duplex* torn between his empirical nature and the latent transcendental faculties of his reason, whose divided nature can only be reconciled through the ongoing inner labor of a genuinely critical philosophy.[16]

Anthropological Difference

It is precisely this figuration of man as *homo duplex* that Laruelle, one of the most interesting philosophical thinkers of recent years, seeks to undermine. In *The Minority Principle* (*Le principe de minorité*, 1981), he declares it imperative "to exorcise what a modern would call the 'empirico-transcendental doublet.'"[17] He does this by appealing to a transcendental truth that "enjoys an absolute autonomy in relation to 'scientific' or 'moral' truth," a truth located in the "pre-ontological and prelogical transcendental seeds" that he refers to as *absolute dispersions*.[18] Enigmatic even by Laruelle's usual standards, this book sets out the rudiments of his project to come, attempting to conceive of the individual (and by association, the multiplicity), otherwise known as "the One," in its most radical manifestation, starting from these individuals themselves (the aforementioned dispersions), rather than thinking them in relation to one

or more universals—which is to say, trying to think the originary giv-
enness of the individual with no concern for determination, individuation, or becoming.

But the stakes of such a reconfiguration of the transcendental
method remain unclear and the nature of these absolute dispersions
elusive. Hence the importance of Laruelle's next book, *Biography of
Ordinary Man* (1985 [2018]), wherein the individual in question
comes to be identified with what he terms the "ordinary man."[19]
This motif is not always Laruelle's focal point. But the notion of
a defense of the human individual, in their irreducible singularity,
against the hallucinations of philosophy and other human sciences—
the question, as Rocco Gangle puts it, of "how ordinary human beings
tend to be denigrated by authoritarian structures in and of the world
with both implicit and explicit philosophical legitimisation"—rears
its head throughout his oeuvre.[20] Maybe, Laruelle proposes in *Theory
of Strangers* (*Théorie des étrangers*, 1995), "it would be fruitful, after
so many systems based on the 'individual,' the 'subject,' '*Dasein*,'
'flesh,' and so on, to return to the former name of 'man.'" To do this,
he continues, is "to force oneself to respect human identity against
the technophilosophical obsession with dividing him up and the
horizon of anthropological difference in which the Human Sciences
still take shelter."[21]

Laruelle holds this *anthropological difference* to be an invariant
characteristic of Western philosophy's relationship to man, "a phan-
tasmatic projection of Greco-Christian ontological prejudices onto
real man" (*BM*, 4). Philosophy posits man "masked and falsified,"
as a divided and doubled being, separated from himself, split between an empirically determined, worldly, or vulgar subjectivity and
a universal exteriority, an inhuman or superhuman transcendence,
the philosopher furnishing the means for not only grasping the latter above and beyond any given man's quotidian existence but
also for grasping the reciprocally determinative relationship between these divided aspects (*TE*, 22). "The essence of the individual," Laruelle bemoans, "has remained unthought by philosophy . . .
denying the conditions of his real experience through the multiplicity of authoritarian universals that it uses to filter him" (*BM*, 5).
Their essence is misrepresented as an expression of difference, a

manifestation of philosophical *decision*—the viciously circular structures and operations to which philosophy subjects the real.[22]

There are several implications of this anthropological difference worth noting. First, philosophy "does not know man except through representations of man," incapable of thinking him as anything other than a shifting set of false figures (*TE*, 105). The proclaimed death of man is thus nothing more than a conflation of man's fate with philosophy's perpetual irresolution. Second, this empirico-transcendental parallelism (or its variations: empirico-ideal, empirico-rational, empirico-metaphysical, etc.) does not belong exclusively to post-Kantian philosophy and the human sciences but is in fact a constituent element of philosophy *tout court*. Lastly, it is fundamentally implicated in the "forgetting of the real or 'finite' essence of man"—which is to say, the forgetting of the "ordinary" man, who does not represent yet another mutation in the figure of man, but who has, in effect, always been there, preceding any such figuration (*BM*, 6). It is this "man" on whom Laruelle focuses his attention: man, in his real essence, distinct from the world (which he may well contemplate but to which he will never belong) and utterly indifferent to the projections, presuppositions, and teleologies of both philosophy and the human sciences (which can only ever posit the possibility of man as such, never his reality). Ordinary man as the real itself, as the absolute that remains utterly indeterminable by philosophy. "A finite or ordinary subject, who, not needing philosophy, has never entered philosophy and does not intend to leave it" (*BM*, 157).

Figuration and Abstraction

In an interview with literary scholar Jean-Didier Wagneur, one of four contained in his book *As One* (*En tant qu'un*, 1991), Laruelle expounds on the use of the expression "biography of ordinary man"—a description of man's interpellation as a divided being, beholden to various authoritarian universals:

> The term "biography" is rare or even nonexistent in philosophy. I have used it to contrast myself against what feels to me like a

certain traditional philosophical contempt for man. Here, "biography" designates the most fundamental, essential events that shape an individual or through which an individual necessarily passes, not in order to become an individual but quite simply in order to continue to be. (*ET*, 209)[23]

Nonphilosophy's appeal to ordinariness here brings to mind the aforementioned ordinary language philosophy—in particular, the later work of Stanley Cavell and his followers, which was, writes Sandra Laugier, a reaction to "the (de)negation of our ordinary language and our ordinary lives, in the philosophical conceit that it can surpass them, correct them, and simply know them."[24] After all, both are defined in large part by a distinction drawn between philosophical discourse and ordinary existence, with ordinary language philosophy aiming, as Cavell puts it, for "a view of words free of philosophical preoccupation."[25] And Cavell's interest in philosophers' proneness to "shun the autobiographical" in favor of a mode of address imbued with necessity and universality would seem, outwardly, to parallel Laruelle's employment of a biographic motif in describing the ordinary man's existence.[26] One would be mistaken, however, in seeing more than a superficial likeness between these two perspectives.

Laruelle himself alludes once in a while to this "English-language usage" of the concept of the ordinary, "a usage partially directed against philosophy" (*ET*, 220–21). But he makes clear that he still deems it philosophical in its character, even if it is a markedly malleable and self-critical variant. Ordinary language philosophy, explains Cavell, arises in opposition to "the logician's wish to translate out those messy, nonformal features of ordinary language," rejecting the positivist representation of a systematic, formalized, and idealized philosophical language in comparison to which the semantic ambiguities and opacities of everyday language use could only be regarded as misleading or nonsensical.[27] Such an approach though, argues Laruelle, does not do away with logicism as such, but only "certain inferior and conspicuous forms"—the most blatantly idealizing or anti-empiricist—with the result that the ordinary language philosopher actually ends up coming to the aid of the logos by "detaching language from formal logic," finding themselves in a long tradition of philosophers who have tried to preserve their discipline's remit by denouncing its more pronounced authoritarian features (*BM*, 172).

So what exactly does Laruelle mean when he speaks of the "ordinary" man? For him, ordinariness is synonymous with radical finitude: the ordinary man is an individual qua individual. He is not an ideal abstraction derived from empirical experience but the real, singular identity of the individual: a *homo simplex*, undivided, foreclosed to any empirical determination and indifferent to any historical, social, and cultural characterization.[28] "Man thinks, acts, or stipulates from within himself, with his own thought," not needing any help from something or someone other than himself (*TE*, 106).[29] Laruelle thus strengthens, rather than dissolves, the distinction between the philosophical, on one hand, and the ordinary, on the other. Castigating the "powerlessness and nihilism" of contemporary philosophy, which has increasingly prioritized concepts such as difference and becoming as a means of loosening and widening its categorial schemas (without ever actually overturning the formal structure within which these schemas are constructed), Laruelle wants nothing to do with such philosophy's attempted rapprochement with quotidian existence (*BM*, 3). Instead, as Andrew Sackin-Poll observes, nonphilosophy "introduces the idea that the ordinary, in the end, resists and does not submit to the order of philosophy," and that "philosophy submits, ultimately, to the ordinary—that is, the fugitive, indeterminate movements of the everyday."[30]

One might object, of course, that this is just apophaticism. Laruelle insists, however, that he is supplying a positive definition of ordinary man, who "is not a residual and shifting figure of philosophy or the Greek episteme, but rather is determined before these and absolutely precedes the philosophical calculation of predicates" (*BM*, 9). Man's ordinariness does not signify the remnants left behind after philosophy's determinations have been subtracted; quite the contrary, for it involves a total absence of the externalities or occasional causes by which man, in his philosophical guise, conventionally comes to be defined. Ordinary man is entirely sufficient in himself. He does not lack anything. He is faceless and solitary. He does not need to venture out beyond himself, into the world, and he is certainly not *in-the-World*, even if he can still contemplate it. He is not alienated, needing to somehow reconcile his divided being, become what he truly is, or needing to seek answers outside himself. He is not social, communicative, or gregarious. He does not need anything to help him know, understand, or reflect on himself. "Precisely because he is 'ordinary,' man does not fall under the determinations of knowledge" (*BM*, 107). He knows himself immediately and unreflectively as *real*.

"But being devoid of predicates," Laruelle clarifies, "does not mean that he is devoid of essence" (*BM*, 9). Indeed, Laruelle frequently, and somewhat unfashionably, refers to the ordinary man's inalienable essence, which is not taken from some prefabricated category (be it philosophical, anthropological, historical, biological, bureaucratic, etc.) but is drawn immediately from himself. His essence "is defined by characteristics that are absolutely original, primitive, internal, and without equivalents in the World," signifying the minimal condition for him to be thinkable qua individual (*BM*, 9). Equally unfashionably, Laruelle's nonphilosophy is premised on an explicit dualism, counterposing ordinary man against the world and its attributes, to which he is condemned but will always remain a stranger—a dualism pitting *minorities* (ordinary men) against the worldly *authorities* that impose these attributes. Laruelle's stated aim is "to tear absolute science, the science of the real, away from the philosopher and give it to he who has not asked for it: ordinary man," establishing a rigorous, nonempirical science of individuals (*BM*, 162; translation altered). A transcendental science, in other words, but not as we usually know it.

While the specifics of how such a transcendental science is effected shift over the course of his work, Laruelle's concern with expurgating the transcendental method of its lingering empirical elements stays consistent. The *strictly* transcendental perspective, as he comes to define it, is not a mode of reflection gazing over empirical experience, trying to describe the latter's a priori conditions or structures; rather, it *is* experience itself—namely, ordinary man's lived experience. It describes the power of man's thought unadulterated by any empirical trappings, drawn only from his own finite immanence, performing operations on philosophical materials and the world they claim to furnish without ever being implicated in them. This expurgation of all such empirical vestiges is patently visible in the very manner in which Laruelle presents his nonphilosophical system, the abstraction and intrication of which is striking. It is certainly not biographical in any recognizable sense.

Laruelle, remarks Ray Brassier, "may well be the first European philosopher in whose work substantive innovation has been whole-heartedly sacrificed in the name of total formal invention."[31] He of-fers no contributions to epistemology, ontology, ethics, aesthetics, politics, history, communication, or any other areas of traditional philosophical interest. He gives no propositions, examples, or case studies, furnishing only transcendental *theorems* that "describe phe-nomena lived by ordinary man, phenomena that are invisible to phi-losophy and its phenomenology as a matter of principle" (*BM*, 15).[32] The result is an intimidating formalism that retains a certain recog-nizable albeit shifting terminology borrowed from various philoso-phers (Plotinus, Kant, Fichte, Husserl, the neo-Kantians, Heidegger, Levinas, Henry, Althusser, Derrida, and Deleuze being particular favorites) but does away with the pretension that his work might tell us anything about the nature of things, about what we can know, how we ought to act, or on what basis we form judgments. By dealing with philosophical materials on purely formal terms, Laruelle at-tempts to reveal the constrictive implications of philosophy's struc-ture of *decision*, which enables the continual fabrication of putatively novel concepts and systems all conforming to a single basic pattern, and of its presumed *sufficiency*, its claim to legislate over and speak for the real (and thus for the ordinary man): "Philosophy is not just a set of categories and objects, syntaxes and experiences or operations of decision and position: it is animated and traversed by a faith or belief in itself as in absolute reality, by an intentionality or reference to the real which it claims to describe and even constitute" (*PN*, 12).[33] While this formalism might seem at odds with Laruelle's emphasis on ordinariness—which, he boldly claims, enables him to "describe the essence of any possible man"—for nonphilosophy, it is only through such abstraction that we can momentarily loosen the yoke of philos-ophy's manifold interpellations, thinking from our own singular finitude in a manner unrecognizable to these hegemonic modes of thought and unassimilable into any kind of universal category (*ET*, 221). Ordinariness comes to represent, more than anything else, an individuality and solitude—a radical immanence—that cannot be defined on the basis of external terms and extrapolated out beyond itself. If the task of ordinary language philosophy, as Laugier puts it, is "to bring us back to ourselves—to bring our words back from their metaphysical use to their everyday use, or to bring conceptual knowledge of the world back to a knowledge of or proximity to ourselves," this still presumes us to be fundamentally social, communicative beings whose essence is defined by the words we use to express ourselves and the knowledge we gain of ourselves and our world.[34] The purpose of nonphilosophy, in contrast, is to bring us back to a solitary mode of thought, comprising nothing but the lonely individual. A biography of ordinary man is equally "a biography of the solitary man" (*BM*, 8).

The Vestiges of Empiricism

To maintain this strictly transcendental point of view, Laruelle argues, "we must distinguish the genuine empirico-transcendental duality from the empiricist-transcendental doublet"—that is, we must separate a transcendental, nonphilosophical mode of thought that deals with philosophical materials on its own terms, in a purely formal and unilateral fashion, from manifold empirico-transcendental or empirico-ideal mixtures in which these terms come to be reciprocally determinative (*TE*, 69). Laruelle himself is, in the context of his own published writings and interviews, very skillful in this exact maneuver, refusing to allow his theorems to be contaminated by empirical examples. Faced with the choice—which Paul de Man once argued, all philosophy seems to come up against—between having to either "to give up its own constitutive claim to rigor in order to come to terms with the figurality of its language" or "free itself from figuration altogether," Laruelle leaves no doubt that he has chosen the latter path, seldom making recourse to metaphors, analogies, tropes, or any other kind of figural expression.[35] A truly individual thought "gives up concrete representations, representation in all its forms" and "defines the essence of individual multiplicities in such a way as to exclude any figuration whatsoever" (*BM*, 20).[36] It involves a "postural and subjective experience of thought from the outset freed from the constraints of the World, from the codes of philosophy, from the norms of transcendent exteriority, from the rules of speculative figuration or the speculative imagination," the notion of *posture* in this description explicitly distinguished from "the *figurative*, but also the *figural*, *relational* and *positional*," being "the necessary kernel of reality that precedes them absolutely" (*PN*, 42). We have already seen just how much of the traditional philosophical schema he is willing to jettison to achieve this formalism.

And Laruelle's nonphilosophical project has, in turn, proven itself quite successful in resisting academic arrogation. In France, though his work has precipitated many theses, monographs, and articles written in a nonphilosophical style, these have tended to replicate rather than ameliorate his own hermetic leanings.[37] And within an Anglophone context, while nonphilosophy has made some inroads into the more speculative corners of continental philosophy, this has not really resulted in its assimilation into the broader canon of "theory."[38] Though one may be inclined to blame this on the stylistic abstruseness of his approach, a cursory glance at the texts produced by the predominant figures in the theoretical pantheon, especially from the (post)structuralist and deconstructionist moment, would suggest that this has never really been a barrier to such assimilation. Indeed, the surmise that, as Chris Kraus once put it, "theory, because it's difficult, must be serious," still exerts influence over the various filtering mechanisms by which humanities scholars differentiate "theory" proper from ordinary, run-of-the-mill theories.[39] Nonphilosophy remains theoretically inassimilable for two basic reasons: first, because it does not offer discrete "concepts" that can be extracted from their original context and incorporated into an eclectic "toolbox"; and second, because its strict formalism and commitment to abstraction offer scant resources for "analysis" in any conventional sense, let alone for the kinds of textual analyses that hold sway in the humanities.

One might still take exception to the claim that Laruelle's work, despite its claimed "refusal of all empirico-ideal experience," can actually escape the "enclosure of representation" (*BM*, 20). Funnily enough, it is probably the very notion of the "ordinary man" that most conspicuously reveals mundane, "worldly" concerns bleeding into nonphilosophical formalism, introducing a contentious, gendered, historically and linguistically situated term into a theory that purports to think ordinary people without projecting any qualities on to them. Of course, Laruelle himself would respond that this term should not be taken as "descriptive" in the philosophical sense, as a signifier that in some way bears on or constitutes the object it signifies; rather, it is a figure extracted from philosophical materials to be reworked, rendered sterile or inert, "an 'abstract' usage" of language "completely distinct from its transcendent or 'figurative' usage" (PN, 130). The One becomes legible via the mediation of contingent discursive materials and the language they offer us, but this manipulation of language in the service of nonphilosophical ends is premised on "the absolute, unreflected precedence of the One or of the real over its description," furnishing purely abstract axioms that point toward an immanent human reality but make no claims to determining or constituting it (PN, 46). This is not to say that the One is ineffable, but that "its description, which is completely possible, is indifferent for it or does not itself constitute it" (PN, 45). This in turn entails two demands: first, that "these descriptions must be multiplied and diversified in accordance with the thematics, whether *philosophical or otherwise*, that are available and chosen as material," and second, that they must be invoked "provisionally, 'against' themselves and in view of making them describe the One's autonomy, self-consistency and indifference to philosophy itself" (PN, 45).

In the most generous reading then, the nonphilosophical usage of the longstanding philosophical concept of "man" (which is considered outmoded in English but, along with the *masculin générique* in a wider sense, is still retained in most French writing), seeks to subvert rather than reproduce its false universalism: the word *man* functions as one of many monikers variously used to describe the One, illustrating just how inadequate philosophy's interpellation of its audience under this umbrella concept is to the lived singularity of human existence and just how indifferent individuals remain to such interpellation. Clarifications of this kind, though, are unlikely to reassure those who take umbrage at the centering of this semantically freighted term, whether because of its gendered character, its humanist connotations, or its historical baggage. In such cases, what is meant to be an entirely abstract axiom is likely to take on a rather concrete appearance. What might, at one time and in one context, seem like a bland, unproblematic descriptor—a commonplace term extracted from philosophy's conceptual armature—can appear to suggest, at another time and in another context, fairly or unfairly, that nonphilosophy has not entirely shaken off the exclusionary presuppositions and practices that have long underpinned so much academic philosophy.

It might also make one wonder why the immanence, finitude, and singularity for which Laruelle has spent so long trying to account must necessarily be indexed back to the individual qua human. For even while Laruelle stresses the importance of multiplying descriptors, he makes clear that a certain humanness nevertheless subsists in the One independent of any such description:

> A text of non-philosophy is constructed around a word, a statement, a philosophical text: this guiding-term must stop functioning as a hierarchizing and ontological unity and not merely as a pole of thematic unification. This is only possible if it is described first as identical, only in the last instance, to a human essence or to a radical lived experience, as a being-immanent *extracted* from the World and even anterior to it. (*PN*, 137)

In other words, while the terms used to express it might differ (*ordinary man* being only one example), the One's inherent humanness does not form part of these contingent descriptions to which it remains indifferent; rather, it is its axiomatic humanness that determines, in the last instance, this very indifference. Such humanness is equated with the singularity and finitude of individual experience, and vice versa—it is made abundantly clear that this individuality is that of the solitary, atomized person (as opposed to, say, that of a community or collectivity of some kind).[40] "This emphasis on 'man' and the 'human,'" argues Ian James, "is both rather arbitrary and, indeed, highly problematic insofar as it appears to contradict Laruelle's own axioms of radical immanence."[41] It suggests that, from the outset, certain preconceived philosophical notions frame Laruelle's attempt to escape the strictures of philosophical discursivity.

The Specter of Philosophy

Laruelle frequently maintains he is not seeking to overturn philosophy but to instigate "a mutation of philosophy's syntax and of its experience of the real," preserving its conceptual heritage and value while utilizing its diverse, contingent materiality for other ends—namely, a science of ordinary men or individuals—unconstrained by the decisional structure (*PN*, 22). But while this science is not limited to working solely on philosophical materials (hence his later engagements with psychoanalysis, theology, photography, ecology, technological science, etc.), it does require materials that conform to said structure and its corresponding presumption of sufficiency.

As a result, this science of ordinary thought, which is supposed to be indifferent to philosophical determination, comes to be expressed in strikingly philosophic terms. Or to put it another way, this science, which is also supposed to be a rigorously scientific biography of ordinary man, supplying a "theoretically justified description of the life he leads," ends up describing this man in terms likely to resonate primarily with those readers who have already undergone inculcation and assimilation into the symbolic codes and logic of academic philosophy, with its watchwords, shibboleths, and revered proper names (*BM*, 1). The audience for nonphilosophy is effectively circumscribed in advance, and thus this "description of the individual without qualities" tacitly speaks to a set of worldly individuals with quite specific, identifiable qualities (*BM*, 37).

Among us mere mortals, of course, communication is never universal—this is not a reasonable benchmark against which any text should be measured. It is always partial, contingent, contextual, and conceived with a particular audience in mind. Every philosopher (a category within which Laruelle includes himself) has their own terminology and syntax, their own means of transmitting their claims, likely appealing to some and off-putting to others. But Laruelle's peculiar use of philosophical materials calls attention to a fundamental ambiguity in his work, and especially in those books where the concept of "man" plays a prominent role: is the science of ordinary men a science *for* all people, or is it a science for philosophers and their ilk bent on demonstrating, or perhaps even convincing themselves, that they are not always shackled to the constraints of academic philosophy? Can this science really remain sufficient to a putative ordinariness when it is occasioned by quite specific materials conforming to a particular formal structure?

In the secondary literature on nonphilosophy, much has been made of Laruelle's stylistic proclivities and the forbidding nature of his writings—"the difficulty of reading to which some people . . . still object in my work," as he puts it himself in one interview, "claiming I have hampered their cherished 'readability'" (*ET*, 227).[42] But the question of philosophical communication involves more than just style or rhetoric, to the extent that the latter is concerned with appealing to or persuading an audience; it also encompasses the more neglected question of who the philosopher imagines their audience to be, and by extension, who the reader, assuming we are dealing with written works, presumes the imagined audience to be. The determinative role played by considerations of audience in the development and articulation of philosophical arguments is rarely discussed, treated as accessory to the intellectual labor of philosophizing itself. As Régis Debray puts it:

> An overly idealist view of the life of ideas comes to obscure the fact that a discursive milieu is constituted by forms of organization that are "materialized" but barely perceptible, even transparent to those whose logical discourse they structure. The presence of something implicitly shared (a community of insinuations) makes the conjunctive milieu prescriptive, through a natural, tacit agreement between members—the "it goes without saying" of those who always know what to say, when to say it, in what order, and in what place.[43]

Nonphilosophy is a perfect example of this unspoken agreement, circumscribing its audience through a set of shared terms, references, and stylistic norms.

After all, despite Laruelle's antipathy toward philosophical discourse and "its spontaneous practices (those of philosophers, of everyone, within the university or elsewhere)," his work is nevertheless written for an audience versed in philosophy—more specifically an audience who will recognize the concepts, methods, and turns of phrase peculiar to that practiced in the philosophy departments of

French universities (*ET*, 253). Indeed, in a much later lecture, admittedly delivered at an English university (albeit one that happened to have, at the time, one of the few philosophy departments in the country that dealt chiefly with modern European philosophy), Laruelle would describe nonphilosophers "inevitably, as subjects of the university, as is required by worldly life."[44] Not that his writings necessarily garner favorable reception even from those who work in such departments (many scholars *au fait* with his influences seem to still find his writings baffling, if not actively obscurantist), but it is hard to shake the feeling that these works, despite their iconoclastic ambitions, are written with a quite limited audience in mind. We end up with an account of ordinary or "nonphilosophical" thought that speaks mainly to professional philosophers and those in proximate academic disciplines.

Philosophy, argues Felski, "remains haunted by the ghost of its own past" as a master discipline, its long-ago abdicated position as queen of the sciences, "an aura that endows it with a lingering authority and prestige."[45] And Laruelle is more than happy to capitalize on this aura at the same time he claims to subvert it. Proclamations announcing philosophy's ongoing decline are a persistent motif within his writings. He complains that this discipline "finds itself lagging behind the arts and sciences," having chosen to disregard any alternative directions that might have prevented it becoming "a conservative and repetitive activity" (*PN*, 31). It contributes, we are told, to "the pain and anxiety, war and violence driving culture, language, and society" (*TE*, 17). Laruelle habitually insists on philosophy's totalizing power, its predominance over thought, to justify the task of delegitimizing it. He simultaneously dismisses philosophy as a reactionary symbol of decline, incapable of producing anything genuinely new, and elevates it to a position of supreme intellectual authority. After all, the suggestion that suspending Western ontological habits will open a "field of realities that have been absolutely hidden since the origin of philosophy," finally breaking through millennia of decadence and stagnation induced by the philosophical paradigm's dominance, is only plausible if one already accepts that philosophy (in the decisional form by which Laruelle characterizes it) maintains a chokehold over contemporary thought (*BM*, 16).

This suspension is not intended as a onetime occurrence; rather, it is an ongoing project, a "labor of thought" that defines "a *philosophically impossible yet complexly real usage*" of philosophical materials, the evolving nature of which is reflected in Laruelle's self-periodization of his own voluminous output (*PN*, 20).[46] Despite Laruelle's ambition of getting beyond the interminable commentary and textual production characteristic of academic philosophy, his writing is often accused of being needlessly repetitive, rehearsing the same formulas over and over again with only subtle variations. In part, this is a consequence of the resolute absence of examples, case studies, and any kind of overtly empirical content, leaving only an abstract framework from which his method is derived. But it is also because, in the absence of said content (which remains, in any case, nonphilosophically inadmissible), nonphilosophy's role—even if it cannot actually express it in these terms—becomes primarily about inducting its readers into a certain ethos, a certain way of thinking, and, most important, a certain posture vis-à-vis the philosophical texts they encounter. It demands continual work from its audience, recapitulating what occurs in Laruelle's texts themselves.

"The performative nature of non-philosophy," suggests James, is decisive in Laruelle's work, "because it is ultimately the sole guarantor of the 'non' of non-philosophy (that is, its distinctness from philosophy itself)."[47] Where the typical philosopher will likely try to persuade their audience (through methodological rigor, conceptual precision, explicative clarity, rhetorical extravagance or whatever else) that they possess some kind of truth, the means for accessing this truth, or, in some cases, a means for undermining the very notion of truth, Laruelle tries to persuade them that his approach, despite appearances, is not beholden to the structure of philosophical decision and does not make any misplaced claims to a sufficiency over the real. His readers must recognize the concepts he invokes but also be convinced that the context of their invocation has radically shifted, far removed from the ways in which philosophers are inclined to deploy them. The nonphilosophical corpus, then, could be described as an ongoing labor of abstraction on the part of the author, a never-ending act of loosening the shackles of philosophy, mutating philosophy's wealth of concepts, methods, and frameworks to gesture toward the One, the ordinary individual within all of us, without ever exhausting its infinite possibilities for further description. Yet another addition to what Cavell describes as the "trail of images" philosophers have left us "of themselves preparing for philosophy or recovering from it."[48] This is an ongoing labor that the reader is then urged to recapitulate for themselves.

A Nonphilosophical Ethos

In many of his books, Laruelle focuses on "the individual, finite, or radical immanence of the subject," which differentiates the latter from any conventional form of subjectivity (*BM*, 14). Indeed, more than anything else, ordinariness in a nonphilosophical context signifies "man considered in his finitude," a real, lived experience of the immanent, undivided individual grounded in nothing other than themselves (*PN*, 23). The image of the finite individual subject remains a philosophical penchant—a covert anthropology, even—from which Laruelle never seems to have recovered. As one would expect, he claims to deploy this concept in a manner quite distinct from that of the post-Kantian philosophy with which we are familiar, depicting the essence of man as "nothing-but-subject or an absolute-as-subject," an identification of "the absolute with finitude rather than with an infinite totality" (*BM*, 8–9). The subject is "impenetrable and constituted once and for all," possessing a self-knowledge as finite as itself, bearing no relationship to the "infinite, unlimited subject that includes objective-scientific knowledge as one of its modes, that borders and extends beyond that knowledge" (*BM*, 107). But this just amplifies what Brassier describes as "the post-Kantian pathos of finitude" and raises further questions about the relationship between the ordinary man and his worldly, philosophically interpellated counterpart.[49]

For Brassier, Laruelle's retention of this theme betrays the extent to which the latter's critique "remains all too beholden to Heidegger's phenomenological radicalization" of this pathos of finitude, dissolving the subject/object divide only to situate immanence "squarely on the side of the subject."[50] I would venture, however, that there is an even more important aspect to this pathos, the origins of which lie in a tradition much older than Heideggerian phenomenology. Specifically, one can still identify in Laruelle the retention of what Ian Hunter calls "the pathos of metaphysical longing and the ethos of intellectual self-purification," the central impetus of a longstanding tradition of university metaphysics whereby the philosopher inculcates a set of ascetic rituals in their followers that, through speculation and abstraction, promise to purify their souls of sensible contaminants and thereby release them from the facticity of their worldly existence.[51] Laruelle suspends the asymptotic relationship between sensible finitude and an inaccessible absolute but does so to instead identify the ordinary subject's finitude *with* the absolute. So whereas Kant, say, amplifies this pathos by foreclosing noumena to theoretical reason, leaving rational beings with the mere prospect of vainly striving toward this inaccessible realm, Laruelle absolutizes it, positing no external ideal toward which one might strive, however fruitlessly, but instead making finitude the ordinary man's essential trait, such that his very existence is defined by a solitude that continually comes into conflict with his position as a being in the world. He presents a world toward which he has to continuously work at maintaining an indifferent posture, lest he remain trapped within philosophical discourse's "practice of aporia" and "culture of malaise" (*TE*, 16).

Now, Laruelle himself would insist that ordinary man does not *have to* do anything of the sort. We must take care, he reminds us, not to project a philosophical teleology on to a project built on "an absolutely infinite *de jure* openness of theoretical labor, knowledge production encountering no ontological limit, no philosophical purpose."[52] Not only does nonphilosophy not claim to change the world, but it also does not even attempt to interpret it. It does not purport to fix any of philosophy's limitations or drawbacks. And it certainly does not claim to equip man with a self-knowledge that he does not already possess. "Real critique," Laruelle states, "is carried out by means of the One, but not for the One, because the One does not need it." A rigorous science of man is grounded in ordinary individuals' fully and sufficiently determined essence, and thus, while it unilaterally proceeds from these individuals, they would not lose or miss out on anything were this science (which is occasioned through man's contingent encounter with philosophical materials) not to exist (*BM*, 136). The ordinary man "knows (himself) as never having been a piece of the authoritarian machine, as never having had any care, concern, interest *of* his own" (*BM*, 144). Nonphilosophy, taken on its own terms, does not succeed or fail—or at least it does not rely on any extrinsic criteria for such a determination. Either its theory works or it does not.

We must separate the express propositions Laruelle puts forward, however, from the tacit stance he takes and the subject position his writings try to cultivate in their reader. Although his science forecloses such analysis, concerning itself solely with individuals who are not "visible on the social, historical, or linguistic surface," there is no reason we need restrict ourselves in the same fashion (*BM*, 19). Again, nonphilosophy may well be a science of ordinary men, but when one gets right down to it, it is not actually *for* the ordinary man, since he is, as we are constantly told, totally powerless, passive, and self-sufficient. What remains illegible within nonphilosophy's narrow analytic boundaries is the question of who exactly *it is* for and how their subjectivity relates to that of the ordinary man. At the very least, it is clear, across Laruelle's writings, talks, and interviews, that nonphilosophy *is* aimed at a specific audience with specific interests, priorities, and kinds of cultural capital—an audience that can effect nonphilosophical maneuvers and can in turn be affected by these same maneuvers. Nonphilosophy, as Gangle observes, is "ultimately *for us here in the world*," and this means it "necessitates stringent conceptual labours."[53]

In a recent interview, in fact, Laruelle remarks on his realization that "in addition to conceptual materiality, there is an affective materiality which is a true 'milieu' of existence," reflecting a "need to communicate" and make his thoughts known.[54] And as is typically the case with philosophers, this communicative imperative tacitly involves inducting his readers or listeners into a particular ethos. It might be the case that the individual qua ordinary man is not, according to Laruelle's dicta, ontologically compelled to work toward nonphilosophical outcomes, but his writings very clearly try to guide the reader (who may well identify with the figure of the ordinary man, but whose worldly existence ensures that they are never identical with him) toward a certain subject position in line with these outcomes:

We are attempting to lead philosophers, rather than to renounce philosophy, to break through the ultimate barriers of philosophical imagery and even the speculative Imagination and to give themselves the means to finally think the unthinkable as unthinkable without contradiction, to describe what is speculatively indescribable without paradox. We are attempting to pass from the One's transcendent figures to its essence. (*PN*, 35; translation altered)

In fact, this outward refusal of all teleology is central both to the articulation of this subject position and to the ongoing work of differentiating nonphilosophy from philosophy, painting the latter as comparatively peremptory and dictatorial, interpellating subjects into its preformed narratives.

To reiterate, then, the true "subject" of nonphilosophy is not the ordinary man (who is nothing more than an abstract axiom) but the imagined reader, the prospective inductee into the nonphilosophical project, who is encouraged to see something of themselves in this axiom and to adopt a nonphilosophical posture, deliberately and continuously recalibrating the way that they think about themselves and their position in the world through the techniques and procedures furnished by the nonphilosophical project.

Despite his staunch refusal to use illustrations and case studies, Laruelle's writings often give hints about his ideal reader or subject. Someone who is "condemned to action" and thus also "condemned a second time, and for the same reasons, to philosophy" (*BM*, 1). Someone who wonders if "the Greeks really are as important and unavoidable as those who have put their faith in them claim" (*ET*, 228). Someone who finds that they have something in common with "gnostics, dualists, heretics, millenarianists, and 'fanatics'—that is, all those individuals who fundamentally proclaim their individuality against philosophy rather than at its margins" (*ET*, 225). Someone dissatisfied with the "coded, repetitive, and fetishistic" nature of "traditional philosophical practice" (*ET*, 240). In other words, a quite particular kind of individual: not necessarily a philosopher by profession, but certainly someone who is involved in these debates and who deals with philosophy, most likely in an academic or para-academic context.

Adopting a nonphilosophical posture would not by any measure "improve" such an individual's philosophical work, which will never escape its ensnarement within the aporetic circle of decision and sufficiency. But it *can* help make room for other ways of thinking, by forgoing the customary gestures of displacing or deconstructing this discipline's norms and boundaries and instead attempting to circumscribe their own radical finitude vis-à-vis all philosophical materials (and accordingly circumscribing the boundaries of these materials, suspending their pretension to not only represent but also in some way constitute the real)—a task that demands an ongoing inner labor, extracting nonphilosophical possibilities from philosophical materiality and employing them as the basis for an open-ended, pluralized, and creative project forming statements and descriptions unconstrained by philosophy's rules. The ordinary man may well be "a radically individual reality who precedes philosophy, who does not need the *logos*' universality in order to realize himself" (*ET*, 250). But the aspiring nonphilosopher, who is condemned to be occupied with worldly pursuits and exigencies, can only hope to constantly work at keeping up a posture congruent with this axiom: a work that, despite all its rhetorical gestures, conveniently promotes an unremitting productivity (often referred to as the creation of *philofiction* and *hyperspeculation*) and is optimally expressed in the form of standard academic outputs (e.g., books, chapters, journal articles, conference papers, doctoral theses, etc.).[55]

Functionally, this subject position differs little from that of many prior philosophies that have proclaimed the need to adopt a specific mode of comportment and manner of speaking in order to think the unthinkable and describe the indescribable.[56] Laruelle's assertion that "it will never be possible for thinkers who exercise the human freedom of thought and those who postulate the authority of texts to come to an understanding," actually fits quite neatly with the skepticism toward erudition and book-learning characteristic of numerous post-Cartesian philosophical systems that exhort their readers to not just learn prefabricated propositions by rote but actively take part in the rational cognition proper to philosophy (*TE*, 201).[57]

Though Laruelle is careful to underscore that no one *needs* to follow the nonphilosophical path, that it has no *stakes* in any conventional sense, he nevertheless makes it clear that, in his estimation, philosophy is a stultifying, unimaginative, depleted force—incapable of "carrying out the theoretical and technical mutations which the sciences and the arts—above all painting and music—have carried out" over the past century—and nonphilosophy holds out the only fruitful and thoroughgoing means of thinking beyond its parameters (*PN*, 4). The ordinary man's finitude is simply given, it is a fact, it does not need to be achieved, he does not need to enter into any process of individuation or becoming, but the supposedly rigorous science offered by nonphilosophy very clearly does require ongoing work (for which it supplies the techniques and procedures), involving "the labor that follows from the rectification of non-philosophical descriptions or formulations" (*PN*, 245). The pathos of continual inner labor, not striving to transcend one's finitude (as in more conventional instances of university metaphysics) but instead striving to keep up a principled indifference to the determinative power of philosophical decision and sufficiency.

The Ordinariness of Philosophy

Laruelle is determined to overcome the divided conception of man as exemplified by the post-Kantian empirico-transcendental doublet, but he still retains two basic postulates undergirding this ambivalent figure: first, that the human subject is condemned to worldly (i.e., philosophical) existence; and second, that the subject is never exhausted by this existence, and recognition of and reflection on its own finitude provides a means of eluding philosophical determination. By positing the One as unreflective and indeterminable, Laruelle can abandon the notion that this analytic of finitude provides the means for reconciling man's alienated nature. But this does not mean that such an analytic does not effectively take place in his own work. If it is the case that philosophy "has not ceased repressing and resisting another way of thinking," one surely has good reason to engage in the nonphilosophical enterprise, even if there is no apparent existential compulsion to do so.[58] And while, at a rhetorical level, Laruelle often seems concerned by how philosophical interpellation arrogates and recuperates the achievements of those who are genuinely capable of creating something new (i.e., something that is not constricted by philosophical decision), his primary concern is still, in the end, the academic philosopher.

Laruelle's preoccupation with the image of the ordinary man is symptomatic of the subject position toward which he tries to guide the reader, "putting them in a new scientific posture or relationship *with their own philosophy*" (*ET*, 13). He is effectively offering a kind of self-help—or maybe a "spiritual exercise," to use a less inflammatory term—for disaffected philosophers.[59] This is an accusation that might seem a shade derisive but is not intended as such. As an intellectual exercise, a peculiar variation on the procedures of transcendental reduction, nonphilosophy offers considerable resources, both permitting reflection on the shortcomings of our own scholarly practices and, hopefully, opening up new ways of thinking. But though its approach is quite original, especially in its assiduous commitment to formalism, there is no reason to believe it has unequaled purchase on the real; on the contrary, it fits quite neatly into a long lineage of similar forms of academic self-cultivation.

"Despite their statements to the contrary (in order to signal the exceptional character of their discipline)," writes Laruelle, "philosophy's existence is a mundane phenomenon."[60] Yet nonphilosophy does not actually treat it is such; instead, it depicts philosophy as *extra*ordinary, a uniquely aporetic, hallucinatory, and domineering form of power, its authorities "at least as powerful as their political counterparts," pitted against the ordinary man, who derives both his validity and his reality entirely from himself (*ET*, 253). This likewise puts nonphilosophy in a uniquely impactful position, offering "our only chance for peace in the midst of ideological, cultural, and moral conflicts" (*ET*, 252). Surely, if we are trying to cut philosophy (or at least its more immodest instances) down to size, it would be more effective, albeit perhaps less methodologically elaborate, to emphasize that it is just one in an endless array of discourses, accompanied by a particular set of formal rules and a distinctive manner of speaking—and as a corollary, just one of many ways of identifying an audience and delimiting an imagined community; just another means of cultivating a particular posture within a particular institutional setting.

To think philosophy in this fashion—treating "its various anthropologies as optional and equivalent means through which certain individuals forge the relation to the self," as Ian Hunter proposes, doctrines "whose historical circumstances, purposes and distribution are matters of historical investigation and description"—is to abandon the pathos of finitude, that lingering trace of the empirico-transcendental doublet, whereby such formal determinations are treated as barriers to be overcome through transcendental reflection, and to instead perceive such reflection as one of the many historically and institutionally contingent discursive technologies through which we are interpellated as invariably bounded subjects and by which we distinguish ourselves from others.[61]

....

THOMAS SUTHERLAND is senior lecturer in media studies at the University of Lincoln. He is author of *Speaking Philosophically: Communication at the Limits of Discursive Reason* (2023).

Notes

1. Han-Pile, "Analytic of Finitude," 125.
2. Foucault, *Order of Things*, 421.
3. Foucault, *Order of Things*, 421; translation altered.
4. Laruelle, *En tant qu'un*, 248 (hereafter cited as *ET*); my translation. I follow Laruelle's usage of the noun *man* and the masculine pronouns that accompany it throughout this article. This is in no way an endorsement of the now-outmoded convention (in English) of defaulting to such language in preference to gender-neutral terms.
5. Laruelle divests this term, *the One*, of its usual Neoplatonic connotations, lamenting that philosophers "have refused from the start to shed light upon the One's essence" (*Philosophy and Non-philosophy*, 33 [hereafter cited as *PN*]).
6. Laruelle, *Biography of Ordinary Man*, 5 (hereafter cited as *BM*); translation altered.
7. For the purposes of this article, I focus principally on a few select books drawn from Laruelle's corpus: *Le principe de minorité* (1981), *A Biography of Ordinary Man* (1985; translated 2018), *Philosophy and Non-philosophy* (1989; translated 2013), *En tant qu'un* (1991), *Theory of Identities* (1992; translated 2016), and *Théorie des étrangers* (1995).
8. Certeau, *Practice of Everyday Life*, v.
9. Frow and Morris, introduction, xxvii.

10. During, *Exit Capitalism*, 96.

11. Felski, *Doing Time*, 156.

12. Probyn, *Sexing the Self*, 146; Ang, *Living Room Wars*, 93.

13. Hartley, *Short History of Cultural Studies*, 121.

14. Kant, *Critique of Pure Reason*, A xiii.

15. Fichte, *Introductions to the Wissenschaftslehre*, 144.

16. On *homo duplex*, see Durkheim, "Dualism of Human Nature."

17. Laruelle, *Le principe de minorité*, 13; my translation.

18. Laruelle, *Le principe de minorité*, 16.

19. For my earlier (slightly less developed, perhaps) thoughts on this book, see Sutherland and Patsoura, "Human-in-the-Last-Instance"; and Sutherland, "Authoritarian and Minoritarian Thought."

20. Gangle, "Laruelle and Ordinary Life," 61.

21. Laruelle, *Théorie des étrangers*, 50 (hereafter cited as *TE*).

22. On the relationship between philosophical decision and the concept of man, see *TE*, 38–41.

23. This book also contains interviews by Didier Cahen and Philippe Petit, both of which are quoted at points in this article.

24. Laugier, "Emerson," 45–46; my translation.

25. Cavell, *Must We Mean What We Say?*, 238.

26. Cavell, *Pitch of Philosophy*, 3.

27. Cavell, *Must We Mean What We Say?*, 126.

28. See Gracieuse, "Laruelle Facing Deleuze," 54.

29. In this way, writes Alex Dubilet, "the human is taken as fundamentally a kind of evanescent solitude, one that can never be fully exhausted or interpellated by the World and by philosophy, which try to identify or fix it with particular universal attributes and generalizations" ("(Non-) human Identity and Radical Immanence," 32).

30. Sackin-Poll, "Ordinary Contested," 246.

31. Brassier, "Axiomatic Heresy," 24.

32. "Laruelle decided at an early moment in his philosophical development," write Alexander R. Galloway and Jason R. LaRivière, "to reject the excessively expressive in favor of the compressive" ("Compression in Philosophy," 140).

33. The French *suffisance* signifies not only adequacy but also vanity, arrogance, and self-importance.

34. Laugier, "Emerson," 46.

35. De Man, "Epistemology of Metaphor," 13.

36. "Just as philosophy is spontaneously 'figurative' in a broad sense, describing a given figure of the World, language, objects, and the like or a

transcendent Being, so non-philosophy is 'abstract,' founded in the being-immanent of the One" (*PN*, 23; translation altered).

37. Anne-Françoise Schmid's "non-epistemological" take on the philosophy of science is an admirable exception to this (see in particular her *Épistémologie générique*, authored with the biologist Muriel Mambrini-Doudet).

38. This is not to discount some very interesting adaptations of non-philosophy in English-language "theory": e.g., Smith, *Non-philosophical Theory of Nature*; Galloway, *Laruelle*; Kolozova, *Cut of the Real*; Ó Maoilearca, *All Thoughts Are Equal*; and Fardy, *Laruelle and Art*.

39. Kraus, "Ecceity," 304.

40. Although Laruelle emphasizes at various points that "minorities only exist in the state of multiplicities" (*BM*, 26), these multiplicities being the basis of the more political aspects of the nonphilosophical project, his aversion to any relative ("stato-minoritarian") conception of unity or difference means that they are still ultimately defined by nothing but their individuality or finitude.

41. James, *New French Philosophy*, 179.

42. See also Sutherland, "Style without Substance."

43. Debray, *Introduction à la médiologie*, 97; my translation.

44. Laruelle, "New Presentation of Non-philosophy," 137. The Middlesex University philosophy department was, amid much controversy, closed in 2010 (for financial reasons, unsurprisingly); its postgraduate research programs, and many senior staff, eventually relocated to Kingston University London.

45. Felski, *Doing Time*, 155.

46. On this periodization, see especially Laruelle, *Principles of Non-philosophy*, 33–36.

47. James, *New French Philosophy*, 175.

48. Cavell, *Pitch of Philosophy*, 3.

49. Brassier, *Nihil Unbound*, 127.

50. Brassier, *Nihil Unbound*, 127.

51. Hunter, *Rival Enlightenments*, 57.

52. Laruelle, *Theory of Identities*, 66; translation altered. "I do not suggest any rules about what to do—everyone should continue doing what they have started to do—I propose no goal, no teleology whatsoever, I merely describe. What do I describe? The real relation between man and philosophy" (*ET*, 236).

53. Gangle, "Laruelle and Ordinary Life," 62.

54. Laruelle, Citot, and Peltier, "Entretien avec François Laruelle," 71; my translation. Laruelle has, on many other occasions, complained about philosophy's incessant recourse to communication; see in particular Laruelle, "Truth according to Hermes."

55. "The finished product of this enterprise: the production of nonphilosophical statements from philosophical statements. This is what we also call philofiction or hyperspeculation. Instead of producing effects that merely have a nonphilosophical appearance, on the basis of procedures that remain philosophical (which is what Heidegger and Derrida do), we propose to produce effects that are really nonphilosophical, but ultimately bear a 'family resemblance' to philosophy" (*ET*, 40). For a contrastive account, underscoring nonphilosophy's antiproductivist ambitions, see Coley, "In Defence of 'Noir Theory.'"

56. For a further exploration of this argument in relation to broader philosophical trends in Western thought, see Sutherland, *Speaking Philosophically*.

57. On this skepticism toward erudition, which begins with Descartes but is articulated more explicitly by Malebranche and carries through at least as far as Hegel, see Gueroult, *Dianoématique*, and subsequent volumes.

58. Laruelle, *Theory of Identities*, 16.

59. This notion of philosophy as a form of spiritual exercise was popularized by Pierre Hadot (see *Philosophy as a Way of Life*), who regards the various schools of Greco-Roman antiquity as prioritizing *paideia* over *theōria*. Ian Hunter views such inner labor as characteristic of university metaphysics more broadly, including in the contemporary theoretical scene (see "History of Theory").

60. Laruelle, *Theory of Identities*, 253; translation altered.

61. Hunter, *Rival Enlightenments*, 24.

References

Ang, Ien. *Living Room Wars: Rethinking Media Audiences for a Postmodern World*. London: Routledge, 1996.

Brassier, Ray. "Axiomatic Heresy: The Non-philosophy of François Laruelle." *Radical Philosophy*, no. 121 (2003): 24–35.

Brassier, Ray. *Nihil Unbound: Enlightenment and Extinction*. Basingstoke: Palgrave Macmillan, 2007.

Cavell, Stanley. *Must We Mean What We Say?* Cambridge: Cambridge University Press, 1976.

Cavell, Stanley. *A Pitch of Philosophy: Autobiographical Exercises*. Cambridge, MA: Harvard University Press, 1994.

Certeau, Michel de. *The Practice of Everyday Life*. Translated by Steven Rendall. Berkeley: University of California Press, 1984.

Coley, Rob. "In Defence of 'Noir Theory': Laruelle, Deleuze, and Other Detectives." *Theory, Culture and Society* 37, no. 3 (2020): 123–44.

Debray, Régis. *Introduction à la médiologie*. Paris: Presses Universitaires de France, 2000.

de Man, Paul. "The Epistemology of Metaphor." *Critical Inquiry* 5, no. 1 (1978): 13–30.

Dubilet, Alex. "(Non-)human Identity and Radical Immanence." In *Superpositions: Laruelle and the Humanities*, edited by Rocco Gangle and Julius Greve, 31–45. London: Rowman and Littlefield, 2017.

During, Simon. *Exit Capitalism: Literary Culture, Theory, and Post-secular Modernity*. London: Routledge, 2010.

Durkheim, Émile. "The Dualism of Human Nature and Its Social Conditions." Translated by Charles Blend. In *On Morality and Society*, edited by Robert N. Bellah, 149–63. Chicago: University of Chicago Press, 1973.

Fardy, Jonathan. *Laruelle and Art: The Aesthetics of Non-philosophy*. London: Bloomsbury, 2020.

Felski, Rita. *Doing Time: Feminist Theory and Postmodernism*. New York: New York University Press, 2000.

Fichte, Johann Gottlieb. *Introductions to the Wissenschaftslehre and Other Writings (1797–1800)*. Translated by Daniel Breazeale. Indianapolis, IN: Hackett, 1994.

Foucault, Michel. *The Order of Things: An Archaeology of the Human Sciences*. Translated by A. M. Sheridan Smith. London: Routledge, 1970.

Frow, John, and Meaghan Morris. Introduction to *Australian Cultural Studies: A Reader*, edited by John Frow and Meaghan Morris, vii–xxxii. St. Leonards, NSW: Allen and Unwin, 1993.

Galloway, Alexander R. *Laruelle: Against the Digital*. Minneapolis: University of Minnesota Press, 2014.

Galloway, Alexander R., and Jason R. LaRivière. "Compression in Philosophy." *boundary 2* 44, no. 1 (2017): 125–47.

Gangle, Rocco. "Laruelle and Ordinary Life." In *Laruelle and Non-philosophy*, edited by John Mullarkey and Anthony Paul Smith, 60–79. Edinburgh: Edinburgh University Press, 2012.

Gracieuse, Marjorie. "Laruelle Facing Deleuze: Immanence, Resistance, and Desire." In *Laruelle and Non-philosophy*, edited by John Mullarkey and Anthony Paul Smith, 42–59. Edinburgh: Edinburgh University Press, 2012.

Gueroult, Martial. *Dianoématique, livre I: Histoire de l'histoire de la philosophie*. Vol. 1. Paris: Aubier, 1984.

Hadot, Pierre. *Philosophy as a Way of Life: Spiritual Exercises from Socrates to Foucault*. Translated by Michael Chase. Oxford: Blackwell, 1995.

Han-Pile, Béatrice. "The Analytic of Finitude." In *The Kantian Catastrophe? Conversations on Finitude and the Limits of Philosophy*, edited by Anthony Morgan, 119–36. Newcastle-upon-Tyne: Bigg, 2017.

Hartley, John. *A Short History of Cultural Studies*. London: Sage, 2003.

Hunter, Ian. "The History of Theory." *Critical Inquiry* 33, no. 1 (2006): 78–112.

Hunter, Ian. *Rival Enlightenments: Civil and Metaphysical Philosophy in Early Modern Germany*. Cambridge: Cambridge University Press, 2003.

James, Ian. *The New French Philosophy*. Cambridge: Polity, 2012.

Kant, Immanuel. *Critique of Pure Reason*. Translated by Paul Guyer and Allen W. Wood. Cambridge: Cambridge University Press, 1998.

Kolozova, Katerina. *Cut of the Real: Subjectivity in Poststructuralist Philosophy*. New York: Columbia University Press, 2014.

Kraus, Chris. "Ecceity, Smash and Grab, the Expanded I and Moment." In *French Theory in America*, edited by Sylvère Lotringer and Sande Cohen, 303–8. London: Routledge, 2001.

Laruelle, François. *A Biography of Ordinary Man: On Authorities and Minorities*. Translated by Jessie Hock and Alex Dubilet. Cambridge: Polity, 2018.

Laruelle, François. *En tant qu'un: La "non-philosophie" éxpliquée au philosophes*. Paris: Aubier Montaigne, 1991.

Laruelle, François. *Le principe de minorité*. Paris: Aubier Montaigne, 1981.

Laruelle, François. "A New Presentation of Non-philosophy." In *The Non-philosophy Project*, edited by Gabriel Alkon and Boris Gunjević, 117–37. New York: Telos, 2012.

Laruelle, François. *Philosophy and Non-philosophy*. Translated by Taylor Adkins. Minneapolis: Univocal, 2013.

Laruelle, François. *Principles of Non-philosophy*. Translated by Nicola Rubczak and Anthony Paul Smith. London: Bloomsbury, 2013.

Laruelle, François. *Théorie des étrangers: Science des hommes, democratie, non-psychanalyse*. Paris: Kimé, 1995.

Laruelle, François. *Theory of Identities*. Translated by Alyosha Edlebi. New York: Columbia University Press, 2016.

Laruelle, François. "The Truth according to Hermes: Theorems on the Secret and Communication." *Parrhesia*, no. 9 (2010): 18–22.

Laruelle, François, Vincent Citot, and Alex Peltier. "Entretien avec François Laruelle." *Le philosophoire* 43, no. 1 (2015): 57–72.

Laugier, Sandra. "Emerson: Penser l'ordinaire." *Revue française d'études américaines* 91, no. 1 (2002): 43–60.

Ó Maoilearca, John. *All Thoughts Are Equal: Laruelle and Nonhuman Philosophy*. Minneapolis: University of Minnesota Press, 2015.

Probyn, Elspeth. *Sexing the Self: Gendered Positions in Cultural Studies*. London: Routledge, 1993.

Sackin-Poll, Andrew. "The Ordinary Contested, Laruelle *contra* Deleuze and Guattari." *Paragraph* 44, no. 2 (2021): 238–56.

Schmid, Anne-Françoise, and Muriel Mambrini-Doudet. *Épistémologie générique: Manuel pour les sciences futures*. Paris: Kimé, 2019.

Smith, Anthony Paul. *A Non-philosophical Theory of Nature: Ecologies of Thought*. Basingstoke: Palgrave Macmillan, 2013.

Sutherland, Thomas. "Authoritarian and Minoritarian Thought." *Parrhesia*, no. 32 (2020): 253–62.

Sutherland, Thomas. *Speaking Philosophically: Communication at the Limits of Discursive Reason*. London: Bloomsbury, 2023.

Sutherland, Thomas. "Style without Substance, Form *qua* Function: The Non-philosophical Unilateralization of Philosophical Style." *Pli: The Warwick Journal of Philosophy* 29 (2018): 113–45.

Sutherland, Thomas, and Elliot Patsoura. "Human-in-the-Last-Instance? The Concept of 'Man' between Foucault and Laruelle." *Parrhesia*, no. 24 (2015): 285–311.

Care for Language
An Interview with Bonnie Honig

ANNABEL BARRY

ANNABEL BARRY: The concept of the ordinary has recently become important to your work. Where does this concept come from, and what does it mean to you?

BONNIE HONIG: The concept figures in the work of Stanley Cavell, which I read as I researched an essay in film studies that just came out in *Cultural Critique* and have returned to as I now write a book about the politics of ordinary language philosophy. That said, the ordinary as a concept was important to me in my earliest work, not by way of Cavell, but by way of J. L. Austin, whom Cavell calls his teacher. In my first book, *Political Theory and the Displacement of Politics*, I noted the commonalities between performative speech acts as analyzed by Austin, the ordinary language philosopher, and Hannah Arendt's account of political action as *action that appears in words*. For Arendt, in *The Human Condition*, such speech acts were extraordinary, while for Austin, in *How to Do Things with Words*, they were ordinary. I wanted to make sense of that difference,

QUI PARLE   Vol. 33, No. 1, June 2024
DOI 10.1215/10418385-11125535   © 2024 Editorial Board, *Qui Parle*

especially since they both treated the act of promising as an exemplary action that appears in words.

I brought Arendt and Austin together, not to make them compatible, but to put them into a conversation that might be mutually illuminating. I contrasted Austin's ordinary with Arendt's account of speech action as extraordinary—like a miracle, she says, referring to its rupture with the causal and the expected. But now I note that both affiliated their work with phenomenology, and both wanted to protect the domain of human action from the intrusions of metaphysics. These are important *shared* points of orientation.

At the time, I was more on Arendt's side of a debate that I set up between Arendt and Austin, comparing his account of the "I do" of the wedding ceremony with hers of the "We hold" of the US Declaration of Independence. Both examples were criticized back then and today, rightly so. Austin's "I do" was said to install a sovereign, heteronormative, masculine "I"; Arendt's "We hold" was said to obscure the vast unfreedoms installed by the slave-owning, supposedly freedom-loving "We" that was brought into being by way of the signing of the Declaration.

Back then I drew on Jacques Derrida's critical appreciation of Austin in "Signature Event Context" and on Derrida's reading of the Declaration (draft) in "Declarations of Independence" to show the imbrication of Austin's ordinary with the extraordinary and to highlight the dependence of the new American "We" on acts of writing, which Arendt also understood to be important to speech acts that endure. But where Derrida saw dissemination and iteration as key features of writing, Arendt insisted there was "permanence" and augmentation.

I now feel that I didn't give the ordinary its due. Perhaps because of my more recent work in *Public Things* and the experience of life in the United States since 2016, the ordinary seems to me precarious, and the task of politics is surely not only to interrupt it but also to sustain it at the same time, not as it is but as it might be. I suppose this might mean treating the ordinary as aspirational, which recalls Cavell. That said, Cavell does not hesitate to invest in the "I do" and the "we hold" that I prefer to decenter in our thinking. Cavell argues, most famously in his book *Pursuits of Happiness*, that the so-called comedies of remarriage are instructive because they show how couples who once thought themselves happy, in an ordinary way, learn to practice a kind of perfectionism when they break up and then reconcile ongoingly by way of their resumed and never-ending conversation. For Cavell, these films model a political reconciliation that is still elusive in the United States.

AB: That relates to another question I have. How does the "ordinary" differ from other terms with which it's associated, like the "everyday," or the "common," which is a term that comes up in your book *Public Things*, for example?

BH: The "ordinary" has a specific Cavellian meaning now—to enter into the ordinary is to relinquish the desire or the pathology to abstract from it, to confront things as they are, we might say in a Nietzschean vein, without metaphysical comforts or illusions. Arendt invites us to think not in terms of the ordinary but the everyday, which is the quotidian, the familiar, what we expect to happen in a recurring way. The common is different. Here, you may be thinking about the work I did in *Public Things* on the overlaps and complementarities between notions like the commons and the public. I think they're really different, but they have similar impulses, which is to attend to objects and pursuits that put us in concert with each other. The public is assumed to align with a politics of organized governance, which distinguishes public from private. The commons is more often affiliated with antistatist or extrastatist forms of politics that are also anti-enclosure. From the perspective of the commons, the public looks like a category of enclosure: it's what is left or reserved after privatization.

Public Things was my effort to think about how a commitment to democracy is a commitment to public things, not as an afterthought but as a centerpiece of democratic life. Public things provide for all, prefiguring fuller democratic arrangements, and they provide affective goods, like the feeling that one is part of a public that enjoys and maintains shared things together. For there to be public things, there have to be people who tend to them. And that's one of the functions for us of public things—they remind us of the importance of maintenance, which is hands-on (maintenance is a work of the hands, from *les mains*, "hands" in French, and *maintenant*, French for "now").

AB: You completed your graduate-school education during the linguistic turn. How has your exposure to philosophy of language influenced your work over the years?

BH: First, for me, theory is about close reading. That comes from my prior training in philosophy of language, where the turn of phrase really matters, and where fine distinctions are the coin of the realm. But that habit of close reading also comes from deconstruction, a later moment in the linguistic turn. Finally, and this is something I will be talking about in my next book, I was prepared for this approach to theorizing by the practices of rabbinical commentary on the Hebrew Bible, which I studied in school. This background prepared me for a view of language as both ordinary and exceptional, human and divine, bounded and boundless. I think Austin and Arendt both resonated with me because of this background training.

AB: It is sort of incredible that these two thinkers are developing a theory of speech as action that is in tandem at the same time and not addressing each other's work.

BH: Perhaps even unaware of each other. As far I can tell, Arendt was at that time, in the 1950s—which is the decade of their overlap in these matters—most known for writing *Origins of Totalitarianism*, which is far afield from Austin's philosophical interests. Austin was working on what would have seemed to Arendt like small questions—had she known of them at all, which I think she did not.

AB: I recently had the pleasure of hearing your Una's Lecture at the Townsend Center for the Humanities at the University of California, Berkeley. You talked about Austin and Arendt in that lecture, but I just wanted to give you a chance to share some of the details, either of that talk or of the book that you're working on, which I understand to be coming out of that talk.

BH: The talk was my effort to think alongside—I was even thinking about Sedgwick's use of the term *beside* in *Touching Feeling* today, as in the work of Noga Rotem in political theory at University of Washington—Austin, beside him. That is a way to characterize what I'm doing with Austin in my new project. While I do offer a reading of his book *How to Do Things with Words*, the text where he introduces the term *performativity*, I think of my own project as working out of a kind of adjacency with Austin. To take one example, Austin quotes from the *Hippolytus* by Euripides early in *How to Do Things with Words*, and I took that rather casual citation to be an invitation to read *Hippolytus* alongside Austin. Austin castigates the title character for considering breaking a promise he has made. Hippolytus says, "My lips swore to but my heart did not." Austin rejects that idea: there'd be no such thing as promising if we could all get out of our promises by saying, "I didn't mean it." It has to be that our word is our bond, Austin says.[1]

But, as Marianne Constable points out in *Our Word Is Our Bond*, Austin goes on to specify a whole bunch of other "let-outs" that put pressure on the "word is our bond" idea. There are many conditions under which promising doesn't hold. It's not just about whether you said it or you didn't. And that's right about Austin. Moreover, in the end, Hippolytus doesn't break his promise anyway. This latter detail leads some of Austin's critics, including Cavell, to say that Austin seems to have misremembered the play. But that seems implausible. Before Austin went to Oxford, he translated Euripides from Greek to English for a school assignment. At Oxford he, like many Oxford undergraduates, performed in many Greek tragedies and a comedy as well. He also studied and then taught Greats. It is hard to imagine he did not recall Euripides's play.

So I have taken a different tack. Rather than adjudicate Austin's reading of the play, I ask what possible reasons there were for Austin to feel drawn to that play. Here's a thinker of the performative, the inaugurator of the term, who never talks about forgiveness (one of Arendt's two exemplary speech acts), even though it's one of the most important lubricants of civil society relations. But the play that Austin chooses to center, even if in passing, happens to be a play famous for its great scene of forgiveness—said to take place between a king and his bastard, disavowed son. Was Austin, perhaps, *in* citing the *Hippolytus*, broaching a topic he did not theorize? There's a politics to the question. The play might have come up again for Austin in 1955 (when he delivered the lectures that would become the 1962 book) because of the treatment of it by Bernard Knox as a parable of forgiveness that appeared in 1952 as "The *Hippolytus* of Euripides." In that same decade, in 1958, Arendt is claiming in *The Human Condition* that promising and forgiveness are the quintessential political speech acts. So, through the 1950s, there's this line of thinking by three thinkers in different disciplines, none referring to the others but all living in a postwar world in which the capacity to make and break relationality through words rather than weapons must have been very appealing.

AB: In addition to ordinary language philosophers, you're also working with Black feminist thinkers, including Spillers, Hartman, and Sharpe. How do these intellectual traditions speak to one another?

BH: I would add Patricia Williams to that list. Her book *The Alchemy of Race and Rights* is also about the politics of language. It is a book about the temptations of metaphysical abstraction that take us away from the concrete realities of race in everyday life, and it belongs to the tradition you refer to. How these two traditions of thinking about language and politics relate is one of the things I'm working out in this new book on performativity. My views may change as I go on, but here's how I'm thinking about it now.

I had mentioned earlier my formation by deconstruction in the 1980s. I was in the PhD program at Johns Hopkins, and Derrida occasionally visited the Humanities Center there. I started working on Derrida because of Austin, whose work I had studied in the analytic tradition. My adviser, Richard Flathman, taught a seminar called Language and Politics, in which we read Locke, Wittgenstein, Austin, and more. But alongside that archive there was another, though I did not know it at the time. It struck me when I read an article by Barbara Christian recommended to me by my colleague in English at Brown, Kevin Quashie. "The Race for Theory," published in 1987, is a rigorous and heartfelt essay about the impact of the linguistic turn at the time on the study of Black literature. Theory that was predominantly written by white male thinkers was, Christian argued, sidelining Black women's writing and demoting those who studied it.

At around the same time, Hortense J. Spillers published "Mama's Baby, Papa's Maybe," which was, as its subtitle said, about an "American grammar book." In the decades that followed, others who undertook the study of the racial politics of language included Williams, Hartman, and Sharpe. I think of this now as a tradition of Black philosophy of language that thinks about race as (also, not only) a grammatical problematic and asks how language might stage or constrain emancipatory or egalitarian possibilities of living.

There is something about that Christian essay, which I really love, that occludes this other tradition. By juxtaposing Black literature versus white theory (which was an observed opposition at the time), does Christian occlude work on the philosophy of language by Spillers, Morrison, Williams, Hartman, Sharpe, and many others? I would add Sara Ahmed to that list as well, since she practices phenomenology in a language-centered way. So we have Austin-Wittgenstein-Cavell, let's say, on one side, and Spillers-Williams-Sharpe-Hartman-Ahmed, on the other: the first finding succor, let's say, in the ordinary; the latter finding horror in the ordinary; and each nonetheless looking to theorize techniques of thinking and doing in language, in all its limitations and promise.

AB: I find that really exciting. I really liked what you said about the idea that there might be a Black feminist philosophy of language that's not being called that. People like Spillers are doing a really rigorous linguistic philosophy, whether or not they are directly responding to Wittgenstein.

BH: Yes. And Spillers may well be directly responding to the linguistic turn. We have from Spillers the idea of a grammar, and we have from Sharpe the idea of the anagrammatical. This is Sharpe, citing Spillers, responding to the power of the "American grammar book." In *In the Wake* as well as in *Ordinary Notes* (which I read as notes on the American ordinary), Sharpe asks: (how) can we break that grammatical hold and take the measure of its violence? Sharpe explores various techniques, like redaction and annotation. And Hartman, of course, also looks for ways to say the unsayable, to negotiate the nonnegotiable. That means being creative with language.

This is why I locate performativity in my book between austerity and extravagance. There's a kind of linguistic extravagance in play in Spillers and the others. They do not follow the Cavell-Austin-Wittgenstein call to return language to the ordinary. For Williams, Hartman, and Sharpe, language must take flight beyond the grip of the ordinary. In Williams's *The Alchemy of Race and Rights*, a chapter on the power of analogy in law seeks to dispel the power of analogical reasoning in our own thinking. I'm sure this tradition is richer than I have said here so far. I know it is. Imani Perry and Jennifer Nash belong to it as well. So does Ainsley LeSure, my political theory colleague at Brown.

AB: Queer theorists have critiqued Austin for positing heterosexual marriage as the paradigmatic speech act. The feminist thinkers that you're working with, like Spillers, have sought to envision alternatives to the conventional nuclear family. You've also talked about Cavell's work on the comedy of remarriage. Does the so-called marriage plot feature in your work, and how?

BH: Yes. In "Grammars of Refusal," a recent short essay in a *Post45* collection of work on refusal, I looked at Spillers's effort to conjugate beyond the conjugal in "Mama's Baby." I compared that move in Spillers to an example in Wittgenstein's *Philosophical Investigations*, often referred to as the "aberrant pupil." The young man in Wittgenstein also conjugates beyond the conjugal, I argue, when he stops counting (Noah-like) by twos and suddenly and without explanation starts counting by fours. Is this a queer aberrancy? I will develop that argument further in the book, drawing on Cavell and Quine.

Austin can be queered too. He got a lot of attention in the 1990s at a formative moment for queer theory. Judith Butler had used the term *performativity* in *Gender Trouble* as a way to describe the constant negotiation of compelled gender performances through gendered acts that were performative (identity producing) and not, say, expressive (of a prior identity). I'm sure I don't need to rehearse that argument for your audience. That was a formative book for me, and I read it with Austin in mind. But it wasn't Austin that Butler was drawing on for "performativity," but Derrida. I didn't concern myself with that at the time, but now I am asking whether it matters where you source "performativity." Butler added to the Derridian position: they reworked the Derridian argument to attend to how performatives sex and gender the subjects of language.

In the first issue of *GLQ*, in 1993, Eve Kosofsky Sedgwick criticized Butler for working with Austin's term, given his reliance on the "I do" of the straight wedding. Butler wasn't citing Austin, Sedgwick noted, but still, the use of the term *performativity* should mean turning to Austin, which Sedgwick did. She criticized *How to Do Things with Words* not only for the marriage example, that "I do," but also for its more general reliance on the first-person indicative "I" in most of Austin's examples. What if we turned to a different kind of performative, one with no "I"? she asked. Her example was "Shame on you," which had the added merit, she argued, of being a constitutive experience of queerness. She said there should be a new class of performatives to capture this example and others like it. She proposed "deformatives," which I consider a brilliant addition to the Austinian repertoire.

In their response, "Critically Queer," Butler agreed with this characterization of Austin but defended a politics of resignification. Just because a term has a history doesn't mean we can't rework it in some politically promising way. The word *queer* is itself an example of this, Butler said. Both Butler and Sedgwick went on to do this, each pluralizing performativity. Sedgwick added the "deformative," and later in *Touching Feeling* the "peri-performative," which I drew on in *Antigone, Interrupted*. And then Butler, of course, turns to hate speech in the mid-1990s in *Excitable Speech* as an example of performative utterance, and later, in the 2010s, in *Notes toward a Performative Theory of Assembly*, they further resignify performativity to mean bodies gathered together in protest. Both conjugated the concept well beyond the conjugal. Cavell, by contrast, seems to do the opposite. He returns conjugation to the conjugal, endorsing the power of the "I do" as (potentially) a scene of perfectionism.

I want to say, though, that there's room for a still different read-ing of Austin. There are in *How to Do Things with Words* speech acts that install the sovereign straight masculine subject, just as Sedg-wick and Butler say. But there are other moments in Austin's book— a red thread of aberrancy runs through the book too. The queer cri-tique of Austinian sovereignty was in the 1990s a key pushing-off point that allowed for a lot of creative thinking as queer theory to enter the academy. I myself didn't question it at the time. It's only now, looking back, that I see queer possibilities in Austin (and in Wittgenstein too).

AB: Much of your thinking grapples with the question of how to preserve the functioning of democratic political institutions in a time of emergency and shock. Does the ordinary suggest something differ-ent now, given the reality of multiple overlapping political crises— imperialist, ecological, patriarchal, et cetera?

BH: Ha! There it is again, the "embarrassed 'etc.'" as Butler once called it in *Gender Trouble*.[2] It's only embarrassed because there aren't enough words for all the things we need to name! The wrongs of empire, political economy, patriarchy, etc.

I'm interested in reconfiguring democratic institutions to support a more fully democratic equality. There are days when I think there's not much point in doing that kind of work, because we're up against so much. The institutions, norms, and habits of liberal democratic cit-izenship are so imbricated in inegalitarian, exploitative, and extrac-tive forces of capitalism, colonialism, and patriarchy that it seems crazy to try. But the last forty years of US democracy have been instructive. This is a time of lost ground for egalitarian democracy in the United States. But noting how effective the Right has been in radicalizing existing institutions—well, there is a lesson there in how quickly things can change if you invest time, money, and con-viction into it.

AB: On a different topic, I want to ask you about your work across political theory and literary studies. You often route your political the-orizing through analyses of artistic objects like plays and films, and you also perform literary readings of traditional political theoretical texts. In the preface to the thirtieth-anniversary edition of *Political Theory and the Displacement of Politics*, you write that "close reading is an agonistic practice of love, debt, and resistance."[3] In addition to developing your theories through close readings of individual thinkers, you often juxtapose two or more very different thinkers and read them alongside or through each other in generative ways. Is this an agonistic reading practice?

BH: Yes. I think it is. One of the mainstays of agonistic study is to attenuate certain (prereflective, I want to say) common assumptions so that people are freed up to dream and realize alternative arrangements. This is on behalf of those who are remaindered by current settlements, whose violences are often naturalized. Unexpected pairings, especially those that cross high and low culture, can help jostle settled assumptions too.

I started thinking with film as I was teaching Intro to Political Theory. I wanted undergraduates to think about why Rousseau in *The Social Contract* introduced a lawgiver from somewhere else to found the social contract. I enlisted Clint Eastwood's spaghetti westerns and later I assigned *Shane*, which follows a similar narrative arc: a gunslinger shows up to a town where the ordinary good people (no concerns about enclosure or settlerism here) are overwhelmed by bad guys. The gunslinger restores democracy through violence. That is why he leaves. He has to leave because he is powerful enough to dominate the town and everyone knows it. It's important in the fantasy of the western that there's someone powerful enough to defeat evil, but good enough to leave. In politics, though, the people who rely on his services will need to figure out how to own their power and make him leave.

Using film, I soon realized, was a great way to get students to talk in class. When you have a hundred people reading political theory, there's a lot of variation in people's comfort level. But there's something very democratizing about movies. Not everybody has an equally good reading, but everybody feels like, "you saw what I saw, and so whatever I saw, I must have something to say." It emboldens everyone to share and habituates people into classroom conversation. I became committed to doing democratic theory with that democratic medium—not via high-culture *cinema*, but movies.

AB: In your most recent book, *A Feminist Theory of Refusal*, you develop a new reading of Euripides's *Bacchae* to describe a feminist arc of refusal that begins with the suspension of the everyday but must culminate in a return to and contestation with patriarchal structures of power. The essays in *Shellshocked* suggest that the virtue of feminist criticism is its ability to reorient us towards the particularities of everyday injustice. For feminism, what is the relationship between suspending the everyday and using it to ground an unsettling of politics?

BH: That's a great question. To me, the *Bacchae* is a great text of feminist refusal. Normally, the women are pathologized and their return to the city is seen as a misstep. Do they expect to be welcomed back? After killing the king? But regicide, figuratively speaking, is a democratic practice, and the play is a democratic, feminist parable: it's about women who engage in work refusal, who do things that look insane from a patriarchal perspective (like abandon their children), and who kill the king who tries to contain (and then spy on) their explorations of an alternative form of life. The bacchants' mistake is to think the king is dead, though as Foucault says, he needs to be "killed" over and over again. So they come back too early, before the city is fully ready for them (which it may never be). They want to share what they've learned. But that is not welcome.

There isn't here, in my view, a normative claim that such fugitive experiments *must* always culminate in a return to the city. It's that in this parable, they do culminate in a return to the city. And really, one of my big questions, teaching that play, was always, Why? And might there be a lesson there for feminism in that return?

The bacchants had everything. They weren't hungry. They were free. So why did they go back to the city? I consider various answers. One is that no fugitive community can be safe from the cities that claim them as long as those cities retain their power. Another, perhaps morally and politically compelling, is that we have reason to come back in order to assist those left behind.

In *Shellshocked* I consider Penelope, who isn't just awaiting the turn of Ulysses. She puts off the suitors, who want to marry her and take Ulysses's place and property, by saying she can't marry until she completes a burial cloak for Ulysses's father. Every day the suitors see her working on it. It takes forever. And they wait. But the reason it takes so long is because she's working on it every day, yes, but secretly unraveling it at night. In *Shellshocked* I treat that as a metaphor for the work of feminism, which must unravel so much while also reknitting the fabrics of understanding, mutuality, and relationality. Many of us are immersed in lives that make us complicit in the things we also oppose and fight against. This means we must unravel and ravel, as it were, and it's a difficult, necessarily communal process.

AB: Sometimes it seems like there's an unraveling of feminism itself that has to happen. It seems to me that feminism is a political movement or an intellectual lineage that uniquely is constantly rewriting some of its key tenets. Attempts to revive or return to second-wave feminism are having a moment right now, in Amia Srinivasan's *The Right to Sex* and Manon Garcia's *We Are Not Born Submissive* and *The Joy of Consent*, or in artworks like Pratibha Parmar's documentary *My Name Is Andrea*. Yet feminism also sometimes struggles to make use of the insights of previous waves that come to be seen as exclusionary, essentialist, and misguided, and that's what Jack Halberstam describes in *The Queer Art of Failure* as feminism's difficulties with inheritance. I say all this because it's my sense that an agonistic notion of politics like yours could position feminism's fractures and disagreements as a critical resource rather than an obstacle. If agonism is essential to a healthy politics, then maybe feminism's constant questioning of its own terms and foundations, its inability to ever get anything finally right, is actually worthy of emulation.

BH: Precisely so! I wrote an article early on, in 1992, called "Toward an Agonistic Feminism," about how to think about feminism not as either based in identity or as rejecting identity but as having a kind of perpetual agonistic engagement with identity. That came out in an important volume at the time, *Feminists Theorize the Political*, which was edited by Butler and Joan Scott. I think we would now say more readily than we might have said in 1992 that the process of working out one's sex/gender identity and coming to be aware of its fluidities and fixities is nonnegotiable in terms of elements of sexuality familiar to many people working in a feminist vein, and certainly, familiar to those working in queer theory. This is an agonistic practice.

That said, after the 2016 election I started saying publicly, "You know, we are all second wavers now." We had to think past the binary for the sake of those minoritized by it. But we also had to find a bulwark for the work in a dangerous misogynistic moment. It felt necessary to occupy feminism in its second wave at that moment without necessarily readopting the essentialism and the rest. Take, for example, a mantra like "believe women." I would've resisted that ten years earlier, but not at that moment.

AB: Or questions of abortion rights, which people thought were over.

BH: Yes! Actually, in my first book, in 1993, I used *Roe v. Wade* as an example of what happens when people take a court win for a *political* victory. Rarely do I find myself right about a political prediction, but I may have been right when I said then that if we allow courts to displace politics and we don't keep working to shore up a judicial decision already made, we could lose it later. I pointed to the *Casey* decision at the time, which had already started to chip away at *Roe*.[4] Relying on courts to decide rights is absolutely necessary to twenty-first-century democracy, but it's also foolish to count on that. There's a kind of raveling and unraveling that has to happen at the same time. We have to build courts into reliable legal institutions that will protect, defend, and expand rights, but we also have to do the popular mobilization work of building alliances and maintaining popular convictions in favor of those rights, so that when things take a turn, people are ready. Fortunately, people are ready right now to be protesting on behalf of abortion rights and reproductive justice, as Dorothy Roberts rightly insists we call it. That's not a silver lining, it's a political possibility.

AB: *Political Theory and the Displacement of Politics* cemented your reputation as a theorist of agonism. Yet your work also considers care in the writings of such thinkers as Adriana Cavarero, Donald Winnicott, and others. Care also has been described as important to a specifically feminist ethics. Is care compatible with agonism?

BH: *Political Theory and the Displacement of Politics* argued in favor of care, albeit in tension with rights, in a reading of Carol

Gilligan's *In a Different Voice*. But Gilligan's and other feminist care ethics are not necessarily what I have in mind when I write about care later on. Winnicott and Cavarero are; you're right to pick them out. Also, to go back to the thinkers we talked about earlier, I would say that Spillers, Williams, Sharpe, and Hartman are all practitioners of care, and of particular interest to me is their care for language.

Care for the agon, though, is very much a part of agonism.[5] Shortly after *Political Theory and the Displacement of Politics* appeared, in which Nietzsche figured importantly, I wrote a short piece, "The Politics of Agonism," in response to a political theorist's critique of Nietzsche as a nihilist. I said, you know, if you read "Homer's Contest," which is an early essay of Nietzsche's, you don't see nihilism. You see a thinker committed to agonism. "Homer's Contest" is about the agon as a space of contest. Nietzsche identifies the legal mechanisms designed to protect the agon, to care for it, to maintain it. One was ostracism, aimed at anyone powerful enough to dominate the agon, lest they shut it down. The possibility of the agon's closure highlights its dependence on maintenance. So, too, democracy requires the care of hands-on engagement. So, too, the public things of democratic life require care and sustenance. As such, those public things are figures for democracy.

I recall how, in New York, after Hurricane Sandy in 2012, the cell-phone towers went down and people suddenly couldn't call their relatives to let them know they were okay or find their missing loved ones. Inexplicably, someone went into a phone booth to see if it worked, even though no one had used a phone booth in ten years. The phone worked. People lined up to use it. That outdated telephone—a public thing, not a private cell phone—is what got some people through. Sheltered by its booth, it survived the storm. It was there because public servants had been tending to it. This neglected old-media telephone, surely disparaged for years, was kept working so that when we, the public, needed it, it was there.

....

BONNIE HONIG is Nancy Duke Lewis Professor of Modern Culture and Media and Political Science at Brown University. Her first book, *Political Theory and the Displacement of Politics* (1993), cemented her reputation as a theorist of political agonism. Her most recent books are *A Feminist Theory of Refusal* and *Shellshocked: Feminist Criticism after Trump* (both 2021). Her current book project reconsiders ordinary language in the analytic philosophy of J. L. Austin, Stanley Cavell, and Ludwig Wittgenstein and the Black feminist theory of Saidiya Hartman, Christina Sharpe, Hortense Spillers, Patricia Williams, and others.

....

ANNABEL BARRY is a PhD student in English at the University of California, Berkeley. Her research focuses on how Anglo-American ordinary language philosophy is extended both by feminist accounts of how power shapes language use and by formal experiments in Irish women's writing that shed light on the constructed ordinariness of English. Her academic articles appear or are forthcoming in *English Literary History*, the *Keats-Shelley Review*, and *Milton Studies*. With Caroline Godard and Jane Ward, she edited a cluster of essays on "heteropessimism" for *Post45: Contemporaries*.

Notes

1. Austin, *How to Do Things with Words*, 9–10.
2. Butler, *Gender Trouble*, 143.
3. Honig, *Political Theory and the Displacement of Politics*, xvi.
4. *Planned Parenthood of Southeastern Pennsylvania v. Casey* (1992) upheld the essential right to obtain an abortion guaranteed by *Roe v. Wade* but permitted multiple provisions limiting abortion access, deeming that they did not pose an "undue burden" to those seeking abortions.
5. For more on "care for the agon," see Honig, "*Twelve Angry Men.*"

References

Austin, J. L. *How to Do Things with Words*. Oxford: Clarendon, 1962.

Butler, Judith. *Gender Trouble: Feminism and the Subversion of Identity.* New York: Routledge, 1990.

Honig, Bonnie. *Political Theory and the Displacement of Politics: Thirtieth Anniversary Edition*. Ithaca, NY: Cornell University Press, 2023.

Honig, Bonnie. "*Twelve Angry Men*: Care for the Agon and the Varieties of Masculine Experience." *Theory and Event* 22, no. 3 (2019): 701–16.

Writing with Bruised Fruit

DARYL MAUDE

A review of Lauren Berlant, On the Inconvenience of Other People *(Durham, NC: Duke University Press, 2022).*

> Books are never finished: one just stops writing them. The exempla
> are beginnings, not hermetic seals.
>> Lauren Berlant

Throughout *On the Inconvenience of Other People,* in both its main text and its footnotes, Lauren Berlant repeats a certain phrase. It takes the formula "From x person I learned to think about y thing." At the end of the introduction, for example, they write: "From [Eve Kosofsky] Sedgwick I learned that it's not an idea until you circulate it, whatever stage it has reached. From [Stanley] Cavell I learned that showing up with the bruised fruit of one's perspective is what the argument requires to reshape the dynamic processes always on the move from and toward forms of life" (30). Beyond the standard citational systems of quotation and footnote, with page numbers and book titles, which allow the curious reader to read more and the suspicious reader to check if the writer is right, this practice calls these

QUI PARLE   Vol. 33, No. 1, June 2024
DOI 10.1215/10418385-11125547   © 2024 Editorial Board, *Qui Parle*

authors to Berlant's own text. It marks Berlant's writing as emerging from a large network of thought and brings in the other as an active participant in the dialogue. To read and write in any academic discipline is to enter into a conversation that has been going on for a long time, well before one entered the room, and that will continue after one leaves. With this writerly quirk, Berlant extends a hand, telling their reader what transpired in the conversation before the reader came through the door. It functions as an anecdote of Berlant's formation as a thinker. Rather than "see *x* on *y*," the verb *learned* in the role of a citation is both a generous methodology and an active act that asserts Berlant's own writing voice. They are cutting up the "bruised fruit of [their] perspective" and sharing a messy slice with the reader. *On the Inconvenience of Other People* has many methodological features like this, where a little quirk of language will reveal Berlant the theorist, showing us what they are trying to do while also doing it.

In mentioning Sedgwick and Cavell in their introduction (as well as in gesturing at Ludwig Wittgenstein with the enigmatic concept "forms of life"), Berlant invokes the traditions of both queer affect theory and ordinary language philosophy (OLP). While both Sedgwick and Cavell draw on J. L. Austin's work on performativity, these two projects seem to be at odds: antinormative queerness and antilinguistic affect meeting the normative, language-centric OLP.[1] But both strands of thought are deeply concerned with the normal; whether in more or less antagonistic ways, both take the normal seriously and listen to what it has to say by opposing the normative or repositioning a descriptive approach to the normal use of words as central for philosophical inquiry. That Berlant draws on these traditions at the beginning also shows their methodological expansiveness, which draws from queer and affect theory, OLP, psychoanalysis, and Marxism, among others. They describe the "space of permission opened by" Sedgwick and Cavell and note that methodologically the two "helped me see a way into writing that would be freeing" (29–30). For me, ultimately, it is their *writing* itself that is the key to untangling their work and their academic project. *On the Inconvenience of Other People* is not easy to read. This is not a transparent type of descriptive academic writing in which the author takes it for granted that you will understand the use of evidence, a school of theory, and academic convention; *On the Inconvenience of Other People* does not aspire to fade into the background and provide a smooth reading experience. Every step of the way Berlant is there, writing aloud about writing and demonstrating the truth for this text of what they learned from Fredric Jameson: "that context is immanent in a text" (15).

Like Berlant's *Cruel Optimism*, *On the Inconvenience of Other People* is a high-concept work that moves outward from a central idea. As in *Cruel Optimism*, it shows their deep concern with the everyday and the ordinary, concepts that they do not disentangle in this book but that are suggested as subtly different from each other in *Cruel Optimism*. There Berlant explains that they move away from Michel de Certeau's and Henri Lefebvre's theories of the everyday, which they take as no longer descriptive of twenty-first-century life, and toward an "ordinary" that is disorganized by capitalism. The ordinary, for Berlant, also links to "crisis ordinariness," a term they prefer over *trauma*, as it eschews the exceptionalism and break that *trauma* implies.[2] At the same time, as they note in the preface to *On the Inconvenience of Other People*, the "crisis convergence" of the moment of the final stages of the book's writing brought the coronavirus pandemic, anti-Black racism, anti-Asian racism, and antimigrant racism to the forefront of public consciousness in the United States (ix–x). Ordinary, for Berlant, is not quiet or easy.

To this scene of ordinariness, Berlant brings the concept of "inconvenience" as a way of thinking through a whole host of things that arise from "the affective sense of the familiar friction of being in relation" (2). To be in the world is to be in relation with other people, and to be in relation with other people is to be inconvenienced and inconvenient as we adjust and shift to those people and their presences and effects. This is neither something that Berlant decries nor something they cheer for; it just is. Always a theorist of scales, Berlant locates inconvenience as "more than 'being affected' and something less than 'being entangled'" (2). It indexes a nonsovereignty. Like attachment, inconvenience is fundamental to being with others, but in a different direction, as Berlant suggests: "Attachment, one might say, is what draws you out into the world; inconvenience is the adjustment from taking things in" (6). This psychoanalytic idiom continues in their coining of the concept of the "inconvenience drive," which they define as "a drive to keep taking in and living with objects" (6). This is a drive in a present progressive tense, keeping us in the world and moving.

The forward movement of the inconvenience drive indexes a futurity that Berlant invokes in their calling themself, after Michel Foucault, a "heterotopian." Unlike a "utopian," a "heterotopian" still believes in alternatives and better possibilities, but they nevertheless err on the side of multiplicity and partial potential: the crack through which you can see the light, rather than the chasm you fall into. For Berlant, heterotopia points to an expansive repertoire of techniques of theory and ultimately a nonreproductive futurity that emerges through the inconvenient, painful, or even close-to-unbearable work of thinking that signals "the copresence of an otherwise" (16). It doesn't all fit together neatly, but it doesn't need to. There are still scenes of mutual care, of love, of fun, and there is a recognition of violence and a different politics.

Along with the preface and the introduction, *On the Inconvenience of Other People* has three main chapters, arranged around sex and jokes, democracy and infrastructure, and the desire for life and proxemics. These are followed by a coda on the unbearable. Taking readings from films, poems, and artworks, Berlant lingers in the theoretical at the beginning of each chapter, drawing it through each of their objects and extending their readings of scenes, passages, and moments for so long that they become almost fractally saturated with meaning. For this review, it is hard to pick out moments in the text in which Berlant states a thesis without also disarticulating their text into a list or quoting them at great length. They note that their own process is "modular," which is to say "built through sections that allow a problem-cluster to be both established and transformed through its contact with specific object/scenes or cases" (11). *On the Inconvenience of Other People* has many moving parts, and its moving parts move other parts: its chapters, Berlant states, "offer concepts as tools with which to loosen other concepts. To loosen an object is to make it available to transition" (12). This idea of "loosening" is carried through the book, with Berlant noting that to loosen an object is "to make it available for different kinds of attachment, use, form, concept, scene, world" (124). The object is not just a work of literature or film to read, nor is it just a person, nor is it just a theoretical concept, but rather, as they set out in *Cruel Optimism* and reiterate in *On the Inconvenience of Other People*, it is something around which affect and meaning is gathered: "clusters of promise, projection, and speculation," and "scenes of attachment" (27). Thinking with the object to loosen it opens up new possibilities for how it, its clusters, and its scenes could be otherwise. This theoretical move, in which the object is already overdetermined as a cluster or a scene or an "object/scene," allows Berlant to move between a series of virtuoso close readings and a heady theoretical idiom. The close reading for them is key as a work of demonstration, but the choice of what to read seems often incidental. They gesture at historical moments, like Paris in 1968, but they do not stay there. For the more historically minded or textually prudent reader, Berlant's expansiveness may come across as profligacy, but for Berlant themself, these objects are just case studies: things that Berlant found were good to think with and in which they located something gesturing toward the heterotopian.

On the Inconvenience of Other People is declarative and aphoristic, full of pithy and pleasing sentences that claim truth through their force. As readers, we are listening as we read; we are being told what's what by Berlant. Style, for the work, is not something to be disarticulated from content: the book is in Duke University Press's Writing Matters! series of expansive conceptual writing, founded by Berlant along with Saidiya Hartman, Erica Rand, and Kathleen Stewart (who was also Berlant's cowriter of a 2019 collection of experimental prose poems, *The Hundreds*). The writing itself as an art, a practice, and a way of thinking through and with the world—"How it matters, how it interferes" (176), says Berlant in the acknowledgments—is foregrounded, and as mentioned above, the writer as the writing agent is ever-present. In the vein of many queer and feminist theorists, Berlant's own writer's voice is loud and foregrounded in this work; it is not hard to imagine them saying these things to you, even as someone who never met them in person. They note that they have tried to write in the "parenthetical voice" (29), in which authors often couch their more intimate thoughts, turning the parentheses inside out to let the voice loose in the main text and subsequently banning parentheses from their writing.

Their voice is part of the joy of reading the book, whipping up the thick theory and creating something still rich but also airier, with room for the reader to move about and think. It has certain familiar quirks, like the frequent use of *what's* to evoke a scene of generality, immediacy, and ongoingness: "being with what's ongoing" (6), "a flattened voice near what's threatening" (99), "without reproducing what's diminishing" (126), "confidence about what's transpiring" (137). The instances of *what's* gesture at a texture of everyday life without getting too specific and allow the audience to read between the lines and fish out their own examples. The text also frequently hails the reader as "you," with more aphorisms: "contact with inconvenience disturbs the vision of yourself you carry around" (3); "It's that you can't be certain how you'll feel about or be able to live on in the disturbance you created" (76); "In this book you never know whether something works, if *work* means contain and repair. But you have to show up to try something memorial, nonreproductive, and forward moving" (171). Grammatically, it would work to replace *you* with *one* in these sentences, but the stuffiness of *one* works against generalizability. "One" is someone else, maybe Berlant themself, or maybe someone blank and featureless. But as it's "*you* can't be certain how *you'll* feel," then I imagine myself in the scene. When has this happened to me? How do I act in this situation? Is Berlant right about this? I am drawn into the scene of thinking by the prose, interpellated by the second person.

Even as I am drawn in and given space to think by the voice, it also feels, at times, unrelenting. The pace of *On the Inconvenience of Other People* is quick, even if at points we are running in place to stay with Berlant's object. I feel excited reading Berlant's words, warmed by both their chattiness and their masterful deployment of a host of texts and scenes to make their points, but I also feel as if I am trying to keep up with someone always at least two steps ahead of me, pulling me by the hand—"you, you, you"—but also keeping me out of breath. As they say, "reading is inconvenient to the reader" (19). But inconvenience is not all bad and has its own pleasures: in their reading of Juliana Spahr's "This Connection of

Everyone," they quote at length from a repeating sequence that builds upon itself, mimicking the in-and-out rhythm of breathing. I know I should read the whole thing, subvocalize and experience the poem as a song, but I am impatient and my eyes slide over to the end of the quote, back to Berlant's prose. The first sentence: "Did you skim?" Oops. Sorry, Lauren. Reading that, I feel abashed that I did, so obviously, and also pleased to have been seen and imagined by Berlant in this way. After such a read they offer a consolation that is also a proposition: "It is hard not to let the incantation fuzz out the demands of staying with what's changing in a rhythmic common" (101). Berlant gives us a model and a lesson in theory and formal analysis, yoking it to the experience of reading and their witty, arch voice.

Aphorism for Berlant is not a gesture of mastery or finality. They are writing theory, but for Berlant, theory is not a grand unified project or a codex of what is true. Rather, it is a creative endeavor, an attempt to get somewhere and figure something out. They note that "work claiming to be theory must be read as propositional" (19), and so, at the same time as we are hailed as readers, pulled into the theoretical abstraction that is the scene of thinking, Berlant also offers us a puzzle. This is an invitation to theorize: What if this were true? What if this abstract conclusion could be drawn from this poem, this film, this piece of art? ("The exempla are beginnings, not hermetic seals" [27].) This spirit runs throughout the book. In the preface, they say, "Everything needs to be tested with humility and focus" (xi), as though offering a note on their general methodology, but this is also a note to the reader. Caveat, reviewer. In the introduction, in the space between two paragraphs, separated from the other text by lines above and below, they insert the following exercise: "So, brainstorm your own examples of structural and affective alienation" (26). After a long list of questions at the end of their first chapter, they note to the reader: "None of these questions is rhetorical; all of them are propositional" (73). We are being asked these questions by Berlant; theory here is also pedagogy, and the reader is being given homework. There is a delight in the gift of being taken this seriously as readers and asked to share in the intellectual work the book is doing.

In my own writing, I have been thinking about futures for a long time, trying to locate my work on Okinawan and mainland Japanese literature written in the shadow of American empire on a map drawn by queer theorists of futurity, one that sketches out a terrain between utopian possibility and nonreproductive antifuturity. In trying to believe in the possibility of something better as a writer—isn't all writing a futural project?—I also want to avoid a tendency to fetishize resistance and protest as the be-all and end-all of every text, assuming that the texts I read have things to tell me that I already know before I open the book. Life and thought are ordinarily complicated, which is to say, there are always too many moving parts to be neatly understood or to lead to a simple solution. At the same time, there is urgency in practices of solidarity. We can't ignore what must be protested. Maintaining this tension is something I continue to struggle with. Turning to Berlant's work then, I take a lot from inconvenience in its indexing of the inevitable difficulty of being together, even as it is a necessary part of being in the world. I also take the heterotopian imaginations of elsewheres we can gather from the practice of loosening the object, and the nonreproductive futurity—the possibility of a future that doesn't replicate the crisis ordinary of the present—that is suggested by this loosening.

Beyond the question of queer futurity, Berlant also engages queerly with the question of sex, which they try to bring back as central to queer inquiry, where it has been pushed out—as they see it—to make room for concerns about sexuality, identity, or love. Sex is something potentially dangerous and definitely inconvenient. In the first chapter of the book, for example, Berlant examines *Last Tango in Paris* (dir. Bernardo Bertolucci, 1972) and foregrounds a problem of writing about a film steeped in sexual violence: how can a writer think about this while also maintaining a sense of sex positivity? Erotophobia in society and in theory arises from bad sex and the possibility of violence, but as a resolution, argues Berlant, it is not adequate, missing out on the potential for overdetermination that allows for a loosening of the object. Sex might be disturbing, but "the disturbance of sex is different from the trauma of sex" (38). Sex is disturbing because people are difficult, and even sex that is desired, they note, can be something we are ambivalent about, wanting and not wanting it at the same time. The "both/and" of this kind of ambivalence around sex may be a dramatic state but might also just be the ordinary messiness of being in relation to other people. This both/and of sex should not be taken as neither/nor, as Berlant states that they aim to find an approach that succeeds at "interrupting the impasse between the affirmative and the aggressive view of sex, one that does not minimize or negate the prospects of happiness or violence" (67). For the couple of Jeanne and Paul in *Last Tango in Paris*, sex is a way to experiment with radicality and an antibourgeois life in the historical moment of a post-1968 Paris, but the experiment fails. There is bad sex, there is rape, and there is death. For Berlant, the attempt and the failure have something to tell us about sex and the political: paying attention to scale again, sex is not just an analogy of the social for Berlant, as if good sex could simply point to a good society and a good society could point back to good sex. Rather, it is something more quotidian: "a training in how simply hard it is to be in the room with another person" (66). So they argue that we need to embrace the "inconvenience of staying in a rebroken social scene" (68) that is the result of being in a world in which political change and revolution is possible and ongoing, as well as understanding the awful normality of sexual violence. *Last Tango in Paris* is a failure of a creation of politics via and proximate to sex, but it "does not mean it was a bad idea to try" (77), says Berlant.

The question of violence is a difficult one in *On the Inconvenience of Other People*. When at the beginning of the book Berlant invokes Fred Moten and Stefano Harney, Achille Mbembe, and Jasbir Puar, or in their discussions of sexual violence and murder, the reader may already be wondering where inconvenience ends and violence begins, or if "inconvenience" isn't a grand understatement. Berlant does try to differentiate between the concepts: for them, this violence is not the same as inconvenience, which is, after all, a state of being with other people. But it is queasily proximate, and even though Berlant states that they have tried to "separate out" the two in their work (x), so that the being with does not equate to the terribly ordinary, the fact that they do not always succeed is instructive. As they say drily and darkly in the coda: "rape/murder: an ordinary thing" (152). This shit is all around us. And so it is important to think about what literature, film, or art could do within the crushing ordinariness of it all. For this, Berlant offers a reading of James Ellroy and Bhanu Kapil's works that discuss the violence of rape and death, and they make the point that the difficulty of their literary form affords the thinker time to go slowly and treat the horror of the violence seriously. The works' experimentation is purposeful "because the incidents involve rape/deaths *for which available genres make too much sense*" (154). In these works, they see a "realism for the nonsovereign" (169), which, rather than an inevitable script or a dour cynicism, allows space to breathe and think in a different mode in a difficult world. The acts of reading, watching, and writing offer something to us all. The world is full of pain. "And yet" (171).

A poignant moment in the book comes when Berlant places *On the Inconvenience of Other People* in between *Cruel Optimism* and their next book, on humorlessness, which they will not write. As the note to the readers at the beginning of the text tells us, Lauren Berlant died in June 2021, when the manuscript was complete but the book was not yet in production; the final work of getting the book finished and into the world was undertaken by the series editors, Hartman, Rand, and Stewart. As a last book, *On the Inconvenience of Other People* is very pleasingly Berlantian: witty, difficult, and theoretical, with attention paid to the ordinary, fantasy, attachment, and sex through a close reading practice that feels like it turns the texts inside out. The line to the book from their previous publications is clear. You and I are left with the rich, pleasurable, inconvenient archive of thought and feeling that is Berlant's work. From Berlant I learned that writing is a way of getting at an ongoing scene, to test out what you think but also to offer other people a hand as they think through the ordinary. From Berlant I learned that showing up in my writing doesn't have to mean a superfluity of the first person, but that it can. From Berlant I learned that theory, like fantasy, is an everyday practice. So, brainstorm your own examples.

....

DARYL MAUDE is a postdoctoral associate in the Department of Asian and Middle Eastern Studies at Duke University. He works on contemporary Okinawan and Japanese literature and on queer and feminist theory. His chapter "Learning Queerness: Pedagogy and Normativity in Tagame Gengorō's *Otōto no otto*" appeared in *Multiple Voices in Japanese Literature, 1989–2019*, edited by Angela Yiu (2024). His translation of Shinjō Ikuo's essay "Male Sexuality in the Colony" appeared in *Beyond Imperial Aesthetics*, edited by Mayumo Inoue and Steve Choe (2019).

Notes

1. For more on the connection between Sedgwick's and Cavell's engagement with Austin, see Annabel Barry's interview of Bonnie Honig in this issue.
2. Berlant, *Cruel Optimism*, 8–10.

Reference

Berlant, Lauren. *Cruel Optimism*. Durham, NC: Duke University Press, 2011.

Space to Breathe

AMBER SWEAT

A review of Christina Sharpe, Ordinary Notes *(London: Daunt, 2023).*

> These intense zones of feeling, thickets of heartbreak and grief,
> eruptions of love, radiant moments of ordinariness, small spaces
> opening inside us . . .
> > Saidiya Hartman, "A Room with History"

> I have found company in the stories of other women, and the
> revelation of all our ordinariness has itself been curative.
> > Melissa Febos, *Girlhood*

Studies in Blackness: A Break

Christina Sharpe's *In the Wake* ushers in a break between the conflicting (but not diametrically opposed) schools of Afropessimism and
Black optimism. While the Afropessimist camp, led by theorists like
Frank B. Wilderson III, argues for an ontological dehumanization
of the Black person after slavery, Fred Moten's Black optimist camp
espouses a resilient belief in collective progress and empowerment

QUI PARLE   Vol. 33, No. 1, June 2024
DOI 10.1215/10418385-11125557   © 2024 Editorial Board, *Qui Parle*

within the Black community. Sharpe's emphasis on the aftermath of slavery and the notion of "the wake" intertwines grief, memory, and the ongoing impact of historical trauma on contemporary Black experience while nevertheless illuminating the preciousness of Black collectivity and existence. Sharpe's dear friend and interlocutor Saidiya Hartman speaks to this theoretical rupture in the Black studies dichotomy: "Christina's work totally unsettles that binary [between Afropessimism and Black optimism]. She addresses the structural conditions of anti-Blackness that condemn Black people on a variety of levels and still attends to the richness of Black social living, and it is an essential contribution."[1]

Sharpe's scholarship contributes to an urgent reevaluation of how we comprehend and confront racialized violence, demanding a reorientation of societal structures toward a recognition of Black humanity. If Black studies flourished as an academic discipline in the twentieth century, broader conversations about anti-Blackness have come to a head following 2020's racial-political uprisings and their many aftermaths, one of them a peculiar and vastly marketable focus on the Black person as someone whose survival is contingent on their being extraordinary. After global movements for Black life in 2020, commodities began popping up in big-box merchandisers across America: Black Girl Magic brand rosé, T-shirts emblazoned with silhouetted Afros, books about how Black children are poised to be exceptional, birthday cards celebrating another year around the sun in tandem with a celebration of Blackness. Yet the year 2020, while anomalous for many reasons, does not exist as a stand-alone moment of racial reckoning. Similar rhetoric circulated in 2016, when products, hashtags, and internet metadata called for #BlackExcellence in the aftershocks of the Trump election. Following the period from 2008 to 2012, the Obamas came to represent a postracial phantasm. Black people are allowed to be extraordinary now (high earners, doctors, lawyers, even presidents, even *magical*), and this has led us to assume that this potential to be extraordinary will save us. But will it? We should put critical pressure on systems that have configured the Black person as one whose worth is directly tied to being magical or super in a society saturated by images and praxes of anti-Black violence—a violence so inextricable from everyday life that it is always already ordinary. The extraordinariness required of Black folks for their survival (largely rooted in Black capitalism and respectability politics) does not save but instead exiles Black people into a more palatably neoliberal but nevertheless violent realm of dishumanity.[2] In a society founded on chattel slavery and its afterlives, spectacularity and magic are marketed as the assumed panaceas to the ordinariness of Black death and subjugation. However, within the ordinary space of the Black quotidian is room for new forms, new beauties, and new methods for celebrating Black life. Sharpe attends to both in *Ordinary Notes*.

A New Wake

Ordinary Notes, Sharpe's third book, is an innovative and imaginative successor to *Monstrous Intimacies: Making Post-slavery Subjects* (2010) and her seminal book *In the Wake: On Blackness and Being* (2016). Sharpe's 360-page text is separated into 248 notes on Black life, all of which are separated into eight sections. On an initial flip through the book, each page varies in both wordiness and form; long, sweeping essays spanning pages are cut through with short reflections, blank spaces, and the occasional image. Diverging from Sharpe's standard, essay-based chapter formats, *Ordinary Notes* takes on an experimental shape to explore quotidian Black life "in the wake." Speaking of the wake: while *Ordinary Notes* is the only of Sharpe's texts that considers the everydayness of Black life in its title, and even though it deviates from her other texts in form, Sharpe's first two books similarly examine the enduring impact of the transatlantic slave trade on the Black quotidian, emphasizing the ongoing violence and trauma that persist in the aftermath of slavery. *Monstrous Intimacies* treats the familiar sexual brutality born of power dynamics deriving from racial subjugation across the Black Atlantic, and *In the Wake*, through a combination of personal anecdotes in tandem with broader sociological commentary, illuminates the pervasiveness of contemporary racial violence, the regularity of Black death, and the artistic methods that imagine new futures despite it all. In a particularly apt chapter of *In the Wake*, "The Weather," Sharpe writes on the all-consuming nature of violences borne on the slave ship and how these violences bleed into contemporary society: "Day after day the stories arrive. Fifty people suffocated in the hold of a ship; three people suffocated in prison over the course of a weekend in the United States. . . . It is not the specifics of any one event or set of events that are endlessly repeatable and repeated, but the totality of the environments in which we struggle; the machines in which we live; what I am calling the weather."[3] This attention to stories told "day after day" might be Sharpe's most primary—and central—interrogation of the ordinariness or normativeness of Black suffering.

Sharpe turns inward toward her own stories with *Ordinary Notes*, but not without losing the polyvocality of her previous texts. Throughout a series of personal fragments that are as tender as they are critical, *Ordinary Notes* sketches out memories, materialities, realities, and potential futures for Black life through the prism of Sharpe's lived experiences and observations. While this is a standout and singular text, Sharpe does not write it alone, often conversing with contemporaries from her personal life, the public sphere, her professional formation, and the interstices of these spaces. (References to writers such as Hartman, Claudia Rankine, Roland Barthes, Toni Cade Bambara, and Toni Morrison are woven together with notes centering on Sharpe's mother, neighborhood kinfolk, and various strangers at sites such as the Legacy Museum of African American History.)

In addition, Sharpe converses with herself; her collection of "ordinary notes" often nods to the publication of *In the Wake* as a critical event in her life. An early note—15—comes from an unnamed former classmate who reconnected with Sharpe after reading *In the Wake* (22). In a separate note Sharpe explains how a reference to Morrison's *Beloved* is an intertextual and everlasting "note on how to live in the *afterlife of slavery*, in the *afterlife of lynching*, and *in the wake*" (67).[4] Sharpe also rereads herself, sketching out how her past voices solicit new interventions, including a reexamination of *In the Wake* in note 74. Sharpe writes, "Rereading 'The Wake,' preparing for a talk, I arrive at this sentence: 'In 1994 the Philadelphia police murdered my cousin Robert'" before explicating the preciousness of their relationship and his nickname, "Bobby." Sharpe continues:

"The addition of the word *cousin* was a gesture of intimacy and re-spect; it was the sound of relation, not estrangement." At the top of the note, Sharpe calls it "a revision, a sound, a correction, an addi-tion" (115). In the wake of *In the Wake*, conversations surrounding Black life—ranging from the disquieting to the discursive—can un-fold with Sharpe's new opus at the center.

As previously mentioned, the collection unpacks the ordinariness of racial violence (which robs Black people of their life, their breath) while finding respite in the ordinary pleasures and potentials of lived existence (the breath-giving fragments of the Black quotidian). While both considerations come to the surface in Sharpe's analyses, the text's shape is as much an investigation of Black life as its written content. This is to say that *Ordinary Notes* is a marvel in form, experimenting with new arrangements for the literary genre of nonfiction. Fragments of varying lengths are interspersed among 360 pages. Shorter notes may take up only one line, such as note 25, "Every memorial and museum to atrocity already contains its failure," and note 85, "A memory that is not mine returns to me" (38, 130). Longer-form, multipage pieces in both prose and verse coalesce in notes such as note 51, wherein Sharpe refers to work born of her text "Beauty Is a Method," alongside photographs of her mother's creative varia, poetic reflections on her childhood, and lists of books (largely Black writing) that molded her relationship to literature (79–86).[5] This stylistic choice enhances the overall effect of Sharpe's text by creating a dynamic and engaging rhythm, catching the reader in the sharp realities of shorter notes or the swelling, affective waves of her longer observations. Multiple photographs—taken from the ar-chives or by Sharpe herself—add a visual dimension to accompany *Ordinary Notes*' written word.

Beyond Sharpe's variations in length and genre, two other formal choices are particularly striking. One is the use of censor bars through-out the text, and the other is Sharpe's employment of negative space. These aesthetic choices are pointed and polysemous. Whereas black-ened omissions draw the eye toward the vulgar, all-encompassing, and interchangeable nature of violence, they also call for a reconsider-ation of the spectacular nature of racial violence. Moreover, Sharpe's artistic use of gaps and negative space encourages corporeal breath for storyteller and reader alike: a respite in the face of this violence. Through these formal choices, Sharpe's sophomore success becomes more than a praxis for storytelling in the wake—it is a life force.

Blacked Out

In initial readings, perhaps the most eye-catching of Sharpe's aesthetic decisions is the use of black censor bars to omit specific words in the text. The first of these bars appears in note 5, wherein Sharpe reflects on a photograph from the integration of Little Rock High School. In the photograph, a group of white students are screaming at Elizabeth Eckford. Tethering Eckford's experiences of violence to her own, Sharpe draws out both difference and similarity by stating, "[At school], I wasn't surrounded by a mob threatening to lynch me and screaming, 'Send that '██████' back to the jungle,' 'go home, ████████! Go back to Africa!' . . . But I heard ████████ almost every day for six years at St. Katharine of Siena" (7). In their first employment, the censor bars perform their usual task of omitting language deemed too obscene for publication. (Given the situation and syntax, the reader is led to believe that Sharpe is censoring racist epithets.)

As the text unfolds, the bars begin to take other semiotic shapes. Notes 15 and 16 detail messages sent to Sharpe by two unnamed interlocutors. The primary, anonymized letter states, "My ██████████ is in a PhD program at ████████████████ and has been reading *In the Wake.* ███ reached out to me because ███ thought I would really enjoy it, especially because ███ noticed so many connections to schools" (22). Sharpe then explains how, "three days later, another note arrives" from a supposed childhood friend, who writes: "Dear Christina, . . . I am ████████████████████████ and we went to school together. I am back living in ███████ after many years outside of the area and drive by your old house frequently" (23). In this instance, different from that in note 5, the censor bar muddies all identifiers of those who see themselves in Sharpe's writing. And whereas the earliest use of the censor bar maintains the same length (emphasizing the singularity of a racist term that connected Sharpe and Eckford), this set of bars begins to vary in tandem with word length.

At first there is room to believe that this censorship is a safety measure, sheltering Sharpe's kinfolk from potential backlash after the text's publication and sparing Black readers the cruelty of racist language. Going farther, however, the bars' disparate lengths and nebulous subjects point to a secondary effect: an amalgam of redacted names begins to create a critical mass, with their effaced, unique identities all coalescing under the shared experience of Black subjugation in the wake. This nameless mass comes to represent the very "totality" of struggle that Sharpe sketches out in both *In the Wake* and *Ordinary Notes*. The suffering of Black life in the wake is so pervasive, present, and powerful that neither it nor its victims need to be named to ensure that it exists. The pain is everywhere. The interlocutor could be anyone; such is the ordinariness of subjugation in the wake. To produce the same effect, Sharpe's most striking use of the censor bar takes place in note 17, which she describes as both "unwritten and unsent" (24). After greeting a censored name, Sharpe writes, "So much rehabilitated and reconstructed into that goodness and perpetual innocence that whiteness extends." The next seven lines are completely blacked out before Sharpe signs her full name at the bottom of the correspondence. It is in the absence of words that the presence of brutality weighs heavy on the page. One need not know exactly what Sharpe is saying—it is enough that the potential for horror exists behind the blackened lines of her prose. In this brutality is Sharpe's orthographic brilliance.

While the names of her personal interlocutors are blacked out in-text, the names of Black lives lost to police brutality and racist violence are not. Sharpe prints the names of Laquan McDonald, Michael Brown, Walter Scott, Marlene Pinnock, John Crawford, Tamir Rice, and Philando Castille (322, 32).[6] While illustrating the importance of saying their names—echoing movements such as #SayTheirName and its variations—Sharpe also displays a deliberate aversion to the naming of their murderers. In a subversive turn, notes containing the censor bar are also where Sharpe most clearly criticizes the "rehabilitation" of "goodness and perpetual innocence" that whiteness affords in the quotidian, especially in contemporary media. Sharpe crystallizes the pervasiveness of this rehabilitation via her notes on racially incited mass killings; in her recollections she explains how the white supremacist perpetrator is often glorified, coddled, or popularized at the expense of their nonwhite victims. In note 63, for instance, Sharpe writes on the infantilizing words that a "sheriff said about ███████████, a white twenty-one-year-old man who is accused of killing eight people, almost all of whom were Asian and women. ██████ murdered six Asian women" (102). Immediately following this, note 64 condemns the *non*condemnation by Christy Wampole, a Princeton University professor, of "████████'s December 14, 2022, massacre of twenty-six people, twenty of whom were children between the ages of six and seven, in Newtown, Connecticut, in the United States," a direct response to Wampole's *New York Times* op-ed that states, "[*These white men] were once our heroes, our young and shining fathers, our sweet brothers*" (103). Note 105 details the harrowing moment when "the police brought ███████ a meal from Burger King after he fired seventy rounds and brutally assassinated nine people in Mother Emanuel AME Church in Charleston, South Carolina" (159). A later note, 225, details a prosecutor's speech after Laquan McDonald's murder at the hands of police: "What ███████ saw 'was a Black boy walking down the street . . . having the audacity to ignore the police'" (322).[7] If earlier uses of the censor bar emphasize the ubiquity of racial violence and the interchangeability of its victims, later uses draw attention to the commonplace nature of mass shootings. However, Sharpe's omissions directly destroy the recognition—and by proxy, the valorization—of its perpetrators.

In a necessary move, Sharpe turns our attention to how the media portrays mass murderers, especially when it comes to racially motivated hate crimes, as ordinary, commonplace, and merely "troubled" young men who came into extraordinary circumstances. This acquittal, at best, diminishes the crime's weight alongside the value of Black life. At worst, it veers racist perpetrators into realms of continual glorification. White male perpetrators are infantilized, and the disproportionate rate of Black death at the hands of police is configured as an anomalous bug as opposed to systemic feature. What's more, sensationalized coverage focuses extensively on the perpetrators as opposed to the victims, providing the perpetrators with an unwarranted platform that can inadvertently serve as a source of inspiration

for others with violent tendencies. The constant repetition of the perpetrators' names and detailed accounts of their actions (in)adver-
tently contributes to a cultlike status, turning them into antiheroes
and martyrs in the eyes of racist audiences. This not only disregards
the suffering of the victims, their families, and the folks who see their
own kin in the victims' faces but also perpetuates a cycle where acts of
violence are sensationalized for the sake of news coverage and at the
expense of Black mental health.[8] Sharpe questions the ordinariness
of this violence, the regularity of its killers, and the normalness of
their actions. Her explicit refusal to name these perpetrators becomes
a praxis of care against the simultaneous glorification and normalization of white supremacy.

Sharpe herself is acutely aware of this mediatized sensationaliza-
tion of whiteness, the digital artification of Black death, and how racial trauma is trans- and intermediated in the present day.[9] Refresh-
ingly, she contends that there is no need for this in healing. As she
pointedly underscores in note 23, wherein she reflects on the virality
of Philando Castile's death video: "The architecture of the memorial
stages encounter. Spectacle is not repair" (36).

Space to Breathe

What, then, is reparative? What is healing? Sharpe seeks to answer
these questions in a few ways, with mentions of love, care, and healing scattered throughout the text. It may be easier to isolate what healing is *not*, and Sharpe lends us a reading in note 20: "One is asked to
assume a certain position; asked to embrace memorial narratives that
offer Black suffering as a pathway to knowledge, national, and 'racial'
healing, reparation, and reconciliation. . . . 'We' are not approaching healing" (31). It is only when the reader combs through the text,
page by page, line by line, that the text's meaning coalesces into an
offering for Black life; the antidote to this embrace of Black suffering is, in fact, the ordinary note. What enables breath is attention to
the complexity of the Black experience, painted with potential for
life even in the normalization of death. Only at the end of the
text—after careful consideration of the book's form—does Sharpe's
first note become clear:

> There are all kinds of ordinary notes: there are unreservedly anti-black notes; there are notes that attempt, but fail, to undo anti-black logics; there are notes that refuse altogether to accede to those logics that simultaneously de/re/and unhuman Black people. *These Black notes may land in silence or a tone, a sound, a pitch, a record, or an observation made with care*; these notes might just reach you across distance, time, and space, and with them you may be "held, and held." (3; my italics)

If we take Sharpe's advice in all of its thoughtful sincerity—that the Black note "may land in silence or a tone"—then we can see how, in retrospect, the entirety of *Ordinary Notes* is a praxis in refusal. The ordinary note, so surrounded by the excess of quotidian suffering in the wake, strikes a liberatory tone in the silence, across distance, through all observations "made with care." It finds a resurgence of Black life in the spaces that are left for breath. Of course, this is merely one interpretation of Sharpe's first note at a largely narrative level. On a formal level, however, this space for breath shows itself in Sharpe's insistence on the pages' blank space. In *Ordinary Notes* each note begins at the top of a page. This means that shorter notes—such as the aforementioned notes 23 and 58—appear as one singular line followed by an entire page of empty, white expanse (38, 130). This configuration stands in opposition to Sharpe's formatting for *In the Wake* and *Monstrous Intimacies*, as well as other enumerated, notelike texts such as Wilderson's *Afropessimism*.[10]

It is toward the end of this review that we return attention to the book's format. The eight sections that make up Sharpe's 248 fragments are mostly bare titles drawn from disambiguations of the word *note*. The only section whose title is not a disambiguation is section vi, titled "preliminary entries toward a dictionary of untranslatable Blackness" (233). It is in this section that Sharpe's meditation on the note exits its formal grammars and definitions, instead creating a space for novel definitions, neologisms, and experimental ruminations on terms of everyday Black life. One of the most central terms—a word that marks "the beginning," per Kevin Adonis Browne—is *breathing*, which is tenderly elucidated in note 167 (237). Through Sharpe, Browne writes that "breathing is the beginning. It is, for us, a first and final movement. In it, we find the prototype of all method, without which: nothing. Breathing, thus, is the foregrounding of all concept—its precursor and first condition, its resolution" (233). In a metaliterary depiction of the book in which it exists, the definition continues to unfold: "Before and after language, and of all that comes and goes unuttered, it is that block of text in the negative space of the page, noticed from the corner of the eye. A premium in these times. Dear. Dearer still. It is how, through the movement of space, life is able to consider itself." Breath is where life becomes attainable, a material reality in the matrix of Black language and existence, for "we, by holding it, are able to grasp a finitude that cannot otherwise be grasped, a meaning that cannot be held" (237). Breathing—the most ordinary and seemingly involuntary act of existence—is the fertile ground on which Black life's potential is at its most legible, its most respirable. Of course, calls for Black breath are necessary in the recognition and negation of violence in the wake. In note 169 Sharpe reminds us of "the man who said 'I can't breathe,'" in a poetic eulogy to those lost in the regular swallows of anti-Black precarity (239). For Sharpe, the necessity of breath is vital, literally and literarily. The genius of Sharpe's *Ordinary Notes* is that it makes us breathe.

Let us return here to the important status of blank space in Sharpe's textual layout. In her work on trauma and memory in Holocaust narratives, literary theorist Anne-Berenike Rothstein sees "blank space as a representation of the unspeakable/the traumatic; blank space as a representation of (lost) space; blank space as a representation of the space of memory and remembrance; and blank space as a representation of the narrative space and the space of reflection."[11] Rothstein's analysis allows us to read Sharpe's employment of blank space in *Ordinary Notes* as an act of reparation that calls for reflection, meditation, and breath. Of Rothstein's four theses on blank space, the fourth, "Blank space as a representation of the narrative space and the space of reflection," merits particular attention. Rothstein, like Sharpe, cites Barthes in her description of aesthetics. While Sharpe cites Barthes's account of the punctum, Rothstein cites his theory of the *mise-en-page* (172).[12] Rothstein argues that texts with blank space "create a form of dialogue with readers and spectators. In this context, the audience becomes even more important and achieves the status of a coproducer of the text."[13] The dialogue, for readers, is not necessarily logocentric. In fact, quite the opposite is the case—it is silent, taken up with nothing but the body's ordinary inhale and exhale. For Rothstein, moments of isolation, blankness, emptiness, and silence become spaces for the reader to pause and reflect. They become moments of meditation and introspection. In the event that a reader does not want to decipher any headier or novel interpretation of the text, they become moments simply to *breathe*. In the disciplinary tapestries wherein Sharpe quilts her work—across Black studies, ethnic studies, feminist theory, media theory, and archival work, to name a few—regular exposure to the nature of one's own marginalization becomes suffocating. For so long it was thought that an escape from this realm of subjugation was some ascension to a new height, an extraordinariness, a magic, an excellence—a type of respectability or success marked by slippery metrics of acceptance crafted by a society steeped in Eurocentric standards and white supremacy.

Sharpe's timely work asks us to reconsider these beliefs. The book's many notes, surrounded by the peaceful void of an empty page, the obfuscated words, the wide margins, the bare topography of nothing but breath—these are the notes that "end in silence." They are the notes that call for a reconsideration of the systems that have constructed our understandings and underpinnings of Black life in the wake. While it's unclear whether or not Sharpe meant for her first note to be a prescription, a disclaimer, or a preface to the work that readers would encounter over the remaining 360 pages, it lives as an undercurrent through the impressive achievement that is *Ordinary Notes*. The escape, the potential, the beauty: it may just be pause. It may just be breathing. It may just be ordinary.

....

AMBER SWEAT is a PhD candidate in French studies at the University of California, Berkeley. Her research examines self-imaging praxis and self-formation for Black girls in both the Francophone diaspora and the larger (digital) Black Atlantic. A Black woman herself, she was taught to be extraordinary but now savors ordinariness.

Notes

1. Quoted in Wortham, "Woman Shaping a Generation."
2. For more, see Robinson, *Black Marxism*; and Chatelain, *Franchise*. Sharpe herself writes on the Obamas and the complications of their image in *Ordinary Notes*, 100n61, 155n104, 307n214.
3. Sharpe, *In the Wake*, 111.
4. Immediately following the citation, Sharpe references herself in a footnote for *In the Wake*.
5. For a greater understanding of note 51, see Sharpe, "Beauty Is a Method."
6. It's interesting that, in the note in which Sharpe names multiple victims of anti-Black brutality, her reflection begins with her witnessing Rankine at a screening of *Situation 8*. Sharpe's naming of these victims harks back to Rankine's famous act of inscribing the names of Black people killed in hate crimes in *Citizen*, 35–36. As Rankine's list of victims continues, each name becomes distinctly lighter before the list ultimately fades into nothingness, mimicking the blank space also present in Sharpe's *Ordinary Notes*. This nod to Rankine (in both naming practice and form) is another stroke of intertextual tenderness between Sharpe and her contemporaries.
7. The citation's truncation is Sharpe's.
8. For more on media psychology, the copy-cat effects of mass shootings' news coverage, and the movement to "not name" perpetrators of violence, see Meindl and Ivy, "Mass Shootings." In recognizing that Sharpe's text indicts police-sanctioned, state-sanctioned, and systemic violences in the wake, I note that this source lends credence to (and sometimes valorizes) state institutions such as the Federal Bureau of Investigation and the Advanced Law Enforcement Rapid Response Training team.
9. In note 225, the same note detailing Laquan McDonald's death, Sharpe writes that violent videos depicting Black death are so pervasive that "since the murder of Michael Brown, I have turned off the autoplay function on all of my devices" (322).
10. I also want to call attention to Sharpe's Wilderson intertext on non-healing on page 31 (note 20).
11. Rothstein, "Presence through Absence," 127.
12. I want to emphasize that Sharpe, while a reader of Barthes, is also an astute critic of his writing. She often complicates his hypothetical readings of her familial portraits by questioning "the ordered hierarchy of the plantation that conditions all his seeing," offering new readings from Black phenomenology and epistemologies (e.g., 178).

13. Rothstein, "Presence through Absence," 139.

References

Chatelain, Marcia. *Franchise: The Golden Arches in Black America*. New York: Liveright, 2020.

Meindl, James N., and Jonathan W. Ivy. "Mass Shootings: The Role of the Media in Promoting Generalized Imitation." *National Library of Medicine* 107, no. 3 (2017): 368–70.

Rankine, Claudia. *Citizen: An American Lyric*. Minneapolis: Graywolf, 2014.

Robinson, Cedric J. *Black Marxism: The Making of the Black Radical Tradition*. London: Penguin, 2021.

Rothstein, Anne-Berenike. "Presence through Absence: The Aesthetics of Blank Space in French Holocaust Literature and Film." In *Narratives of Annihilation, Confinement, and Survival: Camp Literature in a Transnational Perspective*, edited by Anja Tippner and Anna Artwińska, 127–45. Berlin: de Gruyter, 2019.

Sharpe, Christina. "Beauty Is a Method." *e-flux*, no. 105 (2019). https://www.e-flux.com/journal/105/303916/beauty-is-a-method/.

Sharpe, Christina. *In the Wake: On Blackness and Being*. Durham, NC: Duke University Press, 2016.

Wortham, Jenna. "The Woman Shaping a Generation of Black Thought." *New York Times Magazine*, April 26, 2023. https://www.nytimes.com/2023/04/26/magazine/christina-sharpe-black-literature.html#:~:text=Christina%20Sharpe%20is%20expanding%20the,words%20and%20resurrecting%20neglected%20history.

CRITICAL TIMES

Interventions in Global Critical Theory

Samera Esmeir, editor

Critical Times is an open access, peer-reviewed online journal published by the International Consortium of Critical Theory Programs with the aim of foregrounding encounters between canonical critical theory and various traditions of critique emerging from other historical legacies. The journal seeks to showcase the multiple forms that critical thought takes today, presenting essays from different areas of the world; to encourage critical analysis, transnational exchange, and political reflection and practice; and to foster new types of intellectual discourse and reformulate the field by accounting for its regional and linguistic inflections.

6:2
AUGUST
2023

CRITICAL TIMES
Interventions in Global Critical Theory

OPEN ACCESS

Start reading.
read.dukepress.edu/critical-times

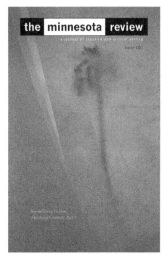

Printed and bound by CPI Group (UK) Ltd, Croydon, CR0 4YY

13/04/2025